ALSO BY ALEX PERRY

The Rift: A New Africa Breaks Free

Lifeblood: How to Change the World One Dead Mosquito at a Time

Falling Off the Edge: Globalization, World Peace and Other Lies

IN E-BOOK

The Hunt for Boko Haram

Clooney's War

Cocaine Highway

Once Upon a Jihad

"Democracy Isn't Working"

Scotland the Brave

The Quake

THE
GOOD
MOTHERS

The True Story of the Women Who Took on
the World's Most Powerful Mafia

❧

ALEX
PERRY

𝒲𝓂
WILLIAM MORROW
An Imprint of HarperCollinsPublishers

HarperCollins books may be purchased for educational, business, or sales promotional use. For information, please email the Special Markets Department at SPsales@harpercollins.com.

Originally published in the United Kingdom in 2018 by HarperCollins UK.

A hardcover edition of this book was published in 2018 by William Morrow, an imprint of HarperCollins Publishers.

FIRST WILLIAM MORROW PAPERBACK EDITION PUBLISHED 2019.

Maps by Martin Brown

The Library of Congress has catalogued a previous edition as follows:

Names: Perry, Alex, author.
Title: The good mothers : the true story of the women who took on the world's most powerful mafia / Alex Perry.
Description: New York, NY : William Morrow, 2018. |
Identifiers: LCCN 2018000498 (print) | LCCN 2018013643 (ebook) | ISBN 9780062655639 (ebook) | ISBN 0062655639 (ebook) | ISBN 9780062655608 (hardback) | ISBN 0062655604 (hardcover)
Subjects: LCSH: Mafia—Italy. | Women and the mafia—Italy. | BISAC: TRUE CRIME / Organized Crime. | BIOGRAPHY & AUTOBIOGRAPHY / Criminals & Outlaws.
Classification: LCC HV6452.5 (ebook) | LCC HV6452.5 .P47 2018 (print) | DDC 364.106092/520945—dc23
LC record available at https://lccn.loc.gov/2018000498

ISBN 978-0-06-265561-5 (pbk.)

19 20 21 22 23   RS/LSC   10 9 8 7 6 5 4 3 2 1

For the good daughters

and for Tess, always

CONTENTS

ACT ONE: *A Vanishing in Milan*

ACT TWO: *Rebellion in Rosarno*

ACT THREE: *Italy Awakes*

CAMPANIA

BASILICATA

Gulf of Taranto

Tyrrhenian Sea

Crati

CORIGLIANO CALABRO

Sila Mountains

COSENZA

Neto

PAGLIARELLE

PETILIA POLICASTRO

CROTONE

LAMEZIA TERME

BOTRICELLO

CATANZARO

Stromboli

VIBO MARINA

VIBO VALENTIA

Lipari Islands

ROSARNO

GIOIA TAURO

POLISTENA

RIZZICONI

PALMI

Aspromonte Mountains

SIDERNO

LOCRI

MESSINA

SAN LUCA

REGGIO CALABRIA

Mediterranean Sea

Sicily

Straits of Messina

Etna

0   20 miles

0   20 km

AUTHOR'S NOTE

To ASSIST THE English-language reader, I have used anglicized place names: Florence, not Firenze, for example. By contrast, I have observed Italian custom when it comes to individuals' names. Maria Concetta Cacciola, for instance, becomes Concetta, or 'Cetta, at the second mention. In another difference from Anglo-Saxon custom, Italian women retain their fathers' surnames after marriage. Thus Lea Garofalo kept her name after she married Carlo Cosco but the couple's daughter was called Denise Cosco.

ACT ONE

❧

A Vanishing in Milan

I

T HE SYMBOL OF Milan is a giant serpent devouring a screaming child.[1] The first city of northern Italy has had other to-
tems: a woolly boar, a golden Madonna, and, more recently, the
designer labels that make Milan the fashion capital of the world.
But the eight-hundred-year-old image of a curled snake sinking
its fangs into the writhing, blood-soaked body of an infant has remained its most popular emblem, adorning flags and bas-reliefs on
the city walls, the Alfa Romeo badge, and the Inter Milan jersey. It's
an oddly menacing standard for a people more normally associated
with family and food, and a strangely crude one for a city whose artistry reaches the sublime heights of da Vinci's *The Last Supper*—and
most Milanese generally profess ignorance of its meaning. In more
candid moments, however, some will confess they suspect that the
image owes its endurance to the way it illuminates a dark truth at
the heart of their city: that the dynamism and accomplishment for
which Milan is famous depends on, among other things, whom you
are prepared to destroy.

In the four days they spent in Milan in late November 2009 before her father killed her mother, then erased any trace of her from
the world, Denise Cosco could almost believe her family had tran-
scended its own special darkness. Denise was seventeen. Her mother
was Lea Garofalo, a thirty-five-year-old mafioso's daughter, and her
father was Carlo Cosco, a thirty-nine-year-old cocaine smuggler.
Lea had married Carlo at sixteen, had Denise at seventeen, wit-

nessed Carlo and his brother kill a man in Milan at twenty-one, and helped send Carlo to the city's San Vittore prison at twenty-two. Denise had grown up on the run. For six years, from 1996 to 2002, Lea had hidden herself and her daughter away in the narrow, winding alleys of the medieval town of Bergamo in the foothills of the Alps. Lea had made it a game—two southern girls hiding out in Italy's gray north—and in time the two had become each other's world. When they walked Bergamo's cobbled streets, an elfin pair holding hands and curling their dark hair behind their ears, people took them for sisters.

One night in 2000, Lea glanced out of their apartment to see her old Fiat on fire. In 2002, after a scooter was stolen and their front door set alight, Lea told Denise she had a new game for them— and she walked hand in hand with her ten-year-old daughter into a carabinieri station, where she announced to the startled desk officer that she would testify against the mafia in return for witness protection. From 2002 to 2008, mother and daughter had lived in government safe houses. For the past eight months, for reasons Denise understood only in part, they'd been on their own once more. Three times Carlo's men had caught up with them. Three times Lea and Denise had escaped. But by spring 2009, Lea was exhausted and out of money, and she told Denise they were down to their two last options: either they somehow found the cash to flee to Australia, or Lea had to make peace with Carlo.

If neither was likely, reconciliation with Carlo at least seemed possible. The state had dropped its efforts to prosecute him using Lea's evidence, and while that infuriated her, it also meant she was no longer a threat to him. In April 2009, she sent her husband a message saying they should forgive and forget, and Carlo appeared to agree. The threats stopped and there were no more burned-out cars. Carlo began taking Denise on trips around the old country in Calabria. One September night he even talked Lea into a date and they drove down to the coast, talking into the early hours about the summer they'd met, all those years before.

So when in November 2009 Carlo invited his wife and daughter to spend a few days with him in Milan, and Denise, her hand over the phone, looked expectantly at her mother, Lea shrugged and said OK, they'd make a short break of it. Lea's memories of Milan in winter were of a cold, dismal city, the trees like black lightning against the sky, the icy winds tumbling like avalanches through the streets. But Denise would love Milan's shops, Lea and Carlo needed to talk about Denise's future, and ever since the summer Lea had found herself wondering about Carlo again. Twenty years earlier, he had held her face in his gorilla hands and promised to take her away from the mafia and all the killing—and Lea had believed him chiefly because he seemed to believe himself. Lea still wore a gold bracelet and necklace Carlo had given her back then. There was also no doubt that Carlo loved Denise. Maybe Denise was right, thought Lea. Perhaps the three of them *could* start over. The idea that Carlo's new geniality was part of some elaborate plot to catch her off guard was just too far-fetched. There were easier ways to kill someone.

LEA GAROFALO HAD outclassed Carlo Cosco from the start. Carlo had earned his position with the clans, but Lea was born a mafia princess, a Garofalo from Pagliarelle, daughter of east coast 'Ndrangheta aristocrats. Carlo was as broad and handsome as a bear, but Lea was altogether finer, her natural elegance accentuated by high cheekbones, a slim frame, and long, thick, curly dark hair. Carlo's stuttering grasp of Italian and his sullen, taciturn manner were never more noticeable than when he was with Lea, who spoke with the sophistication of a northerner and the passion of a southerner, laughing, arguing, and crying all in the same five minutes. In any other world, it would have been the natural order of things for

Lea to have walked out on Carlo a few years into their marriage and never looked back.

At least Carlo was making an effort not to gloat, thought Lea. He had a friend drop around one hundred euros for the train tickets to Milan. When Lea and Denise pulled into the city's central station, Mussolini's opulent glass-and-marble monument to northern order and power, Carlo himself picked them up in a black Audi and took them to the Hotel Losanna, a cozy backstreet place a block from the Corso Sempione, Milan's Champs-Élysées, and a short walk from their old family apartment on Viale Montello. And for the next four days, Carlo refused even to discuss the past. He didn't mention the 'Ndrangheta or how Lea had broken omertà or the way she almost destroyed everything for which he and his brothers had worked. Instead, Denise said the three of them enjoyed a "quiet and pleasant" mini vacation, the kind of family holiday they'd never had. Milan's Ferrari showrooms and Armani stores were a million miles from the goat pastures of Calabria, and Carlo seemed happy for his wife and daughter to enjoy it. With his coat tugged around his shoulders in the Milanese style, and Lea and Denise in jeans and thick down jackets, the three of them wandered the canals and the polished stone piazzas, eating pizza and cannoli and window-shopping in the nineteenth-century galleria across from Milan's flamboyant Gothic Duomo. Carlo paid for everything: clothes for Denise, dinners for the three of them, coffees and gelatos. Carlo even fixed it for the two women to get their eyebrows done at a beauty salon owned by his friend Massimo. Another time, when Lea was out of hash, Carlo summoned a cousin, Carmine Venturino, and made sure she didn't pay.

It wasn't perfect, of course. Denise was busy nurturing a teenage addiction to cigarettes and an aversion to heavy Italian food. Carlo, seeing his wife and daughter for only the second time in thirteen years and noticing how alike they were, couldn't help but be transported to the day, nineteen years earlier, when sixteen-year-old Lea had eloped with him to Milan. Meanwhile Lea was struggling to hold her nerve. She'd asked Carlo not to tell anyone she was in Milan but already he'd gone ahead and introduced her to Massimo and Carmine—and Carmine, for one, seemed more than just a friend to Carlo. She also had the recurrent feeling that they were being followed.

Lea found herself turning to an old habit. Denise's mother had long needed a joint or two just to get to sleep at night and, as the butts Denise found in their room attested, she was now also smoking steadily through the day. Sleep and peace were good, of course, and a real rarity for Lea. But you had to wonder at the wisdom of getting stoned around Carlo, a mafioso who had spent the last thirteen years chasing her across Italy trying to kill her.

Still, the trip went better than Lea might have feared. Initially, she had asked Denise to stay with her when Carlo was around because, Denise said, "if I was there, nothing was going to happen to her." Soon, however, Lea felt safe enough to be left alone with her husband. On the night of November 23, Denise went to bed early, and Lea and Carlo ate out alone. If the years had tightened Lea's nerves, time seemed to have relaxed Carlo. He was now a barrel of a man, with thick ears, a close-shaven head, and a boxer's nose, but his manner was gentle and attentive. When Lea mentioned Denise's plan to go to Milan University, Carlo offered to keep an eye on her. When Carlo volunteered that he'd set aside €200,000 for his daughter and Lea scolded him for the tens of thousands he'd spent trying to track them down—"and for no reason, because you always arrived too late!"—Carlo, unusually, took the slight well. After he paid the bill, Carlo took Lea on a drive through the city, the pair of them gliding through the empty streets in silence, just taking in the sights and each other's company. So distracted was Carlo that he ran a red light, delighting Lea, who was treated to the sight of the big mafioso trying to wriggle out of a ticket.

Watching them together in those days—Lea smoking and laughing, Carlo rubbing his bruiser's neck and letting a smile soften his frown—Denise said you could see they had been in love once. You might even believe it would work out for the three of them. The three of them "ate together as a family," Denise said later. Carlo was showing them how "caring and kind" he was. And there was no denying Lea still had it. Even without a cent in her pocket, and despite everything that had happened, her mother was still a rare and beautiful thing, a Calabrian forest sprite with the same pure spirit that had marked her out from every other girl in Pagliarelle all those years ago. Carlo, Denise felt sure, had to be falling for Lea again. "I had absolutely no bad thoughts about my father," she said.

LEA AND DENISE's last day in Milan was November 24, 2009. The two women were planning to take the 11:30 P.M. sleeper back to Calabria. In their room at the Losanna, Lea and Denise packed. To help take the bags to the station, Carlo brought round a big gray Chrysler he had borrowed from a friend.

As he loaded their cases, Carlo asked Denise whether she'd like to eat that evening with her uncle Giuseppe, her aunt Renata, and their two boys, eighteen-year-old Domenico and Andrea, fifteen. Denise should grab the chance to spend time with her family, said Carlo. A night alone would also give her parents the chance to discuss a few last things.

Denise agreed. She and Lea then walked into town to do some final shopping. It was an overcast day, only just above freezing, and a dull chill echoed off the granite buildings. CCTV later showed Lea in a black jacket with its furry collar turned in and Denise in a thick white jacket with her hood up and a black backpack over the top. Mother and daughter wandered around the arcades, warming themselves in cafés and grabbing lunch at a McDonald's, just happy to be out together in the city and, for once, not looking over their shoulders.

An hour after dark, just before 6 P.M., Denise called Carlo. She and Lea were near the Arch of Peace in Sempione Park, not far from the hotel, she said. A few minutes later, Carlo arrived in the Chrysler, flicked on his hazard lights, and reminded Denise through the driver's window that she was expected for dinner with her cousins. Lea, who had already gotten in the car, didn't want to go. Even if she was getting on better with Carlo, she wanted nothing to do with his family. Carlo suggested he drop off Denise, then return to take Lea out for a quiet dinner. After everyone had eaten, Carlo and Lea would pick Denise up again and all three of them would head over to the station. The women agreed. "See you at the station, Mama," said Denise to Lea, as she jumped into the car. "Later," replied Lea, getting out. "I'm going to have a drink."

Carlo drove Denise to No. 6 Viale Montello on the edge of Milan's Chinatown. A large, grubby six-story walk-up of more than a hundred apartments arranged around a drab internal courtyard, No. 6 Viale Montello had once belonged to the Ospedale Maggiore, one of Europe's first public hospitals when it opened in 1456. But the place had fallen into disrepair and was later abandoned, and in the 1980s the 'Ndrangheta from Pagliarelle had taken it over as a live-in hub for their heroin and cocaine business. The ground floor was now filled with half a dozen cheap Chinese stores—groceries, laundries, *tabacs*—whose metal shutters were decorated with extravagant graffiti. Most of the apartments were home to immigrants from China, Romania, Albania, Poland, Eritrea, and Nigeria, tenants whose own uncertain legal status ensured they were no friends of the law. The rest was given over to around a dozen mafia families. Carlo, Lea, and Denise had lived in one apartment in the early 1990s. Carlo's elder brothers Vito and Giuseppe were still installed in others with their wives and children. It was to these rooms that tons of cocaine and heroin were transported every year before being repackaged and shipped north into Europe.

Carlo left Denise with her aunt Renata at 6:30 P.M. at Bar Barbara, a Chinese-run café on Piazza Baiamonti at the end of Viale Montello, then drove off to fetch Lea. Denise ordered an espresso. Renata said dinner was minestrone and cold cuts. Denise told her aunt she wasn't all that hungry, so she and Renata went to an Asian supermarket a few doors down to buy her a small tray of sushi. Denise tried to pay but Renata wouldn't hear of it.

Looking back, Denise would say it was around then that the make-believe stopped. Back at her cousins' second-floor apartment in Viale Montello, Denise ate her sushi alone. Then she sat with Renata, Domenico, and Andrea as they had their soup and meat in front of the TV. It was far from the family get-together Carlo had described; her cousins were in and out all evening. Her uncle Giuseppe wasn't even home, which was doubly strange as there was a big game that night, AC Milan away at Barcelona. There was something else, too. When Denise had spent time with Renata before, she remembered thinking that her aunt was a jealous wife, always calling Giuseppe to ask where he was, who he was with, what he was doing, and when he was coming home. That night, Denise noticed, Renata didn't call Giuseppe once.

Denise, who after years on the run had developed a sixth sense for these things, began to feel something was off. Around 8 P.M. she called her mother. Lea's phone was unobtainable. That was odd, too. Lea always made sure her phone was charged. Denise sent her mother a text. "Something like 'Where the hell are you?'" Denise said later in court.

The big game started at 8:40 P.M. Barcelona scored quickly. Denise texted Lea a couple more times. Still no answer. Renata told Denise not to worry about smoking in front of the family—no one would tell Carlo—and as the evening wore on, Denise found she was chain-smoking. Her cousins groaned as Barcelona scored a second goal just before halftime. Sometime after 9 P.M., just when Denise was beginning to feel truly unnerved, Giuseppe stuck his head around the door, registered the score and Denise's presence, then left again. A few minutes after that, Denise's phone rang. It was Carlo. He would be over in a few minutes to pick up Denise to take her to the station. She should wait for him downstairs at her uncle Vito's first-floor apartment.

Denise kissed her cousins and her aunt good-bye, then took the stairs to Vito's. Carlo hadn't arrived so Vito's wife, Giuseppina, made coffee. It was after 9:30 P.M. now—more than three hours since Denise had last heard from her mother—and she was fighting a rising sense of panic. After a while, Vito appeared at the door. Behind him, down the corridor, Denise caught a glimpse of her father at the entrance to another apartment. She hadn't even known Carlo was in the building. Instead of fetching her, he was talking to his brother Giuseppe and two other men. Carlo glanced at his daughter, and called over that she should wait for him in the car. Denise went down to the street and found the Chrysler. Lea wasn't in it. By now, it was 10 P.M. When Carlo got in, Denise asked him immediately: "Where's my mother?"

"I left her around the corner," replied Carlo. "She didn't want to come in and see everyone."

Carlo drove in silence to a street behind Viale Montello. Denise regarded him. He looked upset, she thought. The way he was driving, barely focusing on the road. "*Scossato*," she said later. Shaken.

When they turned the corner, Lea wasn't there. Denise was about to speak when Carlo cut her off. Lea wasn't waiting for them, said Carlo, because what had happened was that Lea had asked him for money and he had given her two hundred euros, but she had screamed at him that it wasn't enough, so he had given her another two hundred and she'd stormed off anyway. They hadn't eaten dinner. Actually, said Carlo, he hadn't eaten at all.

Carlo fell silent. Denise said nothing.

"You know what your mother's like," said Carlo. "There's nothing anyone can do."

Carefully, Denise asked her father, "Where is my mother now?"

"I've no idea," replied Carlo.

Denise thought her father was a terrible liar. "I didn't believe him for a nanosecond," she said. "Not one word." All his kindness over the last few days, all the opening doors, fetching coats, and driving them around—his whole Milanese bella figura act—all of it was gone. Carlo appeared to have regressed. He seemed raw, almost primal. He wouldn't even look at her. And suddenly Denise understood. The dinner with her cousins. The calls to Lea that wouldn't go through. The endless hanging around. The urgent discussion between the men in the apartment opposite. Lea had been right all along. Denise, who had begged her mother to let them go to Milan, had been catastrophically wrong. "I *knew*," said Denise. "I knew immediately."

Denise understood two more things. First: it was already too late. Denise hadn't spoken to her mother for three and a half hours. Lea never turned off her phone for that long and certainly not before telling Denise. *It's done*, thought Denise. *He's already had time.*

Second: confronting her father would be suicide. If she was to survive, in that moment she had to accept Lea's fate and fix it in her mind not as possible or reversible but as certain and final. At the same time, she had to convince her father that she had no idea about what had happened, when in reality she had no doubt at all. "I understood there was very little I could do for my mother now," said Denise. "But I couldn't let *him* understand *me*." Inwardly, Denise forced her mind into a tight, past-tense dead end. "They've done what they had to do," she told herself. "This was how it was always going to end. This was inevitable." Outwardly, she played herself as she might have been a few minutes earlier: a worried daughter looking for her missing mother. The speed of events helped. It was absurd, even unreal, how in a moment Denise had lost her mother, her best friend, and the only person who had ever truly known her. She didn't have to pretend she was struggling to catch up. She even had the feeling that if she willed it hard enough, she might bring Lea back to life.

It was in this state, with Carlo in a daze and Denise acting like there was still hope in the world, that father and daughter drove all over Milan. "We went to all the places we had been," said Denise. "Where we'd had a drink, where we'd eaten pizza, the hotel where we had stayed, over to Sempione Park. We went to a local café, a shopping center, the McDonald's where we had lunch and the train station, where my father bought two tickets for my mother and me. We went all over the city. I was phoning and texting my mother all the time. And of course, we found nothing and nobody."

Around midnight, just after the train to Calabria had departed, Denise's phone rang. Denise was startled to read the word "Mama" on the screen. But the voice on the other end belonged to her aunt Marisa, Lea's sister in Pagliarelle, and Denise remembered that she had borrowed her cousin's phone before leaving for Milan.

Gathering herself, Denise told Marisa that Lea was nowhere to be found and that they had just missed their train back to Calabria. "Have you heard from her?" Denise asked her aunt. "Did she call you?"

Aunt Marisa replied she had missed a call from Lea sometime after 6:30 P.M. but hadn't been able to reach her since. Marisa was calling to check that everything was all right. Denise replied that Lea's phone had been dead all night.

"They made her disappear," Marisa told Denise, just like that, with Carlo sitting right next to Denise in the car.

"She was so matter-of-fact," Denise said. "Like she assumed we all expected it. Like we all felt the same."

Denise and Carlo kept driving around Milan until 1:30 A.M. Finally, Denise said there was nowhere else to look and they should file a report with the police. Carlo drove her to a carabinieri station. The officer told Denise she had to wait forty-eight hours to make out a missing person's report. With Carlo there, Denise couldn't tell the officer that she and Lea had hidden for years from the man standing next to her, so she thanked the officer and they returned to Renata's, where her aunt opened the door half asleep in her dressing gown.

Renata was surprised to hear Lea was even in town. "We came up here together," Denise explained. "We didn't tell you because we didn't want to cause any trouble." The three of them stood in the doorway for a second. Denise found herself looking at her father's clothes. He'd had them on all evening. It had been in that jacket, thought Denise. That shirt. Those shoes.

Carlo broke the silence by saying he would keep looking for Lea a little while longer and headed back to his car. Renata said Denise could sleep in Andrea's room. To reach it, Denise had to walk through Renata and Giuseppe's bedroom. "I could see Giuseppe wasn't there," she said later. "And I ignored it. I ignored everything *for a year*. I pretended nothing had happened. I ate with these people. I worked in their pizzeria. I went on holiday with them. I played with their children. Even when I knew what they had done. I had to be so careful with what I said. They were saying my mother was alive even after I hadn't seen her for more than a year. I just made out like I didn't know. But I knew."

II

IN CALABRIA, LEA Garofalo's disappearance needed no explanation. The mafia even had a term for people who, one day, just vanished: *lupara bianca* (white shotgun), a killing that left no corpse, seen by no one. In Pagliarelle, the remote mountain village on the arch of Italy's foot where Lea and Carlo were born, people knew never to speak Lea's name again.

They wouldn't be able to forget her entirely. Lea's modest first-floor studio, its shutters and drainpipes painted bubblegum pink, was only yards from the main piazza. But the four hundred villagers of Pagliarelle had learned long ago to live with their ghosts. In three decades, thirty-five men and women had been murdered in mafia vendettas in Pagliarelle and the nearby town of Petilia Policastro, including Lea's father, Antonio, her uncle Giulio, and her brother Floriano. In such a place, in such a family, Lea's disappearance could seem inevitable, even a kind of resolution. Years later, her sister Marisa would look up at Lea's first-floor window from the street below and say: "Lea wanted freedom. She never bowed her head. But for people who follow the 'Ndrangheta, this choice is considered very eccentric. Very serious. You want to be free? You pay with your life." Really, Marisa was saying, there was nothing anyone could do.[1]

Alessandra Cerreti knew many of her colleagues shared that view. When she arrived in Calabria from Milan seven months earlier as the province's newest magistrate, she had been struck by how many Calabrians still accepted the 'Ndrangheta as an immutable fact of life. Outside southern Italy, the mafia was regarded as a movie or a novel, an entertaining, even glamorous legend that might once have held some historic truth but which, in a time of more sophisticated concerns such as financial crises or climate change or terrorism, felt like a fable from a bygone era. Not so in Calabria. Like their more famous cousins in Sicily and Naples, the 'Ndrangheta had been founded in the nineteenth century. But while the Sicilians, in particular, had seen their power steadily eroded by a state crackdown and popular resistance, the 'Ndrangheta had grown ever stronger. The organization was still run by its original founders, 141 ancient shepherding and orange-farming families who ruled the isolated valleys and hill towns of Calabria. Its foot soldiers were also still quietly extorting billions of euros a year from Calabria's shopkeepers, restaurant owners, and gelato makers—and murdering the occasional hardheaded carabinieri or judge or politician who stood in their way. What had transformed the 'Ndrangheta, however, was a new internationalism. It now smuggled 70 to 80 percent of the cocaine in Europe. It plundered the Italian state and the European Union for tens of billions more. It brokered illegal arms deals to criminals, rebels, and terrorists around the world, including several sides in the Syrian civil war. By the prosecutors' count, by 2009 the 'Ndrangheta's empire took in fifty countries, a quarter of the planet, from Albania to Togo, linking a mob war in Toronto to a lawyer's assassination in Melbourne, and the reported ownership of an entire Brussels neighborhood to a cocaine-delivering pizzeria in Queens, New York, called Cucino a Modo Mio (I Cook My Own Way). By the dawn of the second decade of the new millennium, the 'Ndrangheta was, by almost any measure, the most powerful criminal syndicate on earth.

If ruthless violence was the fuel of this global empire, astounding wealth was its result. The prosecutors' best guess was that every year the organization amassed revenues of $50 billion to $100 billion,[2] equivalent to up to 3.5 percent of Italian GDP, or twice the annual revenues of Fiat, Alfa Romeo, Lancia, Ferrari, and Maserati combined. So much money was there that cleaning and hiding it required a whole second business. And so good had the Calabrians become at money laundering, pushing billions through restaurants and construction companies, small offshore banks and large financial institutions, even the Dutch flower market and the European chocolate trade, that Alessandra's fellow prosecutors were picking up indications that other organized crime groups—Eastern Europeans, Russians, Asians, Africans, Latin Americans—were paying the 'Ndrangheta to do the same with their fortunes. That meant the 'Ndrangheta was managing the flow of hundreds of billions or even trillions of illicit dollars around the world.

And it was this, the 'Ndrangheta's dispersal of global crime's money across the planet, that ensured the Calabrians were in everyone's lives. Millions of people lived in their buildings, worked in their companies, shopped in their stores, ate in their pizzerias, traded in their companies' shares, did business with their banks, and elected politicians and parties they funded. As rich as the biggest businesses or banks or governments, 'Ndrangheta moved markets and changed lives from New York to London to Tokyo to São Paulo to Johannesburg. In the first two decades of the new millennium, it was hard to imagine another human enterprise with such influence over so many. Most remarkable of all: almost no one had ever heard of it.

THE 'NDRANGHETA—PRONOUNCED *un-drung-get-a*, a word derived from the Greek *andranghateia*, meaning "society of men of honor and valor"—was a mystery even to many Italians.[3] In truth, this ignorance was due as much to perception as deception. Many northern Italians had trouble even imagining wealth or achievement in the south. And the contrast *was* striking. The north had Florence and Venice, prosciutto and parmigiana, Barolo and balsamic, the Renaissance and the Enlightenment, AC Milan and Inter Milan, Lamborghini and Maserati, Gucci and Prada, Caravaggio, Michelangelo, Pavarotti, Puccini, Galileo, da Vinci, Dante, Machiavelli, Marco Polo, Christopher Columbus, and the Pope. The south had lemons, mozzarella, and winter sun.

This was, Alessandra knew, the great lie of a united Italy. Two thousand years earlier, the south had been a fount of European civilization. But by the time the northern general Giuseppe Garibaldi amalgamated the Italian peninsula into a single nation in 1861, he was attempting to join the literate, the industrial, and the cultured with the feudal, the unschooled, and the unsewered. The contradiction had proved too great. The north prospered in trade and commerce. The south deteriorated and millions of southerners left, emigrating to northern Europe, the Americas, or Australia.

In time, the provinces south of Rome had come to be known as the Mezzogiorno, the land where the midday sun blazed overhead, a dry, torpid expanse of peasant farmers and small-boat fishermen stretching from Abruzzo through Naples to the island of Lampedusa, 110 kilometers from North Africa. For much of the south, such a sweeping description was a clumsy stereotype. But for Calabria, the toe, it was accurate. The Romans had called it Bruttium, and for 300 kilometers from north to south, Calabria was little more than thornbush scrub and bare rock mountains interspersed with groves of gnarled olives and fields of fine gray dust. It was eerily empty: more than a century of emigration had ensured there were four times as many Calabrians and their descendants outside Italy as in their homeland. When she was driven out of Reggio and into the countryside, Alessandra passed a succession of empty towns, deserted villages, and abandoned farms. It felt like the aftermath of a giant disaster—which, if you considered the centuries of grinding destitution, it was.

Still, there was a hard beauty to the place. High up in the mountains, wolves and wild boar roamed forests of beech, cedar, and holly oak. Below the peaks, deep cracks in the rock opened up into precipitous ravines through which ice-cold rivers raged toward the sea. As the incline eased, woods gave way to vines and summer pastures, followed by estuary flats filled with lemon and orange orchards. In summer, the sun would scorch the earth, turning the soil to powder and the prickly thorn grass to roasted gold. In winter, snow would cover the mountains and storms would batter the cliffs on the coast and drag away the beaches.

Alessandra wondered whether it was the violence of their land that bred such ferocity in Calabrians. They lived in ancient towns built on natural rock fortresses. In their fields, they grew burning chili and intoxicating jasmine and raised big-horned cows and mountain goats that they roasted whole over hearths stoked with knotted vine wood. The men hunted boar with shotguns and swordfish with harpoons. The women spiced sardines with hot peppers and dried trout in the wind for months before turning the meat into a pungent brown stew. For Calabrians, there was also little divide between the holy and the profane. On saints' days, morning processions would be followed by afternoon street feasts at which the women would serve giant plates of *maccheroni* with *'nduja*, a hot, soft pepper sausage the color of ground brick, washed down with a black wine that stained the lips and seared the throat. As the sun began to sink, the men would dance the tarantella, named after the effects of the poisonous bite of the wolf spider. To the tune of a mandolin, the beat of a goatskin tambourine, and a song about thwarted love or a mother's love or the thrill of a hot spurt of blood from a stabbed traitor's heart, the men would compete for hours to see who could dance fastest and longest. "The Greece of Italy," said the newspa-

pers, though in reality that was an insult to Greece. Unlike its Ionian neighbor, southern Italy's legal economy hadn't grown since
the millennium. Unemployment among the young, at more than one
in two, was among the worst in Europe.

THE SOUTH HAD experienced one kind of development, however.
Many southerners saw Garibaldi's creation of a northern-dominated
Italian state as an act of colonization. Already damned for who
they were, they cared little for northern opinions of what they did.
Across the Mezzogiorno, from the birth of the Republic, brigands
were commonplace. Some organized themselves into family groups.
In the century and a half since unification, a few hundred families
in Naples, Sicily, and Calabria had grown rich. And as criminal rebels who claimed to be secretly subverting an occupying state, they
used the intimacy and loyalty of family and a violent code of honor
and righteous resistance to draw a veil of omertà over their wealth.
Even in 2009, Calabria's crime bosses still dressed like orange farmers. It was only in the last few years that the Italian government
had begun to grasp that these brutish men, with their bird-faced
women and reckless sons, were among the world's great criminal
masterminds.

There was, at least, no mystery to who ran the 'Ndrangheta.
The south's lack of progress was social as much as material. Tradition held that each family was a miniature feudal kingdom in which
men and boys reigned supreme. The men granted their women little
authority or independence, nor even much of a life beyond an existence as vassals of family property and honor. Like medieval kings,
fathers paired their girls off as teenagers to seal clan alliances. Beatings of daughters and wives were routine. To men, women were de-
sirable but feckless, not to be trusted to stay faithful or direct their
own lives but to be kept strictly in line for their own good. Women

who were untrue, even to the memory of a husband dead for fifteen years, were killed, and it would be their fathers, brothers, sons, and husbands who did it. Only blood could wash clean the family honor, the men would say. Often they burned the bodies or dissolved them in acid to be sure of erasing the family shame.

Such a perversion of family would have been extraordinary in any time or place. It was especially so in Italy, where family was close to sacred.[4] The severity of the misogyny prompted some prosecutors to compare the 'Ndrangheta with Islamist militants. Like ISIS or Boko Haram, 'Ndranghetisti routinely terrorized their women and slaughtered their enemies in the service of an immutable code of honor and righteousness.

So, yes, Calabria's prosecutors would say, the life of an 'Ndrangheta woman like Lea Garofalo was tragic. And, yes, the 'Ndrangheta's inhuman sexism was one more reason to destroy it. But that didn't mean the women were much use in that fight. Almost from the day in April 2009 that Alessandra arrived from Milan, many of her colleagues told her the women in the mafia were just more of its victims. "The women don't matter," they said.[5] When they heard of Lea's disappearance, they conceded the news was heartbreaking, especially for those who had known Lea and Denise in witness protection. But Lea's death was merely a symptom of the problem, they insisted. It had no bearing on the cause.

Alessandra disagreed. She claimed no special insight into family dynamics. Alessandra was forty-one, married without children, and her appearance—slim, meticulously dressed, with short, straight hair in a sharp, boyish part—emphasized poise and professionalism. When it came to The Family, however, Alessandra argued that it was only logical women would have a substantial role in a criminal organization structured around kin. Family was the lifeblood of the mafia. Like an unseen, uncut umbilical cord, family was how the mafia delivered nourishing, fortifying power to itself. And at the heart of any family was a mother. Besides, argued Alessandra, if the women really didn't matter, why would the men risk it all to kill them? The women *had* to be more than mere victims. As a Sicilian and a woman inside the Italian judiciary, Alessandra also knew something about patriarchies that belittled women even as they relied on them. Most judicial officials missed the importance of 'Ndrangheta women, she said, because most of them were men. "And Italian men underestimate all women," she said. "It's a real problem."

At the time Lea Garofalo went missing, evidence to support Alessandra's views was on display in every Italian newspaper. For two years, the press had filled its pages with the lurid allegations and distinctly conservative attitudes of a state prosecutor in Perugia named Giuliano Mignini. Mignini had accused an American student, Amanda Knox—with the assistance of two men, one of whom was Knox's boyfriend of five days—of murdering her British flatmate, Meredith Kercher. Mignini alleged the two men were in thrall to Knox's satanic allure. Taking his lead from Mignini, a lawyer in the case described Knox as a "she-devil . . . Lucifer-like, demonic . . . given over to lust." Fifty-nine years old, a devout Catholic and father of four daughters, Mignini later told a documentary maker that though the forensic evidence against Knox was scant, her "uninhibited" character and "lack of morals" had convinced him. "She would bring boys home," he mused. "Pleasure at any cost. This is at the heart of most crime."[6]

In the end, Knox and her boyfriend were acquitted on appeal, twice, and the prosecutors castigated by Italy's Supreme Court for presenting a case with "stunning flaws." But at the time of Lea's disappearance, Knox was days from being found guilty for the first time and Mignini's version of events—that an unmarried American woman who had slept with seven men was just the kind of fiendish deviant to have sex slaves murder her roommate—was the accepted truth.

Alessandra didn't lecture her colleagues on female emancipation. In their own lives they were free to hold whatever views they wished, and she wasn't about to let any of them think she was asking for special treatment. But when it came to cracking the omertà that cloaked Europe's biggest mafia, Alessandra argued that the state had pragmatic reasons to care about the prejudice of gangsters. The 'Ndrangheta was as near-perfect a criminal organization as any of them would ever encounter. It had been around for a century and a half, employed thousands around the world, and made tens of billions a year. It was not only the single biggest obstacle standing in the way of Italy finally becoming a modern, united nation, but also a diabolical perversion of the Italian family, which was the heart and essence of the nation. And yet until a few years earlier, the Italian state had been barely aware of its existence. When she arrived in Reggio Calabria, no one at the Palace of Justice could give Alessandra more than rough estimates of how many men the 'Ndrangheta employed or where it operated or even, to the nearest $50 billion a year, how much money it made. The kind of free will and independence that Lea Garofalo had shown, and the murderous chauvinism rained down on her as a result, represented one of the few times the 'Ndrangheta had ever broken cover. At a time when prosecutors were just beginning to understand "how big the 'Ndrangheta had become and how much we had underestimated it," said Cerreti, women informants were an invaluable, untapped source of knowledge with unimpeachable motivations for talking. The 'Ndrangheta's violent bigotry wasn't just a tragedy, said Alessandra. It was a grand flaw. With the right kind of nurturing, it might become an existential crisis. "Freeing their women," said Alessandra, "is the way to bring down the 'Ndrangheta."

III

ALESSANDRA CERRETI WAS born on April 29, 1968, in the eastern Sicilian port of Messina.[1] In twenty-two years away, she'd only rarely visited her hometown. Now she was living in Reggio Calabria, Messina's sister city, three miles across the water, and rarely out of sight of it. She realized she'd never noticed how Messina changed through the day. At dawn, a pink light would lift its piazzas, boulevards, and palm trees out of a purple gloom. At midday, the sun painted the scene in primary colors: blue sea, red roofs, yellow hills, and the white cone of Mount Etna to the south. Sunset was a languid affair, as the wind slackened and Messina sank back into the dusk under clouds edged with orange filigree. Night ushered in a Mediterranean glamour, a fathomless black set off by a necklace of white lights strung like pearls along the coast road.

It was a scene that had drawn artists and writers for generations. Those raised beside the Strait of Messina, however, have long understood that the truth of the place is in what lies beneath. The Strait is a narrow, plunging abyss formed when Africa and Europe collided fifty million years ago and Africa bent down toward the center of the earth. In this underwater chasm, the rushing currents created when the Ionian and Tyrrhenian Seas meet make for some of the most disturbed waters in all the oceans. Boiling whirlpools and sucking vortexes trap yachts and fishing boats. Slewing tides send ferries and freighters skidding sideways toward the rocks. Those peering into the depths can see startled bug-eyed fish, and even sharks and whales, shot to the surface from the seafloor 250 meters below. The swirling winds of the Strait reflect this turmoil, inverting the normal pattern of hot air over cold to create an optical illusion called the fata morgana, in which boats and land on the horizon appear to float upside down in the sky.

On land, human history has mirrored this natural upheaval. Reggio and Messina were founded by Greek colonists whose king, Italos, eventually gave the country its name. But for three millennia, the Strait has been continuously conquered and appropriated, first by Syracusans in 387 B.C., then by Campanians, Romans, Vandals, Lombards, Goths, Byzantines, Arabs, Normans, Hohenstaufen German kings, Angevins, Aragonese, Spanish Habsburgs (twice), Ottomans, Barbary pirates, and reactionary French Bourbons and Bonapartists, before finally, in 1860 and 1861, Reggio and Messina were captured by Giuseppe Garibaldi in the war that unified Italy. The wealth of its occupiers had given Messina and Reggio their ancient, yellow-stone harbors, their Arabic street names, and an early artistry that found exquisite expression in the Riace Bronzes, two sculptures of naked, bearded warriors dating from 450 B.C. discovered by a snorkeler off the Calabrian coast in 1972. But this early globalism also had its costs. It was through the Strait's ports that the Black Death entered Europe from Asia in 1346, going on to wipe out two-thirds of the continent's population. In 1743, by which time humanity's numbers had barely recovered, plague returned a second time, killing 48,000 in Messina alone. Next to those disasters, the deadly earthquakes of 1783 and 1894 were largely forgotten, though not the quake and ensuing twelve-meter tsunami of December 28, 1908, which flattened both Reggio and Messina, killing 200,000 people. Rebuilt entirely, the twin cities were leveled again by Allied bombers in 1943.

Assailed by tempests, consumed by catastrophe, the people of the Strait could be forgiven for thinking they were cursed. Many used magic and folk wisdom to account for their suffering. In the *Odyssey*, Homer had written about two sea monsters that lived on opposing sides of the Strait. Surging out from Calabria, the six-headed Scylla would snatch sailors from the decks of their ships, while from Sicily Charybdis would suck entire boats under the waves with her insatiable thirst. People explained Etna's deadly eruptions by describing the mountain as the home of Vulcan, or sometimes of Cyclops, both of them angry, thundering types with low regard for mortals. The tremors people felt under their feet were said to be the shifting grip of Colapesce, the son of a fisherman who took a deep dive one day, saw that Sicily was held up by a single, crumbling column, and stayed in the depths to prevent its collapse. The floating islands that appeared over Reggio, meanwhile, were thought to be glimpses of Avalon, to which the fairy-witch Morgan le Fay (after whom the fata morgana was named) spirited a dying King Arthur. Up there, too, it was said, was *The Flying Dutchman*, a ghost ship doomed to sail the oceans forever.

Alessandra would carry the feel of the Strait with her all her life. It was there in the way a winter's chill would remind her of the morning breeze off the city docks or how the first days of summer would almost instantly change her forearms from alabaster to honey. It was there, too, in her distaste for the way people often seemed to prefer fiction over truth. While most children were delighted to find themselves growing up in a world of gods and castles in the sky, Alessandra was unmoved. Stories of monsters and fairies were entertaining, but they also obscured the deadly reality of the Strait. Every summer, Messina's coastguardsmen heaved a steady procession of dripping, blanketed stretchers onto the docks. How could these regrettable, preventable deaths be part of some mystical grand plan? There was little logic, either, in the other spurious legends that Sicilians would spin to glorify their island. In 1975, when Alessandra was seven, a twenty-six-year-old from Messina called Giovanni Fiannacca swam to Calabria in thirty minutes and fifty seconds, a record that was to stand for forty years. Alessandra's neighbors proclaimed Fiannacca the greatest distance swimmer in Sicily, perhaps even of all time. The reality, as most Sicilians knew, was that he had timed his crossing to coincide with a particularly strong east–west tide that would have carried a rubber duck to Calabria.

In another life, in another land, Alessandra might have forgiven these illusions and the credulous adults who repeated them. But her home was the birthplace of Cosa Nostra. By the 1970s, the Sicilian mafia was operating all but unopposed on the island. It was a state within a state, extracting taxes via extortion, dividing up public contracts among mafia companies, settling disputes, delivering punishments—and lying, cheating, and murdering to preserve its position. Yet no one said a thing. To inquisitive outsiders, Sicilians would claim the mafia was a fable, a cliché, or even a groundless slur. Among themselves, proponents would characterize it in more mythic terms, as an ancient Sicilian brotherhood built on courage, honor, and sacrifice. Never mind that the mafia itself cooked up these romantic legends and embellished them with more recent folklore, such as their story about how mafiosi rode Allied tanks to liberate Sicily in the Second World War. Never mind that in their hearts most Sicilians knew they were being lied to. Just as the islanders found it hard to accept the indifference shown to their city by Nature and Man, so most preferred not to confront the truth that their fellow Sicilians had grown rich by robbing and killing them.

Alessandra lamented her neighbors' complicity in these deceptions even as she understood it. Decades later, reading sensational newspaper accounts of mafia adventures, she would react the same way she had as a child. The facts about the tyranny and the killing were plain. Why dress them up as something else? What Alessandra truly detested, however, was the way outsiders assisted the mafia's mythmaking. A year after she was born, Mario Puzo, an American pulp magazine writer, sold the screenplay adapted from his book *The Godfather* to Paramount for $100,000. Two years later, Francis Ford Coppola was directing Al Pacino in the movie on location in Savoca, twenty-five miles south of Messina.

The film, one of the most successful of all time, contained elements of truth. The Corleone family *was* a crime syndicate from south of Palermo. There also *had* been a disagreement inside the mafia in the 1950s over whether to enter narcotics trafficking, a dispute that did lead to an internal war. What Alessandra found unforgivable was the way Hollywood used southern Italians' daily tragedy as a device to make its dramas more compelling. She shared none of Coppola's empathy for the men who murdered their wives and girlfriends. She could make no sense of the women, either, passive, giddy creatures who allowed their men to lead them from love to betrayal to an early death. Nor did she recognize any of the film's somber majesty or mournful grandiloquence in the blood that stained the gutters as she walked to school. When Alessandra was ten, two ambitious bosses, Salvatore Riina ("the butcher of Corleone") and Bernardo Provenzano ("the tractor," so called because, in the words of one informer, "he mows people down"), began what became an all-out mafia war by assassinating several Sicilian rivals.[2] The decade and a half that followed, spanning most of Alessandra's adolescence, became known as *la mattanza*, "the slaughter." More than 1,700 Sicilians died. Mafiosi were shot in their cars, in restaurants, as they walked down the street. In a single day in Palermo in November 1982, twelve mafiosi were killed in twelve separate assassinations. Yet through it all, foreign tourists would arrive in Messina asking for directions to the Godfather's village. No, thought Alessandra. This was a hideous, willful delusion. It was a lie. It had to be corrected.

When Alessandra was eight, her teacher asked her class to write an essay about what they wanted to be when they grew up. "Let your minds wander," said the teacher. "You can be anything at all, anywhere in the world." Excited by the chance to escape Messina's violence and fear, most of Alessandra's classmates wrote whimsies about becoming princesses or moving to America or flying a rocket to the moon. Alessandra said she would be staying put. *I want to be an anti-mafia prosecutor*, she wrote. *I want to put gangsters behind bars.*

IT WAS TO pursue her ambition that in 1987, at the age of nineteen, Alessandra took the train north to become a law student. Pulling in to Rome's central station the next day, she found herself in a different nation. But Alessandra quickly assimilated. She graduated in 1990, qualified as a magistrate in 1997, and quickly became a specialist in organized crime. Over the next twelve years, she investigated the 'Ndrangheta's expansion across northern Italy, assisted the prosecution of billion-euro tax evasion in the art world, sat as a judge in a high-profile terrorist recruitment case, and, on a quiet weekend, married a rising anti-mafia carabinieri officer.[3]

No one was surprised that Alessandra married into the job. Few outsiders would tolerate the life of a mafia prosecutor's spouse. The wide autonomy Italy's anti-mafia prosecutors enjoyed in their investigations was about the only freedom they possessed. The constant threat to her life required Alessandra to exist in isolation behind a wall of steel—literally, in the case of her office door and her armor-plated car—and for her to be escorted by four bodyguards twenty-four hours a day. Spontaneity was out of the question; all her movements were planned a day in advance. A normal life—meeting friends and family, eating out, shopping—was next to impossible. "We go nowhere with crowds because of the risk to others," said Alessandra. For the same reason, she and her husband—whose

identity she kept secr[...]
would have to fear fo[...]
me or my husband."

Alessandra didn't [...]
had come to accept [...]
needed to face the [...]
and glamour remai[...]
the facts. To some, [...]
living a gray half-[...]
She told herself sh[...]
victims, even fro[...]
blood and family [...]
was the enemy. She had to be the opp[...]
and dispassionate.

By forty-one, what once had been girlish obstinacy had matured into stoicism and self-possession. In her office in the Palace of Justice, Alessandra kept her desk clear and her office spartan. Besides a photograph of the legendary Sicilian prosecutors Giovanni Falcone and Paolo Borsellino, she hung only a graphite drawing of Lady Justice and a pastel of the Strait of Messina. Among her staff, the young female prosecutor's icy focus was a favorite topic of discussion. She wasn't scared or emotional, as some of the men had predicted. Rather, she was unwavering, scrupulous, and unnervingly calm— *legale*, they said—her rebukes all the more crushing for their dispassion, her smiles all the more disarming for their unexpectedness.

Inside this narrow, monotone life, Alessandra permitted herself a few indulgences. Every August she and her husband took off on a foreign holiday without their bodyguards, telling no one where they were going—"the only time I can be free," she said. On a shelf in her office, she kept a collection of snow globes, sent to her by friends from their travels in Europe. Alessandra also liked to dress well. To court, she wore slim, dark suits over plain white blouses.

To the office, she wore woolen w[...]
stretch jeans with a biker's jac[...]
dress, her toes and fingern[...]
gerine in summer. Thi[...]
Anti-mafia prosecut[...]
about freedom. T[...]
restrictions a[...]
thousand [...]
true st[...]
unyi[...]

nter shawls with leather boots, or
ket, or heels with a sleeveless summer
ils painted chocolate in winter and tan-
was not about looking good to the world.
rs were rarely seen by anyone. Rather, this was
o do her job and not be defined by it, to accept its
d not be beaten by them, to face the threats of ten
afiosi and respond with grace and elegance—that was
le and, in a world of male brutality, a display of adamant and
elding femininity.

THROUGHOUT HER TIME in the north, Alessandra had kept a close watch on the southern battle against the mafia. It had been a long and bloody fight. After the state tried to stem *la mattanza* in the 1980s, judges, policemen, carabinieri, politicians, and prosecutors became targets, too. On May 23, 1992, the mafia detonated half a ton of explosives under an elevated highway outside the city on which Giovanni Falcone, Italy's most celebrated anti-mafia prosecutor, was driving with his wife and three police bodyguards. The explosion was so big it registered on Sicily's earthquake monitors. Hearing the news of Falcone's assassination, his coprosecutor Paolo Borsellino, who had grown up in the same Palermo neighborhood and had always been somewhat in Falcone's shadow, remarked, "Giovanni beat me again." Two months later, Borsellino and five policemen were killed by a car bomb outside the home of Borsellino's mother in Palermo. Six houses were leveled and fifty-one cars, vans, and trucks set on fire.

Falcone's death was to Italians what President John F. Kennedy's was to Americans: everyone can remember where they were when they heard the news. To the tight group of Sicilians like Alessandra who had taken up the fight against Cosa Nostra, the loss of their two champions was deeply personal. At the time, Alessandra was a twenty-four-year-old law graduate in Rome who had just begun training to be a magistrate. Falcone's and Borsellino's sacrifices only made the two prosecutors seem more heroic. "They were the inspiration for a generation," she said. "Their deaths made us stronger." To this day, the two prosecutors remain the titans against whom all Italian prosecutors measure themselves. A picture of either Falcone or Borsellino, and generally both, hangs on the wall of every anti-mafia prosecutor's office in Italy, often accompanied by a famous Falcone one-liner. "The mafia is a human phenomenon and, like all human phenomena, it had a beginning, an evolution, and will also have an end," was one favorite. "He who doesn't fear death dies only once," was another.

In time, even Cosa Nostra would acknowledge that the murders had been a miscalculation. They gave the prosecutors' political masters no choice but to abandon attempts to negotiate a peace with the mafia and try to crush it instead. Tens of thousands of soldiers were dispatched to Sicily. The two prosecutors' deaths also prompted renewed appreciation of their achievements. The chief accomplishment of Falcone, Borsellino, and their two fellow prosecutors, Giuseppe di Lello and Leonardo Guarnotta, was finally to disprove the grand Sicilian lie. After decades of denial, Cosa Nostra was exposed not as a myth or a movie but a global criminal organization, headquartered in Sicily, with extensive links to business and politics in Italy and around the world. The climax of their investigations, the Maxi Trial, saw 475 mafiosi in court, accused of offenses ranging from extortion to drug smuggling to 120 murders.

How had Falcone and Borsellino succeeded? Many of their accomplishments hinged on a new 1982 law, the crime of mafia association, which outlawed a mere relationship with the mafia, even without evidence of a criminal act. That effectively made it a crime just to be born into a mafia family and was aimed squarely at the omertà and close blood relations on which the mafia was built. The new legislation worked. First a handful, then scores, then hundreds of mafiosi turned *pentiti* (literally "penitents"). A host of otherwise innocent family members did the same. From their evidence, Italy's prosecutors were able to construct a picture of Cosa Nostra's internal structure for the first time.

The Sicilians' other innovation was to abandon the mercurial autonomy traditionally enjoyed by individual prosecutors. Independence from political masters, who were often the target of anti-mafia investigations, remained essential. But prosecutors' habitual individualism had often found expression in less helpful fashion, such as fighting each other for position. By contrast, Palermo's anti-mafia prosecutors worked as an indivisible team, the "anti-mafia pool," as they called themselves, which shared information, diffused responsibility, and cosigned all warrants. In that way, they ensured their work was coordinated and efficient, and never depended on the continuing good health of any one of them.

So it was that in the months after the deaths of Falcone and Borsellino, other prosecutors—first Gian Carlo Caselli; then the Sicilians Piero Grasso, Giuseppe Pignatone, and his deputy Michele Prestipino—picked up where their storied predecessors left off. And in a further decade and a half, the Palermo prosecutors and Palermo's elite flying squad largely finished what their predecessors had started. By the mid-2000s, a generation of Cosa Nostra's bosses were in jail, its links to senior politicians were exposed, and its rackets, while they still existed, were a shadow of what they had once been. Capping the prosecutors' success, in April 2006 at a small, sparsely furnished cottage outside Corleone, Pignatone and Prestipino were present for the arrest of Cosa Nostra's remaining *capo tutti*, seventy-three-year-old Bernardo Provenzano, who had been on the run for forty-three years.

ON VISITS BACK to Sicily, Alessandra saw the transformation in her homeland. In the streets of Palermo and Messina, a new popular movement called Addiopizzo (Good-bye *Pizzo*, mafia slang for extortion) united shopkeepers, farmers, and restaurateurs in a refusal to pay protection. Thousands of anti-mafia protesters marched arm in arm through the streets. Cosa Nostra, in its weakened state, was unable to respond. When mafiosi firebombed an anti-mafia trattoria in Palermo, the city's residents found the owners new premises on a busy junction in the center of town where they opened up again and quickly became one of the city's most celebrated destinations. In time, Palermo and Messina could boast city-center shops run by an activist group called Libera (Free), which sold olive oil, sauces, wine, and pasta made exclusively by farmers who refused to pay protection to Cosa Nostra.

But as the war on Cosa Nostra wound down, a fresh threat took its place. During *la mattanza*, across the water in Calabria the 'Ndrangheta had initially toyed with joining Cosa Nostra's war on the state, and even killed a couple of policemen for itself. But the Calabrians soon realized that with the Sicilians and the government so distracted, the strategic play was not to side with Cosa Nostra but to take its narco business. The 'Ndrangheta paid the Sicilians' debts to the Colombian cocaine cartels, effectively buying them out as the Latin Americans' smuggling partners.

Carlo Cosco arrived in the north in 1987, the same year as Alessandra. Carlo's intention was not to fit into northern Italy, however, but to conquer it—and his timing was perfect. The 'Ndrangheta was pushing its drug empire north across Europe. Milan, Cosco's new patch, was a key beachhead in that expansion. And there had rarely been a business like cocaine smuggling in Europe in the 1990s and 2000s. After saturating the U.S. market, South American producers were looking to other territories for growth. Europe, with twice the population of North America and a similar standard of

living but, in the 1980s, a quarter of its cocaine consumption, was
the obvious opportunity. With the 'Ndrangheta's help, the cartels
flooded the continent with cocaine. By 2010, the European cocaine
market, at 124 tons a year, was close to matching the American one.
In Spain and Britain, the drug became as middle-class as Volvos and
weekend farmers' markets.

In the estimate of Italy's prosecutors, the 'Ndrangheta accounted
for three-quarters of that. So rich, and so fast, did the 'Ndrangheta
grow, it was hard to keep track. On wiretaps, carabinieri overheard
'Ndranghetisti talking about buried sacks of cash rotting in the
hills, and writing off the loss of a few million here or there as in-
consequential. At Gioia Tauro port on Calabria's west coast, officers
were seizing hundreds of kilos of cocaine at a time from shipping
containers but reckoned that they found less than 10 percent of what
was passing through. A glimpse of quite how big the 'Ndrangheta
had grown came in the early hours of August 15, 2007—the Ascen-
sion Day national holiday in Italy—when two 'Ndrangheta gunmen
shot and killed four men and two boys aged eighteen and sixteen
who were connected to a rival clan outside a pizzeria in Duisburg, in
Germany's industrial heartland. Northern Europe was apparently
now 'Ndrangheta territory.

Italy, and Europe, had a new mafia war to fight. And though its
empire was now global, the 'Ndrangheta remained as attached to
Calabria as Cosa Nostra had been to Sicily. In April 2008, two of the
prosecutors who had humbled the Sicilian mafia, Giuseppe Pignatone, now sixty, and Michele Prestipino, fifty, had their requests for
transfer to Calabria accepted. Their friend and ally in the Palermo
flying squad, Renato Cortese, went with them. As the three cast
around for a team who might do to the 'Ndrangheta what had been
done to Cosa Nostra, they realized they faced a problem. Many Italian prosecutors balked at the idea of an assignment to what was
universally regarded as both a backwater and enemy territory. In

2008, only twelve of the eighteen prosecutor positions in Calabria were filled, and the province had just five anti-mafia specialists. In Milan, however, Alessandra applied. She was ready to return to the south, she told her bosses. She understood the work would be "riskier" and more "difficult and complicated." That just made it all the more urgent.[4]

IN APRIL 2009, Alessandra and her husband packed up their apartment in Milan and flew south, following the sun down the west coast of Italy. As the plane started its descent, Alessandra saw the Aeolian Islands to the west, then Sicily and the snows of Etna to the south, then the streets of Messina below. As she passed over the broad blue of the Strait, she regarded the white foam trails of the rusty freighters as they rounded the tip of the Italian peninsula and turned north to Naples, Genoa, Marseille, and Barcelona. Not for the first time, it occurred to Alessandra that the lazy arc of this shore would, from a suitable distance, form the shape of a very large toe.

Alessandra's new security detail met her at Reggio airport. They took the expressway into town as a two-car convoy. The road climbed high above the city, skirting the dusty terraces that led up into the Calabrian hinterland. Below were the cobbled streets and crumbling apartment blocks whose names were familiar to Alessandra from dozens of investigations into shootings and firebombings. Somewhere down there, too, were the bunkers, entire underground homes where 'Ndrangheta bosses would hide for years, surfacing through hidden doors and tunnels to order new killings and plan new business.

As they reached the northern end of Reggio, the two cars took an off-ramp and plunged down into the city, dropping through twisting hairpins, bumping over ruts and potholes, plunging ever lower through tumbling, narrow streets before bottoming out just behind the seafront. Once on the flat, the drivers accelerated and flashed through the streets, past abandoned hotels, boarded-up cinemas, and empty villas before turning back up toward the hills and sweeping through the gates of a carabinieri barracks. In its 3,500 years of existence, Reggio had been a Mediterranean power, the birthplace of the kingdom of Italia, a Norman fortress, and a Riviera resort. Now it was bandit country. Entire neighborhoods were off-limits to carabinieri or prosecutors. For Alessandra, home for the next five years would be a bare-walled officer's apartment jammed into the barracks roof with a view of the Strait of Messina.

IV

DENISE SLEPT FOR an hour and a half the night Lea disappeared.[1] The next morning, November 25, 2009, she ate breakfast with her aunt Renata, walked with her to the kindergarten where she worked, then spent the morning silently smoking cigarettes with Andrea and Domenico in a nearby piazza. In the afternoon, Carlo phoned and told her to meet him at Bar Barbara. On the way there, Denise ran into a cousin from Lea's side of the family, Francesco Ceraudo, who lived in Genoa. She told Francesco that Lea was missing and asked him if he had seen her. Francesco blanched. "Do you know anything?" Denise asked. "Absolutely not," he said, and walked on.

The entire Cosco clan were in Bar Barbara: Carlo, his brothers Vito and Giuseppe, and Aunt Renata. Giuseppe and Renata were playing video poker in the corner. Giuseppe won fifty euros and, clumsily, gave the winnings to Denise. After a while, the carabinieri called Denise on her mobile and said they needed to speak to her. During the call, a squad car pulled up outside. Vito asked what was happening. "Lea's missing," Carlo told him.

The Coscos weren't about to let one of their own go to the carabinieri alone. Vito dropped Carlo and Denise at the station around 8:30 P.M., and father and daughter entered together. Inside, however, carabiniere Marshal Christian Persurich told Carlo he had to talk to Denise unaided. Persurich showed Denise to an interview room. He informed her that in Calabria her aunt Marisa had re-

ported Lea missing. Marisa had also told the carabinieri that Lea
had testified against the 'Ndrangheta and that she and Denise had
spent time in witness protection. Lea had now been missing for
more than twenty-four hours. Persurich needed the whole story.
Denise should take her time and leave nothing out. The interview
would be strictly confidential.

Denise nodded. "If my mother's missing," she began, "then it's
probably because she's been killed by my father."

MARSHAL PERSURICH INTERVIEWED Denise for five hours, finish-
ing just before 2 A.M. Denise emerged to find Carlo pacing the waiting room, demanding that the officers let him read her statement.
Seeing his daughter, Carlo confronted her. "What did you tell these
people?!"

"You asked us to Milan," Denise replied blankly. "We spent a
few days together. You were meant to pick her up. But you couldn't
find her. Then we looked for her all over."

Carlo looked unconvinced. Five hours for that?

On the way back to her cousins', Carlo and Denise stopped at
a restaurant, the Green Dragon, named after the symbol of Milan.
Inside was Carmine Venturino, the cousin who had given Lea some
hash to smoke. Carmine had a babyish face and looked like a born
truant, and Denise had liked him from the moment she met him at
a wedding in Calabria the previous summer. But that night they
had nothing to say to each other. After Carmine and Carlo had a
brief, hushed discussion, Carlo walked his daughter back to Viale
Montello. There, Denise slept in Andrea's room for a second night.

The next morning, Carlo, Denise, and a friend of Carlo's, Rosario Curcio, saw a lawyer in town. Carlo told the lawyer he wanted
to see Denise's statements. The lawyer asked Denise what she'd
told the carabinieri. Denise repeated what she had told Carlo: that

she and her mother had come up to Milan to spend a few days with her father, and Lea had vanished on their last night. She began crying. The lawyer said he could arrange to have Lea's disappearance publicized on national television. There was a show, *Chi l'ha Visto?* (*Have You Seen Them?*), which appealed for information on missing people. "Oh, for fuck's sake!" cried Carlo. The lawyer didn't get it at all. Carlo stood up and walked out, leaving Denise crying in the lawyer's office.

After Denise recovered, she, Carlo, and Rosario drove to a beauty salon owned by Rosario's girlfriend, Elisa. Carlo took Rosario aside for another quiet talk. Elisa asked Denise what was going on. Denise burst into tears once more and told Elisa that her mother had gone missing two nights before. Elisa said that was strange, because Rosario had vanished for a few hours the same evening. They'd had a date, said Elisa, but Rosario had canceled, then switched off his phone. When she finally got through to him around 9 P.M., he'd told Elisa something about having to fix a car with Carmine. It didn't make sense. Why the sudden rush to fix a car? Why at night? Denise was about to say something when Carlo interrupted to say he was taking Denise back to Viale Montello. She slept in her cousin's room for a third night.

The next day, three days since Lea had disappeared, Denise detected an improvement in Carlo's mood. He announced that he and Denise would drive to Reggio Emilia, not far from Bologna, to stay the night with another cousin. They left in the early afternoon. While her father drove, Denise watched silently as the winter sun flashed through the poplar trees like a searchlight through the bars of a fence. How could her mother just vanish? How could anyone be there one minute, and there be no sign of her the next? How would she ever talk to her father again?

In Reggio Emilia, Denise went to bed early while Carlo and his cousin went out for dinner. The following morning, Carlo drove Denise back to Milan, changed cars to a blue BMW, and announced that he and Denise were leaving immediately for Calabria with two other friends. As they were packing, Carmine arrived to say good-bye. Denise was struck by his expression. Stiff and formal, she thought. Something about the way he wouldn't look her in the eye.

From the back seat of the BMW, Denise watched as Milan's grand piazzas and chic boutiques gave way to the flat, gray farmland north of Florence, then the rust-colored hills of Tuscany and Umbria, and finally, as the sun sank into the sea to the west, the towering black volcanoes around Naples and Pompeii. It was dark by the time they crossed into Calabria. Denise felt the road change from smooth asphalt to worn, undulating waves. The car negotiated an almost endless succession of roadworks, then plunged into the steep valley of Cosenza, skimming the cliffs as it wound down into the abyss before hitting the valley floor.

Soon Denise felt the car turn left and accelerate back up into the hills. She registered the tighter turns and the sound of tires scrabbling on loose stones. The cold of the window dried her tear tracks to a salty crust. As the car filled with the smell of pines, the conversation between the three men took on a giddy, jubilant tone. "The only thing in my head was my mother," she said. "I was just sitting in the back, crying. But the others—they were so happy. Chatting and smiling and joking and laughing out loud."

After an hour of climbing, the car crested a mountain pass and began to descend. At the edge of a forest, by the side of a stream, they came to a small village. They were heading to the one place where Carlo could be sure Denise would never speak out of turn again. Pagliarelle.

PAGLIARELLE COMES FROM the word *pagliari*, meaning "shelter." The name commemorated how for thousands of years, as the winter snows melted, Calabria's shepherds would lead their sheep and goats up a track into the mountains and find a stream on whose banks they would graze their animals for weeks at a time. Keeping one eye out for wolves and another on the sea on the horizon, the men would collect pinewood, barbecue goat meat, drink wine, and sleep in a handful of open-sided shacks that they roofed with fir and clay. In the twentieth century, the track leading from the nearby town of Petilia Policastro was tarred, electricity arrived, and the shepherds' rest grew into a modest settlement of gray-stone, red-tiled townhouses gathered around a small central square. The name survived, as did the stream, which was channeled into a fountain in the piazza where Lea's and Carlo's mothers would send them as children to fill buckets for the day.

It was here, high up in the frozen, granite mountains of eastern Calabria, that Denise found herself walking a tightrope of pretense in the weeks after Lea's disappearance. Lea hadn't just been Denise's mother. After so many years alone together, she had defined Denise's life. Now Denise found herself back in the place that her mother had tried to escape for so long, adrift among the people she was sure had killed her. It was impossible to know how to behave. With no body and no funeral, Denise couldn't mourn. Carlo was telling people that Lea had run off, maybe to Australia, and Denise found herself having to make believe that her murderous father hadn't really killed her courageous mother at all but that, rather, her fickle mother had abandoned her husband and only child and jetted off to a new life in the sun. Denise knew the way she looked so much like Lea—the same hair, the same cheekbones—made her an immediate object of suspicion. Worse, Carlo was making so much of Denise's return. After years of problems with his wife and daughter, the boss finally had both his women where they belonged—and he wanted everyone to know. Ten days after Lea's disappearance, Carlo organized an eighteenth birthday party for Denise, inviting hundreds of people from Pagliarelle and Petilia Policastro and even buying Denise a car. When Denise refused to go, Carlo went ahead with the party anyway.

Mostly, Denise spent her days trying to learn from her aunt Marisa, with whom she was now living. Ever since Lea had first denounced the 'Ndrangheta in 1996, Marisa had been forced to pull off a daily performance in Pagliarelle. Convincing an entire village they needed to have no doubts about her had required Marisa not just to tell lies but to live them, too. In her mind, Marisa suffocated any affection she had for Lea and focused instead on the resentment she felt toward her sister for the trouble she had caused. Denise realized she would have to learn to hate her mother, too. "I knew my aunt and her family," said Denise. "I knew how they thought. My idea was to understand their mentality and see if I could also work out how to live there. I didn't want to end up like my mother. I wanted to keep living."

V

_____

D ENISE WASN'T THE only one living a lie in Pagliarelle. Watching Lea's daughter offered the carabinieri one of their best leads for finding out what had happened to Lea. But any reminder of the state's relationship with Lea, or any hint that it might continue with her daughter, would be enough to condemn Denise. The carabinieri decided the state's only visible presence in Pagliarelle should remain the lone village policeman. Unseen and unheard, however, scores of officers would watch Pagliarelle day and night.

Over the years, the challenge posed by the mafia had compelled Italy's security services to innovate. To pursue violent 'Ndranghetisti through mountain terrain had led the Calabrian carabinieri to form a unique Special Forces–style squad, the _cacciatori_ (hunters), a unit made up of snipers, bomb-disposal experts, heavy-weapons operators, helicopter pilots, and Alpinists. The sight of a _cacciatori_ helicopter gunship flying low over the Aspromonte mountains was a corrective to anyone who doubted the state was fighting a war in southern Italy.

But even the _cacciatori_'s resources paled next to those commanded by Italy's covert intelligence units. Around the world, only a few specialized police units are permitted to eavesdrop on suspects' telephone calls or spy on them electronically. In Italy, a measure of the mafia threat was that all three police forces—the domestic police, the militaristic carabinieri, and the Guardia di Finanza, which specialized in economic crime—had surveillance divisions that employed thousands. In 2009, the Italian state was tapping a total of 119,553 phones and listening to 11,119 bugs. Almost no type of reconnaissance was forbidden. To establish targets' whereabouts, plainclothes officers followed them, filmed them through hidden minicameras and larger zoom lenses set up at a distance—several miles across the valley, in the case of Pagliarelle—and tracked their phones' GPS signals. To find out what the subjects were saying, they hacked their text messages, phone calls, e-mails, and social media chats.

In Reggio, almost an entire floor of the gracious building that served as the city's carabinieri headquarters had been transformed into a humming, indoor field of electronic espionage. At the center was a control room from which chases and operations were coordinated. Around it were twenty smaller offices, each dedicated to a different surveillance operation. Every room was packed with scores of screens, servers, modems, and snaking, thick black wires. Working without interruption in six-hour shifts that ran continuously, day and night, officers in Reggio and an identical team in Milan had been following bosses like Carlo for years. Chosen for their facility with dialects and their ability to inhabit the skins of their subjects, the operators knew their subjects so well they could decipher the meaning of their words from a euphemism or even an inflection in a person's voice. The Calabrian teams also had a particular skill with bugs. They planted devices in cars, homes, and gardens. They bugged a basement laundry whose underground, signal-cutting location made it a favorite 'Ndrangheta meeting place. They bugged an orange orchard where a boss liked to hold meetings, and for the same reason bugged a forest. One time they even bugged a road where one boss took walks, ripping up the asphalt and re-laying it with tar embedded with listening devices.

Such entrepreneurialism brought results. In early 2008, the squad hunting 'Ndrangheta supremo Pasquale Condello, by then fifty-seven and on the run for eighteen years, observed that every two weeks, as though he were on a schedule, Condello's nephew would shake his surveillance in the center of Reggio, swapping from the back of one motorbike to another in a series of choreographed changes. The carabinieri were convinced the maneuvers were in preparation for meeting Condello. One day, an officer noticed that the nephew always wore the same crash helmet. A few nights later, a carabinieri officer punctured the muffler on a car, then drove it up and down outside the nephew's house to cover the sound of a second officer breaking in and switching the helmet with an identical one implanted with a tracer. When it was time for the next rendezvous, the carabinieri followed the nephew through his usual multiride acrobatics, using the tracer, to a small pink house in a back alley on the south side of Reggio Calabria. Surrounded by more than a hundred *cacciatori*, Condello surrendered without a fight.

THIS WAS THE front line on which Alessandra had imagined herself working when she transferred to Calabria. But a staffing shortfall meant that on arrival she was assigned to Reggio as a city judge. Her knowledge of Milan and Calabria and her interest in 'Ndrangheta women notwithstanding, she was forced to watch the Lea Garofalo case unfold from afar.

Still, there were advantages to such a gentle start. For one, the undemanding hours allowed plenty of time to learn the lay of the land. Alessandra kept pace with active investigations by chatting with officers at the carabinieri's headquarters, a short walk from the Palace of Justice. At other moments, she researched the 'Ndrangheta's history. In her office, she assembled piles of case files, carabinieri surveillance transcripts, *pentiti* statements, academic papers, history books, and even accounts of Calabrian folklore.

To a Sicilian like Alessandra, the origins of the 'Ndrangheta felt familiar. The organization was at its strongest away from the big cities in the hundreds of small mountain hamlets like Pagliarelle nestling in the valleys that led away from the coast. As in Sicily, many of these settlements had been the cradle of some of Europe's first civilizations. Alessandra read how paintings of bulls dating from 12,000 B.C. had been found in Calabrian caves. By 530 B.C., Pythagoras was teaching mathematics in Kroton (later Crotone) on the plain below Pagliarelle while the citizens of nearby Sybaris were drinking wine piped to their homes by vinoducts. Like Sicilians, Calabrians had their own archaic language, in this case Grecanico, a Greek dialect left over from the Middle Ages when Calabria had been part of the Byzantine Empire.

Something else that Calabria had in common with Sicily: from the beginning, it was a land apart. Many of the valleys were accessible only from the sea, naturally isolated behind steep mountainsides, thick pine forests, and, in winter, snows that could cut off villages for months. For thousands of years, there had been no one to defend the families who lived in these valleys. They tended olive trees, fished the ocean, and scanned the horizon as invading armies sailed by from Rome, Germany, Arabia, Spain, France, Italy, and America. They were poor, resilient, and resolutely autonomous, and as Italy's north steadily eclipsed the south, their estrangement from the rest of the Italian peninsula only grew. When in 1861 a group of northerners began to send bureaucrats, teachers, and carabinieri into the valleys to proclaim the rule of a newly united Italy, the families repudiated, thwarted, and occasionally killed the colonizers.

At first, the families had no connection to the mafia. The phenomenon of organized crime first emerged in Italy in the 1820s with the Camorra in Naples and then in the 1840s and 1850s with what became Cosa Nostra in Sicily. In both cases, ordinary criminals found themselves in jail with educated, bourgeois revolutionaries who were fighting foreign domination and feudalism, and who often organized themselves in masonic sects. As patriots, the rebels taught the future mafiosi the importance of a righteous cause. As freemasons, they taught them hierarchy, and the power of legend and ceremony.

When Sicily simultaneously unified with the north of Italy and ended feudalism, the ensuing chaos gave Sicily's criminals a chance to put these new lessons to work. Though the northern dukes and generals leading unification described it as an act of modernization, many southerners regarded it as another foreign conquest. Adding to the discontent, the immediate effect of the advent of private property in Sicily was a rash of property disputes. To protect themselves, landowners, towns, and villages set up vigilante groups who, for a fee, protected their assets, hunted down thieves, and settled disputes. To be effective, these groups required men who could intimidate others. Jail-hardened criminals were a natural choice.

Soon these bands of enforcers were calling themselves mafiosi, a term derived from the Sicilian word *mafiusu*, meaning "swagger" or "bravado." Their new name was, in effect, a rebranding. Violent criminals had always been able to inspire fear. The mafiosi wanted respect, too. While they didn't deny a criminal self-interest, the mafiosi insisted theirs was an honorable endeavor: protecting poor southerners from rapacious landowners and an oppressive north. Of course, Sicilians soon learned that the people from whom they needed most protection were the mafiosi themselves. The protection racket was born.

When organized crime reached Calabria a generation or two later, Alessandra read, it had repeated many of the same patterns. Like Cosa Nostra, Calabria's mafia began in jail. One of Calabria's main administrative centers was Palmi, a hill town with views out over the east coast that, as the provincial capital of the Gioia Tauro *piano*, the estuary plain, possessed a police station, a courtroom, and a prison. In the spring of 1888, gangs of hoodlums, many of them

graduates of the town jail, began staging knife fights in Palmi's tav-
erns, brothels, and piazzas. As the heat rose with the coming summer, it seemed to stoke a violent hooliganism among the ex-cons,
who began rampaging through the streets, slashing citizens with
knives and razors, extorting money from gamblers, prostitutes, and
landowners, rustling cattle and goats, and even threatening magistrates, the police, and newspaper editors.

In those early days, the prototype gangsters called themselves
camorristi, a straight copy of the Naples mafia, or *picciotti*, a word
that the British historian John Dickie translates as "lads with attitude."[1] If they were united, it was chiefly by their dandyish style:
tattoos, extravagant quiffs, silk scarves knotted at the neck, and
trousers that were tight at the thighs and flared at the ankle. In his
history of the three big Italian mafias, *Mafia Brotherhoods*, Dickie de-
scribes how *picciotto* culture spread across Calabria in months.[2] Like
all young male fashions, it might have died just as rapidly had it not
penetrated the hill valleys. There the families had little taste for the
picciotti's dress. But the remote and defensive interior of Calabria
was fertile territory for a movement whose methods were mostly
physical and whose distrust of the state was pronounced. And just
as they ran everything in the valleys, the families were soon running the *picciotteria*.

A central goal for all mafias was to create a consensus around
power. Whenever the question of power arose—political, economic, social, divine—the answer had to be the mafia. It was the
peculiar luck of the Italian mafias that circumstances conspired
to graft their enterprise onto the most durable of southern Italian power structures: the family. In Sicily, the mafia came to be
known as Cosa Nostra, meaning "our thing," and Our Thing was,
really, Our Family Secret, an outsmarting of the northern state
built on the intimacy and obedience of kin. Likewise in Calabria,
the valley families gave the *picciotti* a ready-made hierarchy, or-

der, legitimacy, and secrecy. It was this—loyalty to blood and homeland—that was the foundation of all the horrors to come.

By the turn of the twentieth century, Calabria's street hoodlums had been organized into local cells called *'ndrine*, each with its own turf, ranks, and boss. At first, *picciotti* were useful for small matters: appropriating a neighbor's field for the boss's cows, resisting rent demands from fussing landlords, or extracting protection money from the neighborhood trattoria. Highway robbery, smuggling, kidnapping, and loan-sharking were lucrative earners for more enterprising *picciotti*. Bosses also took on additional duties like adjudicating property disputes or defending women's honor.

But as the *picciotti* endured successive crackdowns by the authorities, some wondered how they might turn the tables on the state. If the source of the wider world's power came from money, they reasoned, then maybe the way to attack that outside world was to venture out into it, steal its money, and take its power?

The Calabrian mafia was soon using its money to buy favors from the carabinieri and the judiciary. After that came bribes to political parties, mayors' offices, the state bureaucracy, and the Italian parliament. In time, the families were also able to infiltrate these institutions with their own men. The insiders then defrauded and embezzled, diverting public funds to mafia-owned contracting businesses such as construction firms, refuse collectors, and dockers. Elections were rigged and more allegiances bought. Those who could not be corrupted or intimidated were beaten, firebombed, or killed.

All this felt familiar to a Sicilian like Alessandra. But the Calabrians outdid their peers in two respects. Where the Sicilians recruited from a particular area, the Calabrians relied on family: almost without exception, *picciotti* were either born into an *'ndrina* or married into it. And while the Sicilians certainly spun stories about themselves, the Calabrians dreamed up legends that wove together honor, religion, family, and southern Italian separatism into an elaborate and almost impenetrable veil of misdirection.

By the early twentieth century, 'Ndranghetisti were tracing their origins to three medieval knights-errant. These figures crop up in mafia creation myths from Asia to Africa to Europe.[3] In the 'Ndrangheta version, the knights were Spanish brothers—Osso, Mastrosso, and Carcagnosso—who had fled their homeland after avenging their sister's rape. Landing on the tiny island of Favignana off Sicily's west coast and taking shelter in damp and cold sea caverns, the trio nursed a sense of righteous grievance and steadfast family loyalty for thirty long and uncomfortably damp years. Eventually their discussions became the basis for a brotherhood founded on mutual defense. With the Honored Society sworn to protect all members, and they it, no outsider would ever think of shaming the brothers and their families again. And when the brothers felt ready to take their creation to the world, Mastrosso traveled to Naples to set up the Camorra in the name of the Madonna, Osso sailed to Sicily and founded Cosa Nostra in the name of Saint George, and Carcagnosso took a land between his two brothers—Calabria—where he established the 'Ndrangheta in the name of Saint Michael, the Archangel.

The story is, of course, bunk. The Calabrian mafia is not hundreds of years old but barely 150. The story of the three knights also seems copied from that of the Garduña, a mythical fifteenth-century Spanish criminal society whose founding legend would have been familiar to 'Ndranghetisti from the time when Spain ruled Calabria. The irony is that most historians have concluded the Garduña was itself a fabrication.[4] This, then, was mafiosi trying to fool others with a piece of gangster fiction that had, in fact, fooled them.

This was far from the only example of mafia make-believe, however. The 'Ndrangheta's ancient-sounding name did not derive from a venerable heritage but, as Dickie uncovered, was a modern artifice that first surfaced in police reports in the 1920s and in newspaper stories in the 1950s.[5] Alessandra found more recent mafia fictions in the form of Internet videos ripping off scenes from American gangster movies like *The Godfather* and *Goodfellas* and set to Calabrian folk songs. The lyrics to these melodies were hardly poetry but no less chilling for that:

> *Keep the honor of the family.*
> *Avenge my father.*
> *I have to get good with guns and knives*
> *Because I can't stop thinking about it.*
> *The pain in my heart—*
> *It can only be stopped if I avenge my father.*

Then there were the "ancient" rituals. For a boss's son, Alessandra read, these could begin soon after birth. A newborn boy would be laid kicking and screaming on a bed, a key next to his left hand and a knife by his right, denoting the state and the mafia. An 'Ndrangheta mother's first duty was to ensure, with a few careful nudges, that her boy grasped the knife and sealed his destiny. In *Tired of Killing: The Autobiography of a Repentant 'Ndranghetista*, Alessandra read about the early life of Antonio Zagari, the son of an 'Ndrangheta boss who turned informant in 1990.[6] In his book, Zagari described a probation of two years, during which a teenage *picciotto* was expected to prove his worth by committing crimes and even killing, as well as learning by heart the fable of Osso, Mastrosso, and Carcagnosso and a set of rules and social prescriptions. After that came a formal initiation ceremony. The ritual began when Zagari was led into a darkened room in which a group of 'Ndranghetisti were standing in a circle. At first, Zagari was excluded. The boss addressed the 'Ndranghetisti, asking if they were "comfortable."

"Very comfortable," they replied. "With what?"

"With the rules," said the boss.

"Very comfortable," came the reply once more.

The boss then "baptized" the meeting in the name of the Honored Society "as our ancestors Osso, Mastrosso, and Carcagnosso baptized it . . . with irons and chains." He ceremoniously confiscated any weapons. The congregation confirmed their loyalty to the society on pain of "five or six dagger thrusts to the chest." The boss then likened their common endeavor to "a ball that goes wandering around the world as cold as ice, as hot as fire, and as fine as silk." After the members of the circle affirmed three times that they were ready to accept a new member, they opened their ranks to admit the newcomer. The boss then cut a cross on Zagari's finger so that it bled over a burning image of Saint Michael while he intoned: "As the fire burns this image, so shall you burn if you stain yourself with infamy."

That was the cue for Zagari to take his oath: "I swear before the organized and faithful society, represented by our honored and wise boss and by all the members, to carry out all the duties for which I am responsible and all those which are imposed on me—if necessary even with my blood."

Finally, the boss kissed Zagari on both cheeks, recited the rules of the society, and delivered a homily to humility, the island of Favignana, and blood—which, in case anyone was lost, was the essence of the icy, fiery, silky, and world-wandering ball he had mentioned earlier.

It was a wonder anyone kept a straight face, thought Alessandra. Certainly, the phony medievalism of the 'Ndrangheta's performances made serious historians choke. Dickie likened the "solemn ravings" of its initiation ritual to a scout ceremony that crossed *Lord of the Flies* with Monty Python. One of Italy's most eminent mafia historians, Enzo Ciconte, was just as dismissive of the 'Ndrangheta's "Red Riding Hood fantasies."[7] But Ciconte cautioned that ridiculous did not mean meaningless. "No group of people can last long just by using violence, just by killing, stealing, and rustling—they need some sort of faith or ideology," he said. "The 'Ndrangheta had no tradition. They had to invent one."

It was a good point, thought Alessandra. What mattered with faith was not plausibility but belief. Most of the main religions clung to unlikely myths and holy stories, which they called miracles or acts of God. Few of them were ever hurt by others laughing at them—quite the opposite. More to the point, a lie was just that: a fib, a fiction, a deceit. No one was claiming the 'Ndrangheta's bosses believed it. After all, they were the ones telling it.

A better question was why the 'Ndrangheta chiefs found such decorous fantasies expedient. The answer was to be found in their spectacular rise. However contrived and derivative the cult of the 'Ndrangheta might appear to academic examination, it had gained the organization the loyalty and secrecy of its members, the fear and respect of ordinary Calabrians, and, as a result, a thick cloak of opacity under which it hid from the world. The 'Ndrangheta's stories might have appealed to Calabrians because of their own distrust of the state or their sense of theater, or simply because they were handed down from father to son with the solemn conviction of a sacred truth. The point was they worked. Myth was how the 'Ndrangheta assumed a moral purpose when it was self-evidently immoral, how it colored itself romantic and divine when it was base and profane, and how it convinced others it was their righteous champion even as it robbed and murdered them. Myth was how those inside the organization were persuaded they were following a higher code and those outside it found themselves stumped by even the simplest questions, such as who was who. It was all an enormous lie. But it was a lie that explained how, almost without anyone noticing, a small group of families from the wild hills of Italy's south had become the twenty-first century's most formidable mafia.

ALESSANDRA BECAME FASCINATED by the intricacies of the deception. The 'Ndrangheta was an extraordinary puzzle, a multilevel mosaic. From transcripts of tapped phone calls and bugged conversations, she discovered 'Ndranghetisti had their own language, *baccagghju*, a slang based on Grecanico whose meaning was obscure to almost everyone but initiates. Even when they spoke Italian, 'Ndranghetisti used a code of metaphors to disguise their meaning. An 'Ndrangheta family in criminal partnership with another would describe itself as "walking with" that other family. Rather than demand protection money outright, 'Ndranghetisti would request a "donation for the cousins," an allusion to those men in jail whose families needed support. For a boss to describe a man as "disturbing" or "troubling" was for him to pass an oblique but unequivocal death sentence on him. The euphemisms could be highly contorted. *Pizzo*, the word for an extortion payment, was a term whose origins were the subject of academic dispute, but according to one explanation, was the "piece" of ground on which a nineteenth-century prisoner had slept in jail, which were ranked according to their proximity to the boss. Outside jail in the twentieth century, it had come to denote the tribute that a boss expected from real estate inside his territory.

Deciphering the true meaning of 'Ndrangheta speak was a constant struggle. "You have to become more perceptive, more capable of decrypting," Alessandra would tell her husband over dinner in their apartment. "Mafiosi very rarely make a direct threat. Instead, they send messages with a dual meaning." Even the smallest gesture could carry the utmost importance. "They can order a murder just by looking at someone from the prisoner cage in court," she said.

One of the 'Ndrangheta's most audacious lies was its relationship with the church. The 'Ndrangheta was plainly an unchristian organization. But since it came from the most Roman Catholic of lands, it simply insisted the opposite was true. It invoked the saints, especially the Madonna and Saint Michael, the Archangel. It mimicked prayer and church services in its rituals. And it co-opted and bred priests. At Mass, some priests in 'Ndrangheta areas would exhort their congregants to resist outsiders. On saints' days, they directed celebrants to bow statues of the Madonna before the *capo*'s house, while at Easter the honor of bearing statues of Jesus, Saint John, and the Virgin was reserved for *picciotti*. The most stunning example of the 'Ndrangheta subverting Christianity happened on September 2 every year, when crowds of thousands gathered at the small town of San Luca in the Aspromonte mountains for the festival of the Madonna di Polsi. Among the pilgrims were hundreds of 'Ndranghetisti, including the heads of all the clans, who since at least 1901 had used the event as a cover for the 'Ndrangheta's annual meeting, the *gran crimine*. In plain sight, the bosses would sit at a table laden with pasta and goat sauce, present their annual accounts—what they had earned, who they had killed—and elect a new *capo crimine* for the coming year. "The church is very responsible in all of this," Alessandra would say. "It's guilty of some terrible, terrible, *terrible* things."

Though the organization found Christianity useful, Alessandra concluded that at its core the 'Ndrangheta was more of a blood cult. Blood was the bond between the families that were the 'Ndrangheta's strength. The act of spilling blood was also revered as a source of fearsome power. That had led to some unforgiving 'Ndrangheta feuds. The Duisburg massacre of 2007—which police identified as an attack on an 'Ndrangheta initiation celebration when a burned picture of Saint Michael was found in the pocket of the dead eighteen-year-old—was the latest atrocity in a quarrel between two clans from San Luca. The feud had begun in 1991 when a group of boys from one family threw rotten eggs at the window of a bar owned by another. Including Duisburg, nine people had since died. Many more had been injured. To avoid being shot, 'Ndranghetisti in San Luca would hide themselves in the trunk of a car just to travel one hundred yards. Killings were timed for maximum horror. The year before Duisburg, a boss from one clan was paralyzed by a bullet that passed through his spine as he stood on a balcony cradling his newborn son. In revenge, a rival boss's wife was shot dead in her family home on Christmas Day.

Why the ruthlessness? For the 'Ndrangheta, the answer was easy: to instill fear and reap power. For individual 'Ndranghetisti, the question was more vexing. Why be an 'Ndranghetista if your fate was to spend lengthy stretches in prison, inflict unspeakable violence on your neighbors, and, in all probability, die young? Alessandra decided it came back to the lie. The 'Ndrangheta had used its fantasies about honor, sacrifice, loyalty, and courage to build a prison around its young men, trapping them in a claustrophobic sect based on blood and butchery. Pride in the 'Ndrangheta's rural heritage even encouraged some 'Ndranghetisti to imbue their violence with a rustic aesthetic. Pigs often featured. A family targeted for intimidation might discover the throats of all its male pigs had been slit. On one occasion, the carabinieri recorded an 'Ndranghetista boasting how he beat another man unconscious, then fed his living body to his own pigs. The bloodthirstiness could also be literal. More than once, men loyal to an assassinated boss were observed to rush to the scene of the killing, dip their handkerchiefs in the departed *capo*'s blood, and press the dripping cloth to their lips.

ALESSANDRA REALIZED THAT the 'Ndrangheta's cult of blood, family, and tradition also accounted for its oppression of its women. That misogynist tyranny was real enough. Driving through small-town Calabria, Alessandra rarely saw women out of doors and almost never unaccompanied. Nevertheless, it was with a sinking sense of inevitability that she read that the 'Ndrangheta's conservative values were yet another affectation.

As long ago as 1892, the 'Ndrangheta had admitted two women highwaymen into its ranks. John Dickie found court records from the 1930s showing that the *picciotti* once had a pronounced personal and professional attachment to prostitution as both pimps and johns. But it seemed that the 'Ndrangheta later dispensed with prostitution because, though the trade was lucrative, it was built on qualities like infidelity, loose discipline, and double standards, which were inimical to order and control. The closed, buttoned-up, isolated family culture of traditional Calabria, on the other hand, was perfect for organized crime. Family ties were also how the 'Ndrangheta fashioned a global criminal octopus out of the pattern of Calabrian emigration to the United States, Canada, Australia, South Africa, and Latin America in the 1920s.

The more she read, the more Alessandra realized that the 'Ndrangheta's true genius had been in co-opting the Italian family. The more the 'Ndrangheta made itself indistinguishable from traditional, family-based Calabrian culture, the more anyone thinking of leaving the organization had to consider that they would be abandoning all they knew and all they were. For most, it would be impossible to see beyond it.

But by basing itself around family, the 'Ndrangheta hadn't merely been bolstering secrecy and loyalty. It had understood that family itself was a source of corruption. The undeniable love of a mother for a son or a daughter for a father—these were the sorts of bonds that ensured even the most law-abiding broke with principle and the law. Fathers would advantage their families however they could. Children would never betray their parents. Mothers, above all, would do anything to protect their children and wreak terrible revenge on those who harmed them. The 'Ndrangheta was the family augmented and accentuated into a perfect criminal entity. It was, of course, a diabolical transformation. The use of children was plainly child abuse, while to pervert the family in a country like Italy was to poison the soul of a nation. But it was also a masterstroke. If family was the basis of its power, and family was the essence of Italy, then family was how the 'Ndrangheta could corrupt the country.

For such a clan endeavor to work, Alessandra was convinced women had to have a role. And from her reading of case files and investigations, she soon discovered they had several. Women acted as messengers between men on the run or in jail, passing along tiny, folded notes—*pizzini*—written in a code of glyphs and addressed by the use of a code of numbers. If a man was killed or inaccessible in jail, his widow could become his de facto replacement and continue the family business. Some women acted as paymasters and bookkeepers.

Most significantly, women ensured the future of the 'Ndrangheta by producing the next generation of 'Ndranghetisti, raising children with an unbending belief in the code of honor, vendetta, and omertà, and a violent loathing of outsiders who, the mothers whispered, were weak and without shame with their loose talk and looser women. "Without women performing this role, there would be no 'Ndrangheta," said Alessandra. Secrecy and power were the goals. Male misogyny and female subservience, forced or even willing, were the means.

What confirmed women's influence inside the 'Ndrangheta was that, though they were often the victims of its violence, they also instigated some of it. Alessandra was astonished to hear about one mother from the Bellocco clan who outdid all the men for bloodthirstiness. The carabinieri had managed to bug a family meeting convened to discuss how best to avenge the death of one of their men, killed in a clan feud. The men proposed killing every male member of the rival *'ndrina*. Then the woman spoke up. "Kill them *all*," she said. "Even the women. Even the kids." The woman wanted an entire family of thirty wiped from the face of the earth.

There was no way any of it worked without the mothers, thought Alessandra. And to a resourceful and open-minded prosecutor, that held out an enticing possibility. In the twenty-first century, there had to be other Lea Garofalos out there, mafia mothers who were unhappy with their lives and the destiny of their children. The mother, the madonna, was a holy figure in Italy, and the 'Ndrangheta had corrupted her and bent her to its criminal will. Some women inside the organization must have hated the way they were being used. It had to be possible for Alessandra to offer these knowledgeable figures a different life and persuade them to betray their husbands and fathers. And imagine if she could. "It would break the chain," she told her fellow prosecutors. "It would remove the guardians of the 'Ndrangheta's traditions. If they took their sons, too, then they would be removing future soldiers. It would be very special, very important. It would impoverish the entire mafia family. It would undermine the whole culture and the mind-set."

Alessandra was refining her theory. The way to destroy The Family, she was beginning to realize, was through its mamas.

VI

I N JANUARY 2010, Pignatone and Prestipino finally gave Alessandra the job she wanted.[1] From the New Year, she would be lead anti-mafia prosecutor for Calabria's west coast, taking in the villages on the Gioia Tauro *piano*, the town of Rosarno, and the port of Gioia Tauro. She would report directly to Pignatone and Prestipino. She would also have a second prosecutor as her junior, Giovanni Musarò, a thirty-seven-year-old on his first big posting.

Like Alessandra, Musarò was attracted by Pignatone and Prestipino's dynamism. "I was very young, they had this huge experience from Palermo, and they brought with them a completely different way of working," he said. Borrowing from Falcone and Borsellino, Calabria's new anti-mafia team ensured the old model of prosecutors as "lonely heroes" was out, said Giovanni. The new watchword was collaboration. "They put a great effort into creating a team, sharing information with colleagues, and behaving like a democracy," he said. Each member brought different strengths. "Alessandra was driven by ethics and very determined. Pignatone had a great ability to predict events. Prestipino was very clever and very pragmatic. He knew all his investigations and all his investigators. He was able to go to each of us and say: 'Maybe go to Alessandra and you'll find this.' Or 'Maybe go here and ask this investigator, and they'll help you with this.'"

For Alessandra, the prize was her new territory. Palmi, on the southern end of the Gioia Tauro estuary, was where the 'Ndrangheta

was born. A century and a half later, the *piano* remained the heart
of the empire. Though you wouldn't know it to look at the place,
thought Alessandra. The 'Ndrangheta was richer than most global
corporations, and in Rosarno even the most minor 'Ndrangheta family was thought to have three, four, or five million euros stashed away.
Yet somehow in a country of amber cornfields, olive hills, and blue
mountains sprinkled with red-roofed villages and magnificent Roman and Renaissance cities, the 'Ndrangheta had contrived to make
their towns into verrucae of unkempt, concrete ugliness. Touring
Rosarno for the first time, Alessandra felt like she'd arrived after
an apocalypse. Everything looked scorched. The trees were dying
and their leaves orange and brittle. The single park was just chalky
pebbles and dry, spiky weeds. The streets, whose asphalt resembled
spilled lava, were strewn with refuse. Everything was covered with
crude graffiti. And the town was dead. Shops were shut or deserted.
Many of the cinder block houses were unfinished and empty, their
gardens building sites, and their glassless windows as vacant as the
eyes of a skull. In the main piazza, no one sat on the benches, no one
ate in the restaurants. To one side, a children's playground consisted
of a rusted swing, a broken slide, and a shattered piece of concrete
littered with wrappers, cigarette butts, and broken glass. Alessandra could feel it. The fear. The omertà.

Unpicking the paradox of how this desperate place could be home
to such a rich criminal empire was key to the story of the 'Ndrangheta's modern rise. It began at 3 A.M. on July 10, 1973, when a
small gang of 'Ndrangheta toughs from the villages around Gioia
Tauro kidnapped John Paul Getty III, the sixteen-year-old grandson
of the billionaire Jean Paul Getty, from outside his home in Piazza
Farnese in central Rome. The gang held the boy in the Calabrian
mountains for five months. His father, who had been in a heroin-
induced haze at the time his son was taken, initially thought the
kidnapping was a hoax staged by his son to obtain money. The kid-

nappers called the family patriarch, Jean Paul Getty Sr., and threatened to cut off his grandson's fingers unless they received a ransom of $17 million. The elder Getty refused, arguing: "If I pay one penny now, I'll have fourteen kidnapped grandchildren." To press their case, the gang cut off John Paul III's left ear and sent it to a newspaper in Rome. It was accompanied by a note threatening that the second ear would be arriving in ten days unless the ransom was paid. Getty Sr. relented and paid $2.2 million, the maximum his accountants advised him was tax efficient. He loaned the final ransom balance of $700,000 to his son, the boy's father, at 4 percent interest.

John Paul Getty III never recovered from his abduction or his grandfather's indifference. He died at fifty-four, an alcoholic and a drug addict in a wheelchair, having been crippled at the age of twenty-five by a near-lethal combination of Valium, methadone, and cocktails. But for the west coast 'Ndrangheta, these grubby beginnings were the seeds of an empire. They went on to stage 150 more kidnappings. In Gioia Tauro, they used the ransom money to buy construction trucks. 'Ndrangheta men inside local government ensured these trucks were contracted for the building of a steel plant near the Gioia Tauro port. When the government abandoned that project as uneconomic, the trucks went to work on a bigger site: the expansion of the port itself.

State construction contracts—building motorways, high-speed rail links, and even wind and solar farms, while loan-sharking at extortionate rates to force rivals out of business—went on to become a giant, profitable 'Ndrangheta business in its own right. By the time Alessandra was posted to the west coast, a project to widen and repair the arterial highway running from western Calabria up Italy's coast to Salerno had somehow ended up costing the state $10 billion in three decades for what was still little more than a succession of roadworks.[2] The biggest earner, however, was the Gioia Tauro port itself. Once its expansion was finished, the port was the largest container facility in Italy and the sixth largest on the Mediterranean, with a capacity to load and unload millions of containers a year on a quay that ran for three and a half kilometers and was backed by an avenue of towering cranes. The 'Ndrangheta, as the only power in the area, had total control. The group "taxed" every container passing through the port at $1.50 a time. It charged the port operators fees amounting to half their profits, an annual income that ran into several billion dollars. It used the port to send weapons around the world. And in the 1980s and 1990s, during *la mattanza*, it was through Gioia Tauro that the 'Ndrangheta built its cocaine empire.

But aside from a single street of new houses nicknamed Via John Paul Getty in a small town to the south, there was no sign of the 'Ndrangheta's wealth. To the 'Ndrangheta, a facade of poverty was crucial to the lie. It helped it escape the attention of the state and added credibility to its claim to be championing a deprived south against an oppressive north. The 'Ndrangheta went to mulish lengths to service its pretense. When Alessandra first visited Rosarno, Domenico Oppedisano, a seventy-eight-year-old 'Ndrangheta big shot, could still be seen in his battered trilby and dusty suit, driving around in a three-wheeled van and delivering his oranges and lemons to market.

For the 97 percent of Gioia Tauro's population who were not 'Ndrangheta, however, the deprivation was real. Calabria was the poorest province in Italy. Incomes were around half those in the north, unemployment ran at 28 percent, and even in 2009, roasted dormice were considered a delicacy. The provincial government, meanwhile, was so dysfunctional that in 2008, a U.S. embassy fact-finding mission concluded that were it an independent state, Calabria would be a failed one.

As she was driven around the estuary delta between Rosarno and the port, Alessandra found it easy to guess who had ruined it. The area was latticed by a series of two-lane highways connected by

a spaghetti of looping off-ramps and roundabouts, a modern industrial grid built with tens of millions of euros donated by the European Union and the Italian government. Economists and bureaucrats
in Brussels, it seemed, had imagined a new warehousing zone to
support the port that would help reverse the economic fortunes of
one of Europe's poorest areas. Initially, 'Ndrangheta construction
companies had been happy to take what public money was on offer.
Then the 'Ndrangheta squashed the project. Threats, violence, and
demands for crippling protection payments had ensured all but one
of the international transport and logistics businesses proposed for
the site had either closed or never opened. Weeds and thickets of
bamboo edged far out into the road. Asphalt roads and concrete
bays cracked and splintered in the sun. Giant bougainvilleas surfed
out over the walls of empty business parks. Once-luxuriant palms
were grotesquely overgrown, their green starbursts turned sickly
yellow by a layer of sticky dust. Streetlights were ubiquitous but
lifeless, connected to a field of large black solar panels fast disappearing under long grass. Rusted signs, some peppered with shotgun blasts, pointed the way to now-defunct enterprises whose gates
were decorated with sun-bleached strings of international flags. In
front of one grand entrance, a giant brass globe on a spike stood at
a crazy angle, a dream of world domination turning, continent by
continent, into a small pile of rusted metal on the ground. The only
sign of life was a herd of goats grazing in drainage ditches choked
with poppies, buttercups, and pink and purple flowers and, to one
side, a tented camp of several thousand African migrants, whom the
authorities, or possibly the 'Ndrangheta, had peevishly kept off-site.

The place felt like a war zone. And in a way it was. Covering the
entire summit of a hill high above the port was a complex of sprawl-
ing villas and gardens once owned by the Piromalli clan, in whose
territory the port lay. From here, the Piromallis had surveyed their
empire like generals. The state had eventually confiscated the prop-

erty but, since no one was willing to buy it, the houses and gardens were empty, an obstinate and unmissable reminder of where real power lay. Below the villa walls were a chapel and graveyard filled with baroque 'Ndranghetisti graves. Since it had been built without permits, the local authority had ordered the chapel demolished, only to discover that no local contractor was available to do the work.

In all of Gioia Tauro, a few lone entrepreneurs had taken a stand. One was Antonino de Masi, who in the 1990s decided to diversify the family agricultural machinery conglomerate into transport logistics. The business had foundered under 'Ndrangheta pressure, and de Masi now pursued other ventures, such as marketing earthquake shelters and smokeless pizza ovens, both of which he had invented himself. But he refused to leave his offices. That simple act of defiance had cost him dearly. After receiving numerous death threats, de Masi had sent his family to live in northern Italy. De Masi himself was obliged to move around in an armored car, flanked by two bodyguards. Two uniformed Italian army soldiers with automatic rifles and a camouflage jeep stood guard in his office parking lot. De Masi described himself as "living in enemy territory."[3]

Why would the 'Ndrangheta ruin its own homeland? Because de Masi was right. As a wealthy businessman with the means to pursue his ambition and the courage not to ask the 'Ndrangheta's permission, he was its sworn foe. It wasn't that the 'Ndrangheta hated development. It was that it tolerated no power other than itself. Inside its territory, there could be no intrusion by the outside world and no escape from the world the 'Ndrangheta had created. Education, especially the kind that encouraged free thinking, was discouraged. The sort of exit offered by gainful employment with a figure like Antonino de Masi also had to be crushed. The 'Ndrangheta even restricted physical ways out of the place. There was just one bus a day to Reggio Calabria. Roads built by 'Ndrangheta construction firms didn't connect to provincial highways, or to each other. Bridges over highways and rivers joined nothing to nowhere. The railway that connected Gioia Tauro to Europe stopped 1.5 kilometers short of the port, meaning all the cargo from one of the biggest Mediterranean container ports had to be loaded onto mafia-owned trucks and driven three minutes to the station. This was the suffocating magnificence of the 'Ndrangheta. The point wasn't money. The point was power.

BY 2010, THE Calabrian anti-mafia prosecutors were finally piecing together quite how much influence the 'Ndrangheta had accumulated. Even veterans of *la mattanza* like Pignatone and Prestipino were astonished. Where once the 'Ndrangheta had been outmatched by Cosa Nostra in drug smuggling, it now dominated the entire European trade in illicit narcotics. Cocaine was produced and refined in Colombia, Peru, or Bolivia, transported east, generally to Brazil or Venezuela, and from there across the Atlantic to Europe via the Caribbean or West Africa, before being landed in Holland, Denmark, Spain, or Italy. Though other criminal groups were involved at each stage of its journey as producers and traffickers, the 'Ndrangheta had assumed a position of broker, overseer, and employer across the entire supply chain.

Inventiveness was a consistent characteristic of this empire, especially in trafficking methods. For sea routes through the Caribbean, the 'Ndrangheta or their partners would conceal cocaine under trawlers full of frozen fish or inside tins of pineapple, or by sewing it into bananas or even dissolving it in bottles of whiskey. Another trick was to secrete a load together with duplicate security tags inside a shipping container carrying other cargo. The drug could then be removed after crossing the Atlantic, generally in customs storage or at a refueling stop, and the containers resealed with the copied tags and sent on their way without detection. To further confuse customs agents, two ships might rendezvous in the middle of the ocean and make a further swap between containers.

Aircraft offered further options. On commercial flights—across the Atlantic to West Africa, and from West Africa to Europe—the smugglers used passengers who would swallow up to thirty plastic bags, amounting to a total load of a kilo each. They would then pack as many as forty "swallowers" onto a plane, sometimes using an entire class of African exchange students who could pay for several years at a foreign university with one trip. Plane crews, who generally sailed through customs without checks, were another good option. Mostly the traffickers would enlist individual stewards, but on occasion they recruited entire crews, including the pilots. When private planes were available, freelance pilots flew small props fitted with custom-enlarged fuel tanks at low altitude thousands of miles across the Atlantic from Latin America to touch down in West Africa. A few times, the smugglers had used an aging Boeing 727, which could take ten tons of cocaine at a time and which in 2009 had been found by the authorities in Mali in the middle of the Sahara, abandoned and torched by the traffickers after snapping its wheels on landing. The onward land route through the Sahara to the Mediterranean was perhaps the most dramatic drug lane of all, involving convoys of twenty to thirty 4×4s driving north for four or five days right across the desert, navigating by the stars and refueling at a string of camouflaged outposts.[4]

Once the drugs reached the Mediterranean, they might be taken from Tunisia to Europe on cruise ships or driven counterclockwise around the coast, across Libya and Egypt and on through Israel and Turkey, a journey facilitated by border guards and army officers. To move cocaine across Europe required a high degree of subterfuge. Tons of cocaine were trucked from Gioia Tauro to Holland hidden under flowers destined for Europe's biggest flower market, where florists served a second purpose as 'Ndrangheta money launderers. Payment going the other way was also disguised. Billions of euros in credit might be uploaded to hundreds of online betting accounts. One time, €7.5 million was sent in the form of 260 tons of Lindt chocolates.[5]

The prosecutors knew which *'ndrine* were so trusted by the Colombians that they were allowed cocaine on credit. They knew which families had diversified into dealing arms. They'd investigated who used smuggling ships on their return journey to dump hazardous chemicals and nuclear waste by sinking boats off the coast of Somalia. The investigators knew which customs services, armies, rebels, Islamists, officials, ministers, prime ministers, and presidents along the smuggling routes took a cut of the profits. Mozambique's customs, the midpoint on an otherwise little-traveled, entirely Portuguese-speaking route from Brazil to Portugal via Africa, had been bought almost whole. So had the entire government of Guinea-Bissau, a tiny West African state and another former Portuguese colony, where soldiers would clear traffic from public highways to allow narco-planes to land.

What gave the prosecutors most pause was how as the rewards of power had multiplied, so had the struggle for it. As 2010 dawned, West Africa was in the midst of an unprecedented wave of coups, civil wars, revolutions, and assassinations driven by the struggle to get rich from drug smuggling. Surveying the chaos created by cocaine, the prosecutors realized the 'Ndrangheta hadn't just ruined Calabria and undermined the Italian state but had done the same to significant parts of the planet. This lent new urgency to their mission. This wasn't the old story about how drugs messed you up. This was about how the 'Ndrangheta's drugs had messed up the lives of hundreds of millions of people in countries on the other side of the world, places that few Europeans had even heard of.

Nor was even that the most worrying part. By 2010, Calabria's

anti-mafia prosecutors were picking up indications that the 'Ndrangheta's money-laundering operations were undermining the world's
financial markets and even the sovereignty of nations. Giuseppe
Lombardo, a prosecutor who specialized in tracking its money, said
that alongside the 'Ndrangheta's growth had come increased financial sophistication. Faced with a need to launder ever-increasing
amounts of money and observing how the world's stock markets
were increasingly lightly regulated, a few 'Ndrangheta families had
made their first few forays into the world of international finance in
the mid-1980s. A generation later, what had begun as an experiment
in diversification and legitimization was now a giant multinational
asset management business run by 'Ndrangheta lawyers, accountants, and bankers in Milan, London, and New York through a maze
of offshore financial centers that specialized in secrecy and low tax:
Cyprus, Malta, Gibraltar, Mauritius, Switzerland, Luxembourg,
Holland, the British Virgin Islands, and other British dependencies.
The global recession of 2007 to 2009 had been a particular boon. As
legitimate finance dried up, businesses, banks, stock markets, and
even political parties found themselves suddenly short of money.
For the 'Ndrangheta, this credit crunch had proved to be a once-in-
a-lifetime chance to convert criminal power into legal economic and
political might around the world.

The 'Ndrangheta was driven by two motivations. It needed to
safely launder its riches. And it wanted to become so indispensable
to the international economy that tackling it would be an act of
self-harm for any government. According to Lombardo, the 'Ndrangheta had largely succeeded in both endeavors. "They have become
one of the main interlocutors in the criminal field," he said. "But
much more broadly, they have become a world power."

Initially, said Lombardo, the 'Ndrangheta had bought politicians
who offered state protection, and created a network of accountants,
lawyers, traders, and other facilitators inside the banking system,

which allowed the 'Ndrangheta to clean and invest its money. But in a crucial second stage, the 'Ndrangheta had opened its financial structure to organized crime groups around the world: Cosa Nostra and the Camorra, but also Chinese triads, Nigerians, Russians, Colombians, Mexicans, and criminal groups from every part of the planet. "The 'Ndrangheta plays the role of service agent to the other mafias," said Lombardo. "They make this network of financial professionals working for them available to other mafias. And after that, when it comes to finances, all the mafias move together as one big mafia."

That meant the 'Ndrangheta had hundreds of billions of euros at its command. Such a tsunami of money had elevated it to a "fundamental and indispensable position in the global market," said Lombardo, one that was "more or less essential for the smooth functioning of the global economic system." This new centrality afforded the 'Ndrangheta the level of protection it sought. It also offered it an opportunity to indulge in typical mafia behavior—bullying, intimidating, extorting, and blackmailing—on a whole new scale. Lombardo had indications that the 'Ndrangheta regularly manipulated stock prices or markets to its advantage and had even caused mini financial crashes to create buying opportunities for itself.

Most remarkable was what the prosecutor had discovered about the mafia's taste for government debt. "I found a huge amount of capital deployed by the mafia to buy government bonds and Treasury debt," he said. At first, this revelation confused Lombardo. There was no sound financial imperative to buy bonds: yields were typically low and far better opportunities were available in other financial instruments. But then he realized the 'Ndrangheta's motivations were more than merely financial. "They don't need to become any richer," he said. "They're rich enough. But alongside the goal of making money is the goal of limiting national sovereignty." The 'Ndrangheta had always sought to undermine Italian state power and authority. Now it was doing the same across the world. It did this by buying up large tranches of foreign countries' debt, then threatening those countries with dumping their debt and prompting a financial default. A debtor nation's only option was to allow the 'Ndrangheta to use its territory as a base and a money-laundering location. So far, the prosecutors had collected evidence that the 'Ndrangheta had blackmailed Thailand and Indonesia in this way. Lombardo expected China and India to be next. "This is about conditioning the global economic system, conditioning the global citizenry, and conditioning the political choices of nations," he said. "This is how the 'Ndrangheta become the rulers not just of territory in Italy but whole other countries."

Lombardo's investigations revealed the 'Ndrangheta not merely as a menace to southern Italy but as a global monster. Though other mafias were better known, the 'Ndrangheta was the most powerful. In the name of profit and power, it was sowing the seeds of war, chaos, and corruption from Rio to Rotterdam to Reykjavík. It was the dark underside of globalization made real in flesh and blood. Of paramount importance to Italy's anti-mafia prosecutors, however, Calabria remained the key to the entire enterprise. Any big business decision—to expand territory, to enter a new business, to eliminate a rival—was referred back to the old country. In their bunkers buried beneath Reggio Calabria and Rosarno and the orange groves of Gioia Tauro plain, the bosses were deciding the fates of nations. As she read through the latest case files, it dawned on Alessandra that with their new crackdown on the 'Ndrangheta, the prosecutors held the destiny of hundreds of millions of people in their hands.

THE STIMULI TO the Italian state's new campaign against the mafia were various: the outcry at the Duisburg massacre of 2007, the

2008 election of a new government publicly committed to ending the threat from organized crime, and, the same year, the arrival in Calabria of Giuseppe Pignatone and Michele Prestipino. The fight against the mafia was quickly reinvigorated with fresh energy and resources. Over 2008 and 2009 the carabinieri bugged millions of conversations. 'Ndranghetisti still habitually spoke in riddles and metaphors, and in isolation the meaning of any one conversation was obscure. But taken together and over time, the mass of recordings added up to a true revelation: the authorities' first-ever complete picture of the internal structure and dynamics of the 'Ndrangheta.

There were several surprises. Hitherto, the prosecutors had understood the 'Ndrangheta as a loose alliance of family firms, each with its own territory. Surveillance of Reggio Calabria and the surrounding towns and villages revealed that the horizontal structure of hundreds of *'ndrine*, each run autonomously by a family boss, was still the 'Ndrangheta's foundation. But it emerged that above it was a new vertical, unifying hierarchy of eleven ranks. Several *'ndrine* together made a grouping called a *locale* or *società*, managed by a paramount chief, assisted by an accountant and a "head of crime" who oversaw all illegal activities. Above the *locali* were three regional authorities called *mandamenti*, one each for the Tyrrhenian and Ionian coasts and another for Reggio Calabria. Together these three groups made up a council variously called *la provincia* or *il crimine* or—something that made Alessandra do a double take—*La Mamma*. Overseeing all of it was a *capo crimine*, or boss of bosses, who could convene a court, or *tribunale*, of senior bosses to judge a peer accused of transgressing the code.[6] "We'd always thought of the 'Ndrangheta as a lot of local, smaller organizations," said Alessandra. "Suddenly we realized it had a federal structure and was being run almost like a military organization."

In the 1990s, carabinieri had picked up word of an attempt by the 'Ndrangheta to unite the clans. That had ultimately failed. From what the carabinieri were hearing now, this time the reorganization had succeeded. Why? The old arguments in favor of better coordination to improve efficiency and discipline still stood. But in 2009, the carabinieri were detecting a more ominous motivation: to coordinate a concerted assault on the authorities through a series of assassinations and bombings. On October 31, 2009, the carabinieri filmed an especially brazen 'Ndrangheta summit outside Milan at which twenty-two bosses raised their glasses to toast the new city boss inside a memorial dedicated to Giovanni Falcone and Paolo Borsellino.[7] The 'Ndrangheta was abandoning its decades-old policy of discreet infiltration in favor of direct confrontation. Why the change? From what the carabinieri could gather, the 'Ndrangheta felt their hand was being forced. The new push against organized crime had resulted in the arrests of hundreds of mafiosi, including twenty-one of Italy's thirty "most wanted," and the confiscation of assets and businesses worth €9 billion.[8] Though the operations had hurt the Camorra most of all, the 'Ndrangheta knew it was next. Its bosses had decided on an aggressive and unified response.

For Alessandra, one episode captured by the new intelligence was especially significant. Officers watching a mafia wedding in the hill town of Platì on August 19, 2009, between two powerful clans, the Pelles and the Barbaros, were amazed to spot a who's who of the 'Ndrangheta among the two thousand guests. These included bosses not only from across Calabria but also from northern Italy, Europe, and as far away as Canada and Australia. "They came from all over the planet to this tiny little town in the middle of nowhere," said Alessandra. The reason for this unprecedented summit was soon clear. Wiretaps and bugs picked up numerous references to the election of a new *capo crimine*, Rosarno boss Domenico Oppedisano, appointed to spearhead the 'Ndrangheta's war on the state. That seemed to confirm the importance of a well-attended meeting of bosses held a few days earlier in Oppedisano's orange orchard. Two weeks after the wedding, Oppedisano's promotion was formally confirmed at the annual 'Ndrangheta meeting, held at the festival for the Madonna di Polsi at San Luca.

What interested Alessandra was not Oppedisano himself but who he represented. She knew the *capo crimine* was elected by a kind of criminal meritocracy, based on who inside the organization was deemed "most charismatic, most admirable, and most ruthless." The boss had to be someone the entire 'Ndrangheta could agree outdid them all for criminal excellence, a leader who would ensure they wasted no more time and blood fighting each other.

On the face of it, seventy-eight-year-old Oppedisano, with his farmer's tan and a family that was outranked by at least two others in Rosarno, was an eccentric choice. But with her burgeoning knowledge of the clans, Alessandra could see its logic. More than advancing the Oppedisanos, Domenico's new position confirmed the ascendancy of the west coast clans inside the 'Ndrangheta. Specifically, it attested to the dominance of a particular Rosarno crime family to whom Oppedisano was related by marriage. It was this family's domination of the cocaine trade with two other Gioia Tauro families that, more than anything, accounted for the 'Ndrangheta's spectacular growth over the last three decades. Its reputation for ruthless violence ensured that as well as being one of the richest and most powerful crime families in all Italy, it was also one of the most feared. "Through Gioia Tauro, they were running all the drugs and all the arms," said Alessandra.

So spectacular had been this family's progress and so naked their ambition to dominate the 'Ndrangheta, however, that they were resented by almost every other *'ndrina*. An earlier attempt to force the election of their own family *capo* had been fiercely resisted on all sides as an unacceptable affront. The other families might be diminished by comparison, but honor demanded they save face by pretending otherwise. Nominating Domenico Oppedisano was a shrewd compromise, combining the signature 'Ndrangheta characteristics of strategy and willful delusion.

Still, Alessandra had no doubt who now held power inside the 'Ndrangheta. She had seen video surveillance of family members toasting Oppedisano with champagne on the night he was elected. In any new war on the 'Ndrangheta, this family would be target number one. They were called the Pesces.

VII

L EA GAROFALO WASN'T the first 'Ndranghetista to turn on the
organization, nor even the first woman.[1] But she was one of a
mere handful of 'Ndrangheta *pentiti*, and only the second woman,
and the story of the Pagliarelle mama and boss's daughter who
had crossed over to the state had reverberated like a cannon blast
around the valleys. Seven years later, Lea was most likely dead. The
message that sent to places like Pagliarelle and Rosarno was that
there *was* no alternative to the 'Ndrangheta. You leave, you die. It
was a disaster for the Italian state's new war on the mafia. What had
gone wrong?

Lea's long struggle with Carlo and the 'Ndrangheta was
well documented. She had made lengthy statements against the
'Ndrangheta and Carlo three times, in 1996, 2002, and 2008. From
these, the picture that emerged of the rural Calabria where Lea
and Carlo had grown up was of a lost world, cut off from the rest
of humanity by a wall of violent tyranny. For most 'Ndrangheta
children, it was enough just to be born in a place like Pagliarelle
to know their destiny.

But Lea had been different. Her father, an *'ndrina* boss called
Antonio Garofalo, was killed by three brothers from a rival clan
on New Year's Eve, 1974, when he was twenty-seven and Lea was
just eight months old—and, for Lea, none of it made sense after
that. The feud, or *faida*, that her father's murder set off between the
Garofalos and the Mirabellis, another Pagliarelle family, lasted all

through her childhood until Lea was eighteen. When she was seven, in 1981, Lea's uncle Giulio tried to avenge his brother by opening fire on a Mirabelli funeral. A few months later, Giulio was killed in retaliation. In 1989, when Lea was fifteen, another of her relatives was shot dead, right in front of her and in broad daylight, in the center of Petilia Policastro. That same year, the Garofalos began taking their revenge, killing one of the three Mirabelli brothers. They shot a second in 1990 and the third in 1991, then in 1992 they murdered Mario Garofalo, a cousin who—illustrating the incestuous nature of the feud—worked for the Mirabellis.

Lea's older brother, Floriano, directed much of the bloodletting. He involved his nine-year-old sister, asking her to hide a pistol belonging to their uncle when a police raid was imminent.[2] But despite Floriano's instruction in the duties of vendetta, despite Marisa's warnings about the need at least to pretend, despite all the anger she felt over her father's death, and barely knowing that any other life even existed, Lea couldn't remember a day when she hadn't seen through the lie. "Lea was born into a family where violence was the rule," said her former lawyer Vincenza Rando, known to everyone as Enza. "It was 'Kill one of mine and I'll kill one of yours.'" Lea saw the world differently, said Enza. To her, "the 'Ndrangheta was a cult of death, and Lea was a woman who loved life. The 'Ndrangheta writes your destiny for you. Lea wanted to write her own."

Lea's independence might have come from her mother. Though her mother had married an 'Ndranghetista, she had always worked, mostly as a cleaner at a school in Petilia. "Our mother had a completely different mind-set from people around here," said Marisa. "She was a decent woman." It was Lea's mother who taught her what Lea always used to tell Denise: that education was freedom, and that providing for her family was what gave a woman dignity.

Still, their mother wasn't affectionate, said Marisa. She, Floriano, and Lea grew up mostly in the care of their grandparents, who might as well have been from another century. Of the three children, Marisa said it was Lea, the youngest, who felt their parents' absence most keenly. She was always asking for pictures of her father, who, since she had never known him, she was free to imagine as perfect: caring and loving and cruelly taken from the daughter he adored. As a teenager, Lea had a small "A" for Antonio tattooed onto her hand. While the violence raged on around them, Lea couldn't imagine her father wanting her to spend her life carving out brief moments of peace in a dead-end job as her mother had done. "You don't *live*," Lea told the carabinieri in 2002. "You just survive in some way. You dream about something—anything—because nothing's worse than that life." As Lea grew up, it dawned on her that the freedom she craved would be impossible unless she left Pagliarelle.

Lea's tragedy was that, like many 'Ndrangheta women, she thought love was her way out. When she was fifteen she fell for a village boy she had known all her life, a thick-set bruiser with a flattened nose and cropped hair called Carlo Cosco. Carlo, nineteen at the time, was back from his new life in the north and visiting Pagliarelle for the holidays. What Lea especially liked about him was that he seemed to have no ambition other than to work an honest job and raise a family. And he lived in Milan, "a big city where she could start again," said Enza. Lea and Carlo eloped after a few weeks. When she was sixteen, in 1991, they married and moved to Milan, where Carlo had an apartment in a large, drab building on Viale Montello.

Almost immediately, Lea realized her escape was a mirage. No. 6 Viale Montello was in the possession of the 'Ndrangheta and Carlo turned out to be one of several 'Ndranghetisti using it as a base from which to traffic cocaine and heroin. Lea had rejected the 'Ndrangheta code, but it transpired that her new husband's embrace of it had been so wholehearted, he thought nothing of tricking Lea into marrying him. Worst of all, it emerged that Carlo was working for Lea's brother, Floriano, whose bloodthirstiness in Pagliarelle had propelled him to the head of the Garofalo 'ndrina. Lea had thought she courted Carlo. Now it occurred to her that Carlo had sought her out—because she was the sister of an 'Ndrangheta boss. Marriage to her had been a promotion for Carlo. For Lea, the love she had imagined would free her had trapped her even deeper.

Lea sank into depression. According to Enza, she made several attempts at suicide. When she got pregnant in the spring of 1991, Lea tried to abort. "She did not want to give her son or daughter the same future," said Enza. In December, heavily pregnant, she left Viale Montello and took a bus to a hospital deep in the country. She gave birth alone, to a baby girl. Lea had imagined she might give her baby up for adoption, somewhere Carlo would never find the child. "But when Denise was born," said Enza, "Lea fell in love all over again. Denise gave Lea a reason to live."

LIKE EVERYONE WHO had worked mafia cases in Milan, Alessandra knew all about No. 6 Viale Montello. A vast and historic building in the middle of the Italian business capital, *il fortino delle cosche* (the fort of the clans) wasn't just a mafia base but a six-story challenge to Italy's claim to be a modern, unified, lawful state. The 'Ndranghetisti paid no rent on its 129 apartments, nor any tax, nor any bills for municipal services like water or electricity. They treated the Renaissance mansion with disdain. A spaghetti of wires hung from its walls and collapsing balconies. Its courtyards and central garden were filled with refuse and rusted, broken appliances. The stairwells and corners stank of urine. Not only was the building a hub of the European drug trade, it was the source of supply for hundreds of Milan's street dealers, especially those in the notorious Piazza Baiamonti, and a focal point for other criminals of every type: enforcers, smugglers, and killers; political corrupters and state contract fixers; wayward policemen, judges, and politicians. And all of it in flagrant plain sight. Viale Montello was an arterial thoroughfare just a kilometer from the city center and yards from a city police station. Unsurprisingly, No. 6 Viale Montello was something of a preoccupation for Milan's anti-mafia prosecutors, who had it under near-permanent surveillance.

For the prosecutors, the relationships inside No. 6 Viale Montello in the 1990s—between brothers, in-laws, and even husband and wife—and the way those dynamics eventually played out became an important early case study of this newly ascendant mafia. It was from watching events there that the prosecutors would be able to assemble a picture of what Alessandra described as a "modern, efficient, present-day organized crime syndicate" whose strength lay in "enforcing a respect for medieval rules." In the end, the prosecutors would conclude that they were fighting a culture, and that in No. 6 Viale Montello they had a peculiarly instructive petri dish. Among the most informative events they watched there was the rise of an ambitious young 'Ndranghetista called Carlo Cosco, and his eventual undoing by his wife.

Carlo's first big step up the ladder had been to marry the boss's sister. On his return to Milan in 1991, the surveillance teams watched as Floriano's lieutenants in Milan, Silvano Toscano and Thomas Ceraudo, duly catapulted Carlo and his brothers, Vito and Giuseppe, to prominence, granting them control of the lucrative dope and protection rackets in Piazza Baiamonti and nearby Quarto Oggiaro. As a medium-level drug smuggler, dealer, and extortionist, Carlo wasn't above manual tasks. Sometimes he would ask his new wife, Lea, to help cut and package heroin, cocaine, and hashish. He asked her for other favors, too, like spying on Antonio Comberiati, a rival 'Ndranghetista who lived in the building with his wife, Gina.

Comberiati was a hothead and troublemaker. His nickname was *il lupo*, "the wolf." He resented most of the families in Viale Montello, seemingly aggrieved by his and Gina's inability to conceive. But he was especially incensed by Carlo's promotion.

One day in February 1994, Lea was dressing Denise, then two, for her first Milan city carnival, when Carlo interrupted to say he had seen Comberiati talking to the Chinese shop owner who "employed" Carlo as a security guard. This arrangement was standard for the men at Viale Montello. Whenever carabinieri asked for proof of occupation, they would be shown contracts of employment claiming a job providing security for the Chinese traders on the ground floor. Carlo was concerned by what might be transpiring between his sponsor and his rival and asked Lea to listen in from the street. Lea soon overheard Comberiati insisting that the store close because it was being watched by the carabinieri. If Carlo lost his "job," said Comberiati, that was too bad.

This was too much for Lea. "I couldn't help myself," she said in testimony years later. "I interrupted and tried to defend Carlo, saying we had a daughter and Carlo had the right to remain there to work." Comberiati, outraged at being confronted by a woman, and his rival's wife to boot, shouted back that he outranked Carlo. Then he threatened to kill Lea for daring to face him. "I'm the boss around here!" he shouted. "I'm in charge! It's my right!"

The fight continued inside the courtyard of Viale Montello. Eventually, Gina and several other women intervened. Lea ran back up to her apartment. Carlo was waiting. He had heard everything. "Don't worry," he reassured Lea. "One day Comberiati will pay."

In the event, it was Comberiati who made the first move. In simultaneous assassinations on the night of November 30, 1994, Thomas Ceraudo was gunned down in Quarto Oggiaro and Silvano Toscano was abducted from his mother-in-law's house in Petilia and killed, his body dumped in a field outside town. Comberiati barely bothered to deny he was to blame. The surveillance teams at Viale Montello reported that he immediately installed himself as the new king of Milan.

But with Carlo's backers dead and Floriano looking weak, Comberiati was daring Carlo to respond. Six months after the double murders, just after midnight on May 17, 1995, Lea was sleeping in bed with Denise when she heard several shots ring out in the courtyard below. When she opened the door, she could see Comberiati's body lying prone on the concrete. It was raining. Gina was screaming for an ambulance and shouting that the killer was still in the building. She started smashing the windows of a Chinese shop in which she was convinced the gunman was hiding. Lea observed her. Then she watched the ambulance and carabinieri arrive. After twenty minutes, Carlo's brother Giuseppe appeared at her door, exhilarated.

"He's dead," said Giuseppe.

"You sure?" asked Lea.

Giuseppe giggled. "The bastard just wouldn't fucking die," he said. "It was like he had the devil in him or something. But, yeah, he's dead now, for sure."

Giuseppe left for his apartment. Carlo arrived seconds later.

"Where were you?" asked Lea.

"Karaoke," replied Carlo.

"Liar," Lea shot back.

Carlo laughed. "Well, then, I've been over at the shop getting a sandwich."

Lea later told the carabinieri that she had surmised that Carlo had stood watch for Giuseppe while his brother shot Comberiati, then the two men had dumped the gun in the street. It made sense for Giuseppe to pull the trigger, said Lea, because he "needed the points." "Carlo doesn't need them," she explained to the prosecutors. "He's already Floriano's brother-in-law. But Giuseppe's no one. A killing like this gives him position. He becomes somebody."

With his rival dead, Carlo's accession, and the elevation of the Cosco family, was complete. Previous generations of Coscos had been goat herders and fruit farmers. Now, through luck and ruthlessness, they were players in an exploding international criminal empire. Carlo himself was right hand and brother by marriage to Floriano Garofalo, one of the most powerful 'ndrina bosses in all Calabria.

For Lea, however, something died with Comberiati. Her husband had brought violence into the home where she lived with their daughter. Years earlier, she had tried to escape and it hadn't worked. For Denise's sake, she had to try again. Looking at her daughter was like looking at herself in the third person, thought Lea. She could see everything clearly: all the troubles around the two of them and what they needed to do to move past them. "She wanted Denise to have other possibilities in her life," said Enza. "The chance to be part of the cult of life and friendship and respect and to be part of another kind of family."

Lea tried one more time to convince Carlo to leave the 'Ndrangheta. The three of them could begin again somewhere new and raise their baby to be anything she wanted to be, she said. Carlo's response was to beat her. That was the last straw for Lea. "So she decided to go to the carabinieri and tell them all about the drug trafficking," said Enza.

In May 1996, Carlo, Floriano, Giuseppe, and several others were arrested at No. 6 Viale Montello. The operation to detain them—using four hundred men to seal off the street and storm the building—confirmed the Coscos' new status in the European drug trafficking elite. Carlo was transferred to San Vittore prison, on the other side of town.

Though she had played a key role in his arrest, Lea decided she would give Carlo one last chance. In September 1996, Lea, now twenty-two, took Denise, five, to see him in prison. "I want to stay with you," she told him, "but on one condition: you collaborate with the carabinieri and denounce the 'Ndrangheta. When you come out of jail, we can start a new life. Or you continue this life and you will never see me or Denise again."

Carlo leaped over the screen between them and grabbed Lea. He had his hands around her throat by the time the prison guards pulled him off. He expected his wife to stand by him. After all the work and all the blood, Carlo's maneuvering had paid off. He was king of Milan. Now Lea was betraying him and taking it all away: his link to the boss in the old country, his standing in the brotherhood, even his self-respect as a man. Lea had broken the code. There was only one remedy. From that day, said Enza, Lea knew she was living under "a death sentence."

Lea returned to Viale Montello for a final time. She packed a suitcase, then called a friend to drive her and Denise to a convent in Bergamo where they would be safe. Renata, Giuseppe Cosco's wife, saw Lea leave. "I remember the day Lea left Milan well," she said in court fifteen years later. "Lea looked at me with anger. She spat on the ground. She swore she would never again set foot in that shitty place. She yelled that she wanted a different future for herself. A different future for her daughter." And just like that, Lea and Denise were gone.

THE NEXT SIX years were the happiest of Lea's and Denise's lives. Initially, the pair stayed in an Ursuline convent in Bergamo dedicated to the education of women and girls. In Mother Grata, who ran the convent, Lea seemed to discover the parent she'd never had. She began reading for the first time in years, learning about Giovanni Falcone, Paolo Borsellino, and Giuseppe Impastato, a Palermo anti-mafia activist who had been born into a Cosa Nostra family and was assassinated by them at thirty. After a few months, Lea and Denise moved into a small apartment on Via Alfieri, a quiet street of bungalows and two-story houses painted yellow and pink.

Later they moved into town to another small place on Via Mose del Brolo, a dead-end street full of pensioners and students. Lea found work in factories and bars. She met a man. She and Denise adopted a dog. Lea even went skydiving.

Every June, Lea and Denise would go down to Pagliarelle to spend the summer holidays with Marisa and their relatives. Perhaps it was those breaks in Calabria, unmolested by Carlo's men, that lulled Lea into thinking her escape was real. When they were back home, Lea even allowed Denise to visit Carlo in Catanzaro jail, to which he had been transferred from Milan.

But Carlo never had Lea out of his sights. When the officers investigating Lea's disappearance tracked down Salvatore Cortese, an 'Ndrangheta killer who had shared a cell with Carlo in Catanzaro from 2001 to 2003 and had since turned *pentito*, Cortese told them Carlo never forgave Lea. Carlo, he said, was always talking about how Lea had betrayed him and betrayed the 'Ndrangheta. Carlo was especially incensed that she still stayed with her family in Pagliarelle and walked around the village alone and in front of everyone. She was flaunting her freedom, said Carlo. He knew about her affair in Bergamo and suspected, since Lea never came to visit, that the other inmates in Catanzaro had deduced the same thing. Worst of all, her brother Floriano was doing nothing about any of it. Carlo had been wronged and wronged again. It was intolerable. "And," said Cortese, "according to the 'Ndrangheta's rules, Floriano's silence allowed Carlo to appeal to other men of honor for permission to kill Lea."

Nonetheless, killing the sister of a boss was a tricky business. Carlo told Cortese that Lea had to be dispatched in such a way that Floriano would believe she had run off with her new lover. "The plan to physically eliminate Lea Garofalo and get rid of her body by dissolving it in acid grew in Carlo's mind since at least the early 2000s," said Cortese. How, the carabinieri asked, did Cortese know that? Because, Cortese replied, he was among those Carlo asked to help him.

Carlo knew he might fool Floriano but not the entire 'Ndrangheta. If he was to pull off such an audacious killing, he would need approval from higher up. Approaching two bosses in the prison yard, he explained how his honor and that of the wider 'Ndrangheta had been so impugned that it could only be restored by washing it in blood. The two bosses knew Carlo was right. But they had their own clan feuds to pursue. Calculating that Carlo's vendetta would anyway have to wait until he was released from jail, they stalled.

Carlo still held out hope that Floriano would choose his duty over love for his sister. Getting his brothers to set Lea's car alight in Bergamo in 2000 was Carlo's way of reminding Floriano of his obligation. It had some effect. One summer's day two years later, when Lea and Denise were back in Pagliarelle, Lea took Denise to buy a gelato from the shop off the main piazza. Vito Cosco drove up in his car. He was agitated. He told Lea he was tired of taking Denise to see Carlo. Carlo was sick of it, too. It wasn't right, said Vito. Lea had to get in line.

Lea refused. As the argument grew more heated, Floriano, by then out of prison and back in Pagliarelle, arrived. Vito was right, Floriano shouted at Lea. What kind of woman let her husband rot in jail alone? What kind of sister was she to him, Floriano, an *'ndrina* boss? Then, in the middle of the square, Floriano held Lea by her shoulders and slapped her across the face for everyone to see. He leaned over his sister, looking as though he was about to strike her again. As he did so, however, he whispered in her ear: "Lea! You have to escape! Because, really, I have to kill you!"

TWICE LEA HAD run from the 'Ndrangheta. Twice it had clawed her back in. For choosing freedom over murderous criminality, her husband wanted her dead, the 'Ndrangheta required it, and her brother had told her he would be the one to do it. Lea felt like the world was closing in on her. On July 29, 2002, a few days after the argument with Vito and Floriano, the door of Lea's grandmother's house was set alight while Lea and Denise were inside. It was an especially blunt 'Ndrangheta message. There was no way out.

Perhaps because it was so unthinkable, the 'Ndrangheta had overlooked one exit, however. The same morning as the fire, prosecutor Sandro Dolce in the nearby city of Catanzaro received a call from the chief of the carabinieri in Petilia Policastro. "He told me that in front of him stood the sister of Floriano Garofalo. She had a ten-year-old girl with her. She wanted to give evidence about a number of facts and events concerning her family. She wanted to break with her past and the environment in which she had been living."

Dolce immediately understood the significance of what he was hearing. In 2002, the authorities knew very little about the 'Ndrangheta. Despite prosecuting several 'Ndranghetisti for their roles in the Pagliarelle feud, their knowledge of what had happened barely extended beyond the body count. Though they had successfully prosecuted Carlo and Floriano for drug trafficking, they also knew little about the structures and hierarchy of the wider 'Ndrangheta. "Up until that time, we had very poor knowledge of the workings of the 'Ndrangheta," said Dolce. "State witnesses are our main source of knowledge for any mafia and we just hadn't got that many from the 'Ndrangheta. The 'Ndrangheta was known, of course—its existence was no big secret—but its internal dynamics were not known."

Dolce knew immediately what he had to do. "I did not go to Petilia," he said. "It's a small town. The fact that she had gone to the carabinieri would have already alarmed people there. So I could not go personally to listen to her statement there. Instead, I had the carabinieri move her urgently to a hotel one hundred kilometers away, and I went to see her there. And I did nothing but listen to her talk for two days."

What particularly impressed Dolce was how different Lea was from the stereotype of an 'Ndrangheta woman. Most were submissive, ignorant, and poorly educated. Lea was assertive, knowledgeable, and articulate. "She had a different outlook," said Dolce. "She was open-minded. She wanted her own life. She did not want to depend on a man or to stay at home. She wanted her independence. She wanted to be the protagonist and the subject in her own life. Lea had grit." Just as impressive, said Dolce, "she was very honest. If she hadn't told us she had been involved in the drugs, we'd never have known."

Lea's testimony began from her father's death when she was eight months old and ran through everything that had happened in the previous twenty-eight years. She spoke about the Pagliarelle feud. She gave an account of all the murders and named all the killers. She detailed how her brother Floriano had shot and knifed his way to the top, and how that had enabled him to take over the protection and cocaine rackets in Milan, especially Quarto Oggiaro. She talked about packaging and distributing cocaine inside No. 6 Viale Montello. She described Antonio Comberiati's murder and how Carlo and Giuseppe had spoken about killing him. Finally, she said she had decided to turn state's evidence because she felt time was running out. Her greatest fear was that someone would break into her house and shoot Denise.

Reading through Lea's statements years later, prosecutors investigating her disappearance were amazed by the detail. Dolce had reacted the same way at the time. "I have had experience of false *pentiti*—men who just say a few things but not everything," he said. "They make a utilitarian choice. They decide to collaborate because they are facing life sentences." But Lea was different, he said. Her collaboration was "more genuine, and more effective. She said everything she knew. She hid nothing. You could feel how her choice had put her through suffering and pain. But she had a very dignified look. She was very determined and proud of what she had done."

The more the new team of Calabrian prosecutors read about Lea, the more they were struck by how, seven years before, in two days of interviews and on her own initiative, Lea had single-handedly proved Alessandra's theory that mothers were the key to undoing the 'Ndrangheta. Lea's testimony amounted to an unprecedented insight into the 'Ndrangheta. Her motivation—to give Denise a better life—was untainted and unstoppable. Lea should have prompted a complete rethink inside the Italian judiciary of the value of women in the fight against the mafia. There was certainly every reason to imagine that July 2002 had been the start of a whole new chapter in the war on the mafia. That made the investigation into Lea's disappearance even more critical. What had happened?

VIII

L EA WAS A beguiling mix of the carefree and the purposeful.[1]
She laughed easily, because life was for living, but she would
erupt if she felt her freedom or Denise's were threatened. She and
Denise would have been safer, she knew, if she had been able to accept the meek, servile existence of an 'Ndrangheta mother and wife.
But to Lea, that meant dying anyway. If the happiness she enjoyed
as a free woman and the possibilities Denise enjoyed outside the
'Ndrangheta were often eclipsed by terror, it was a price Lea felt
they had to pay.

The day Lea walked with Denise into a carabinieri station in
July 2002, she was petrified. Annalisa Pisano, then thirty-four, was
a public defender on call. "There was a list of lawyers to deal with
witness cooperation," she said. "I think they picked me because I
lived close by and I was a woman." Tall with short blond hair and
the businesslike bearing of a young criminal lawyer with her own
practice, Annalisa arrived at the station, rang the bell in the waiting
room, and sat down, unaware that the mother with a small child
sitting quietly next to her was her new client. "But then the carabinieri officer came and said: 'This is the girl who has asked for your
help. She has made the choice to talk.' And we had fifteen minutes
to prepare before the procedure began."

Annalisa remembered thinking how Lea was "so small, so skinny,
and Denise so tiny." She wondered how they would handle the giant
step they were taking. "There's almost no words to describe the

choice Lea was making," said Annalisa. "I could see she was blinded by terror, in a condition of high anxiety and stress. She had an idea about her brother, that he could take some action to reconcile with Carlo and preserve the status quo. But she was trying, like all mothers, to be courageous because she had her daughter with her." Annalisa tried to be sympathetic, telling Lea that she would get help and support from the state. The provincial carabinieri guarding her were no help. "Are you really interested in cooperating?" asked one officer, gruffly. "Because if not, you'll stay here."

The state's first task was to assess whether Lea and Denise were worth protecting. After two days of testimony, Lea was judged genuine, and she and her daughter were granted state protection. The process, bureaucratic and banal, was at odds with the momentous nature of what was happening. This, after all, was how a *pentita* gave up allegiance to family and homeland, abandoned everything and everyone they had ever known, accepted that forever after they would be at war with one of the world's most ruthless mafias, and put their faith in a state that they had been taught to despise from birth.

Initially, Lea and Denise were moved to Ascoli Piceno, a small, quiet province east of Rome. Lea told Denise they were to pretend they were sisters. They'd even had new make-believe names: Alessandra de Rossi and her younger sister, Sara. But Denise kept forgetting the rules, calling Lea Mama or Ma, and after a few weeks, Lea changed their names to Maria and Denise Petalo so that anyone overhearing them could excuse Ma as Lea's nickname.

Though safe from harm, Lea and Denise found their new life hard. They were rarely in one place long enough to put down new roots, moving six times in six years. Lea, for whom freedom meant the opportunity to be gregarious, found the isolation especially difficult. Her one connection to the outside world was a mobile given to her by the prosecutors, which she used to talk to Annalisa. "We spoke every day for the next six years, even on Saturdays and Sundays," said Annalisa. "For all that time, I was her only point of contact on the outside."

Despite the state's efforts, Lea also felt a constant threat around the corner. One day in August 2003, she read in the newspaper how Vito Cosco, then thirty-four, had shot and killed two small-time drug dealers who had insulted him. One of Vito's shots had also killed a two-year-old girl. A fourth victim, a sixty-year-old man who witnessed the shooting, had collapsed and died on the spot. Vito holed up at No. 6 Viale Montello for three days before phoning the carabinieri and telling them to come and arrest him. The newspapers called the killings "the massacre of Rozzano" after the small town outside Milan where they took place.

The Garofalo-Mirabelli *faida* raged on as well. In September 2003, Lea's cousin, Mario Garofalo, was shot in his car at a junction outside Pagliarelle. In June 2005, Floriano, by then forty, was walking to his front door in Pagliarelle when a man stepped out of the shadows carrying a shotgun. Floriano ran. Sprinting through a vegetable plot, he tore across the main road and up a side street. The gunman ran after him and shot him in the back. Floriano fell against a fence. The gunman reloaded, walked up to Floriano, and shot him several times in the face, blowing his head back to a stump.

Though Lea had often lived in fear of Floriano when he was alive, now she was convinced her brother had died because he had refused to kill her. Carlo had been released from prison in December 2003. Floriano's murder eighteen months later couldn't be a coincidence. "It's my fault they killed him," she told Marisa. The guilt destroyed her. Just as bad, in her safe house her protection officers would grin at her and tell her that the threat to her life was gone. They didn't understand anything. Not that it had probably been Carlo who had killed Floriano. And not that with Floriano dead, Carlo now not only ruled the Pagliarelle 'Ndrangheta but had also inherited the task of restoring its honor by killing Lea. The threat to Lea had soared. She took to staying awake through the night and sleeping during the day while Denise was at school. Even then, she kept a knife under her pillow.

Lea was right to be scared. Carlo began his search for her the day he left jail. He dropped by the convent in Bergamo, explaining he was a relative and asking the nuns if they had any contact with his cousin. In November 2004, Gennaro Garofalo, a member of Carlo's *'ndrina* who had once worked as a police auxiliary, showed up at his old station in Monza, asked his old colleagues out for pizza, then casually logged onto the witness protection system to search for Denise's address, which came up as No. 9 Via Giovanni Ruggia, Perugia. Later in court Gennaro would claim he saw nothing sinister in a father's desire to know his daughter's whereabouts. "Carlo always treated Denise well," he explained. "In Pagliarelle, he made sure Denise ate and dressed well. She always had earrings."

Early in 2005, Carlo sent two of his men, Rosario Curcio and Giovanni Peci, to find Lea in Perugia. The address in Via Giovanni Ruggia turned out to be a police station. When the men returned to Carlo empty-handed, he sent them back in a fury. By then, however, word had circulated in Pagliarelle that Carlo was closing in on Lea and a cousin had traveled to Perugia to warn her. Lea and Denise were quickly moved to Florence. But Carlo was relentless. In 2006, he sent another cousin, Genevieve Garofalo, to meet Lea with a message that Carlo wanted to see her and had set aside €200,000 for Denise. "It's a trap," Lea told Denise. "He's trying to get us back to Calabria." Lea was right, no doubt. Still, Carlo's persistence was having an effect. Lea could feel herself increasingly enclosed in a prison of paranoia.

ALESSANDRA HAD ENOUGH experience of witness protection not to be surprised by Lea's experience of it. The system wasn't perfect.

The mafia had always had its men inside the judiciary, who passed it information on the whereabouts of *pentiti*. There was also an inherent contradiction between trying to protect someone and simultaneously giving them their freedom. Sometimes that need for personal liberation led witnesses to put themselves in harm's way. Lea's motivation was always to give Denise a different life. But she also longed to free herself—and she had hardly achieved that. She couldn't go out unaccompanied. She couldn't talk to strangers. She was to live meekly and quietly, dependent on meager handouts. It was eerily similar to 'Ndrangheta life. Some of the officers guarding her seemed to regard her as little more than a lowlife Calabrian hick who'd conned the state and struck it lucky. The truth was that the sacrifices she had made in her fight against the mafia—risking her life, abandoning her family and friends—were far greater than any nine-to-five provincial cop would ever make.

Lea began to push back. She demanded to see her boyfriend from Bergamo. She asked not to be placed in towns with Calabrian populations. She wandered off into town without telling anyone. She refused to accept her protection officers' complaints about her behavior. "Why do I have to defend myself against the state that is supposed to be defending me and my daughter?" she asked. Denise, as a growing girl, was also becoming difficult. "Lea would explain to her daughter why they were moving and why they had to change their names," said Sandro Dolce, the prosecutor, "then the daughter would talk about it at school, and they would have to move again."

As months turned to years, the state began to have doubts about Lea and Denise for other reasons, too. The procedure for mafia turncoats was to keep them closely guarded while their evidence was evaluated and corroborated, and any trials conducted. Only after that would the government give them a permanent new identity, home, and job. But not only was Lea proving tiresome to handle, without other *pentiti* to confirm her evidence, the investigators were having trouble building a solid case against Carlo. Lea's statements, mostly describing what she had heard but not seen, weren't enough on their own to make arrests or secure convictions. "We investigated for a long time but we never found enough confirmation," said Dolce. "Then a colleague replaced me and was very severe in his assessment: how what we had was not enough for arrests, and the silly things Lea did. So in February 2006 Lea and Denise were ejected from the program."

Annalisa immediately won Lea and Denise a temporary reprieve while she appealed the decision to throw them out of witness protection. But Lea was shattered. The state had reneged. It had promised her and her daughter a new life. Then it had betrayed them. She had expected the state to prosecute every crime she had revealed. It hadn't prosecuted any. Worse, by taking her testimony, the state had needlessly exposed Lea and Denise to even more danger than before. The Italian state, Lea decided, was little better than the 'Ndrangheta. The irony was that if Lea had been an actual 'Ndranghetista—if she had taken part in the dealing and the thieving and the killing—she would have been of more use to the authorities. It felt like they were punishing her for being honest.

That July, she phoned Annalisa. "I've changed my mind," she said. "I'm getting out of the program." Denise said later, "My mother decided to give up on the state. She had lost all confidence in them. Our life was exhausting, and for what? Her statements turned out to be useless."

Annalisa, aware that Lea was now suffering increasingly dramatic mood swings, managed to talk her client around. "More and more, she was finding herself lost in a reality that was bigger than her," said Annalisa. "You have to remember she was just a girl, only thirty-two years old. She thought her world and all her plans were collapsing around her." But Lea had already submitted a formal request to leave the program, and until Annalisa could get her readmitted, she and Denise were on their own. It was terrifying, said Annalisa. The state had washed its hands of Lea and Denise. Her mafioso husband was trying to kill her. Lea had no one. "And so," said Annalisa, "it fell to me."

Annalisa did her best. In November 2006, she moved close to where Lea and Denise were living. She became, as she said, "less a lawyer than a mother." But Lea remained volatile and mistrustful. Denise, who turned fifteen in December 2006, was also no longer a girl playing a game of hide-and-seek with her mother but, increasingly, had become a teenager with her own opinions. Lea had shielded her daughter from much of the truth about Carlo. The price of Denise's innocence was that she didn't understand why, now that she and Lea were out of witness protection, she couldn't see her father. "Denise kept asking," said Annalisa. "She would insist, pressing and pressing. Lea would call me every day because she couldn't manage Denise—you know how teenagers are." Annalisa tried to mediate between mother and daughter. Denise responded by demanding that the lawyer find a way for her to meet her father. Annalisa refused point-blank. "I told Denise it was completely unacceptable for her to meet her father. I only had to see the terror in Lea's eyes when the name of Cosco came up. But I think Denise started hating me after that."

Looking for help wherever she might find it, Lea briefly moved with Denise back to Bergamo, where Lea sought the advice of Mother Grata and found a job in a bar. Then they moved to Fabriano, where they had also lived before and Lea had an old boyfriend. At the end of 2007, Lea went to a café in Rome run by the anti-mafia group Libera. She met Libera's president, Don Luigi Ciotti, who put her in touch with a lawyer who volunteered for the organization.

Lea met Enza Rando at her townhouse offices in the center of Modena. The two women were very different. Lea, now thirty-three, was free-spirited and passionate, and the knowledge that she might die any day had given her a determination to live each one as her last. Enza was in her fifties, small, neat, and conservative. But at their first meeting, Lea brought pastries, then sat down and poured out her life story. Almost immediately, Enza loved her. "Lea was beautiful," she said. "Very intelligent and very courageous."

Annalisa had often been hard on Lea, especially when it came to Denise. Though Enza couldn't offer Lea much more than Annalisa, to Lea, after six years in isolation, she was a fresh face ready to listen. And from the moment Enza appeared, Annalisa sensed a new distance between herself and Lea. "There was a change," said Annalisa. "I could tell another lawyer was giving her advice. Something was wrong. I felt I was losing Lea. And I thought it was best to stop right then. Overlaps like that—inconsistencies, conflicting advice—could be very dangerous for Lea."

Heartbroken, Annalisa wrote a letter to Lea, offering her resignation. "In my mind, I was hoping this would shake Lea up and she would change her mind," she said. "We'd had ups and downs, but six years is a long time." Instead, in June 2008, Lea accepted Annalisa's notice.

IN SEPTEMBER 2008, largely as a result of Annalisa's years of appeals and applications, Lea and Denise were readmitted to the witness protection program. They were moved to Boiano, a small town near Campobasso in central Italy. Denise settled in well at her new school, and soon had a new group of friends. But by now Lea's state of mind had graduated from paranoid to disturbed. She was still staying awake all night, sleeping through the day, and keeping a knife under her pillow. Now she bought a guard dog and began taking lessons in martial arts. Nothing could soften the loneliness, however. She had no friends in Boiano and, with Annalisa gone, no one to talk to. Without government papers giving her a new identity, she also couldn't risk working, lest her name on an employee record identify her whereabouts. "It's all been a pile of crap," she would tell Denise. "Just a giant waste of our lives."

"It was so lonely for her," said Denise. "And without a job, she couldn't be independent, she couldn't provide for us by her own efforts and, for her, this was a real defeat."

One day in April, Lea decided to write to the president of Italy, Giorgio Napolitano:

> *I am a young mother at the end of my tether. Today I find myself together with my daughter isolated from everything and everyone. I lost everything. My family. My job. I lost my home. I lost countless friends. I lost any expectations of the future. I had reckoned on all of this. I knew what I was getting when I made my choice.*

But her sacrifices had been for nothing, wrote Lea. Her statements had led to no arrests and no convictions. She and Denise had suffered for seven years for no reason. And then the state cast them out. Lea wrote that she was losing her faith in justice. "The worst thing is that I already know the fate that awaits me. After poverty comes death. Undeserved and unearned but unavoidable." Who else would make the choice she had? she asked.

"Today, Mr. President, you can change the course of history. I still believe that a person can live with integrity and decency in this country. Please, Mr. President, give us a sign of hope. Help innocent victims of injustice."

But when Lea went to post the letter in Boiano, she spotted a couple on a street corner who seemed to be watching her. The woman was wearing an earpiece. As Lea approached, the woman reached into her bag. Lea thought she was going for a gun. "I didn't believe her," said Denise, when Lea told her later, "but I wasn't there and I didn't see it and my mother certainly believed there was someone who wanted to hurt her. She was very frightened. She decided not to send the letter and told me that we were leaving the protection program once again."

Lea's second request to leave the state program was the final straw for its administrators. They gave her and Denise two weeks to vacate their safe house and advised her never to reapply. Lea and Denise were on their own once more, and this time forever.

LEA, HOWEVER, HAD a new plan. She phoned her sister Marisa and asked her to pass on a message to Carlo. "She basically said: 'OK, I said some things that were inconvenient for you,'" recalled Denise. "'But I retracted everything and there will be no trial and no one will be shamed. So you have to leave me alone and leave my daughter alone.'"

Lea wanted out of witness protection, said Denise, because the process had been "absolutely pointless." The one upside was that if the state wasn't using her evidence, then Carlo had no reason to kill her. She just wanted to return to Pagliarelle and be left alone to quietly bring up their daughter. In return, she said Carlo would get to see Denise whenever he wanted. "She just didn't want to have to worry about her life and my life anymore," said Denise.

Carlo agreed. In a few days, Marisa came to pick up Lea and Denise from Boiano and take them back to Pagliarelle. Lea refused to see Carlo and stayed in the house with the curtains drawn. For Denise, it was the first chance she'd had to see her father in nine years. "He took me for drives, to restaurants, to see his friends, to eat at his house," she said. "He said we should move to Pagliarelle and that I could finish high school down there." Denise said she wanted to finish school in Boiano, where she had friends. She asked Carlo to rent an apartment there, because she and Lea had nowhere to live. Carlo agreed to that, too. After Easter, he and Denise drove to Campobasso, a short bus ride from Boiano, and rented the first apartment they were shown near the school in the old town for one month. Carlo then installed Denise; his mother, Piera; and his nephew, Domenico—Uncle Giuseppe's son—in the apartment. Since he was paying for it, Carlo moved in himself for a few days.

Lea was furious at the way Carlo was insinuating himself back into their lives. She had no choice but to accept his money for her daughter's sake. Nevertheless, while Denise, Carlo, Carlo's mother, and Carlo's nephew slept in the apartment, Lea refused to meet Carlo and spent the nights outside in the car. "We'd slept in the same bed for years," said Denise. "She found it hard."

The pressure eased slightly when Carlo returned to Milan. But the atmosphere in the apartment remained poisonous. On April 24, Lea's thirty-fifth birthday passed without celebration. Another day, she fought with Carlo's mother, Piera, saying she shouldn't be there and that she, Lea, should be taking care of Denise, seeing as she'd managed for seventeen years. Shortly afterward, Lea had to take Piera to the hospital for what looked like hypertension. When Carlo heard his mother was sick, he drove back down from Milan.

The night that Piera was released from the hospital, Lea, worried about her mother-in-law and unable to deny a son's love for his mother, found herself at supper with the entire Cosco family. It was the first time Carlo and Lea had been in the same room for thirteen years. Lea was primed to explode. When Piera yelled that Lea was making her unwell—"she's killing me with her shouting"—Lea, who was holding a bread knife, blew up. What was Piera even doing there? Why were any of them there? What the fuck was *Carlo* doing there? Lea and Denise had done fine by themselves all these years. She waved the knife at Carlo and shouted at him. "You have to go," she said. "Get the fuck out of here right now! Go now! Go now!"

"I was crying through all of it," said Denise. "But my father didn't say anything. He just took the two suitcases he'd brought with him, kissed me on the cheek, and left."

WITHOUT MONEY, LEA and Denise were still dependent on Carlo. They needed him even for small things like fixing the broken washing machine in the apartment. In early May, Denise and Lea went to a four-day pop festival in Rome, returning to Campobasso early on May 5. At 9 A.M., Carlo called Denise to say a repairman was coming that day to fix the washing machine. Denise said OK and went to bed. Lea fell asleep on the couch.

A few minutes later, the doorbell rang. Lea stuffed a knife in her back pocket and answered the door to a clean-shaven man in jeans and a blue jacket with a tattoo down one side of his neck, carrying a toolbox with a Winnie the Pooh sticker on the side. The man said he had come to fix the washing machine. Lea let him in and showed him to the kitchen. She watched him as he pushed a few buttons on the machine. He didn't open his toolbox. He asked Lea how the machine worked. Lea regarded him. "If you have to kill me, do it now," she said.

The man flew at Lea and she pulled the knife from her back pocket. He stuck two fingers down her throat, trying to choke her. Lea kicked him in the crotch. The toolbox fell onto the floor. Upstairs, Denise heard the crash. "I came down and this man and my mother were wrapped around each other," she said. "At first I thought it was my father, because he was dark-skinned and wearing the same jacket my father had."

Denise jumped on the man and started punching and kicking him. She saw his face: it wasn't Carlo. Still, the man seemed to recognize Denise. He looked at her with shock, threw the two women off, and ran for the door. Denise chased him and grabbed him by the throat. "Who sent you?!" she shouted. "Who sent you?!"

"Let me go!" the man yelled, and ran out.

Denise went to help Lea, who was bleeding. The two of them examined the toolbox that Lea's attacker had left behind. Inside were no plumbing tools but, instead, duct tape, wire, rope, scissors, a saw, and latex gloves. Lea called the carabinieri, who interviewed her and Denise and took fingerprints. Once they left, Lea told Denise that though it was important to have an official record of the attack, they couldn't count on the carabinieri to keep them safe. They packed, ran down to Lea's car, and drove to a B&B, taking care to park on a different street. After staying in their room all day and all night, they left early the next morning without paying and drove to the main piazza, where Lea pitched a tent opposite the town hall. They were safer where everyone could see them, she said.

Lea and Denise were convinced Carlo had sent an assassin to kill Lea. Still, when Carlo called, Denise arranged to meet her father in town. "I had no choice," she said. "If a person wants to hurt you or kill you, either you let them or you pretend to be their friend."

When Denise saw Carlo, however, she couldn't control herself. She flew at him. She accused him of trying to kill her mother. Carlo shouted back that the attack had had nothing to do with him.

"But you were the only one to know about the broken washing machine!" said Denise.

"Your phones are tapped!" shouted Carlo. "You were in the protection program! Anyone could have known about the washing machine! Anyone could have sent that guy!"

Denise was caught off guard for a second. Then she said: "I never want to see you again. I'm going with my mom."

LEA WISHED THAT the two of them could have ridden off into the sunset as Denise wanted. But with no money, no state protection, and no lawyer, their only option was to follow their original plan, move back to Calabria, and try again to secure a truce from Carlo. They packed up their tent, caught the train to Calabria, and moved into Lea's mother's house in Petilia, all three women sharing a kitchen, a single bedroom, and a tiny bathroom. Lea replaced the old wooden front door with a new metal one. Aside from walking a few meters to buy cigarettes, she stayed indoors.

For Lea, life in Pagliarelle was more claustrophobic than ever. She had to assume that most of the village might be trying to kill her. She quarreled with the few people she did see.

Denise quickly couldn't stand to be in the apartment with her mother. Almost without realizing it, she found herself falling into the routine of clan life, taking drives into the country with her father when he was down from Milan, eating lunch with him and his friends. In Pagliarelle, there was no way to behave differently. But when she returned to the house with new jeans, new trainers, or a new jacket, Lea, who had raised her daughter to despise materialism, would throw a fit.

What surprised Denise was that Carlo seemed to find the situation just as hard. One day he asked his daughter to go on holiday with him. When Denise asked Lea, and her mother initially agreed only to change her mind at the last minute, Carlo erupted. "On that occasion, I really understood how deeply my father loathed my mother," said Denise. "He insulted her in front of me and said that for my entire life, my mother had made all the decisions for me and that she still did. He couldn't stand that. It was intolerable. He couldn't allow my mother to decide whether or not I spent time with him." Marisa, who overheard, took Denise aside after Carlo left. "He really wants her dead," said Marisa. "He truly hates her."

Toward the end of summer, however, Lea began to think that Carlo might be softening. In September 2009, she asked to meet him and Carlo came to the house. Denise was there. "They were talking for more than an hour, just the two of them," said Denise.

"At one point, I couldn't see them anywhere and I got scared. But when I looked out from the balcony, they were in the garden under a tree, just talking. They waved at me." Lea announced that she and Carlo were going for a drive to Botricello, a small holiday town built around a medieval castle on the coast where they used to go as teenagers. It was already 11 P.M., and she and Carlo didn't return until 4 A.M. When Denise asked Lea the next morning what her parents had been talking about for so long, Lea smiled coyly and said: "You know, old times. Mind your own business."

It might seem strange to others, said Denise, but she believed her parents had loved each other once. Now she began to imagine that they would again. A lot of their conversation that night had been about where Denise should go to university. Lea favored Catanzaro while Carlo was pushing for Milan. Lea was hurt that Denise might want to leave her. "After all she had been through, after everything she had done for me, she said I was being ungrateful," said Denise. Still, it was everyday parent chat. Meanwhile, Denise and Carlo were getting used to each other's company again. "We spoke on the phone, we went to the beach, we ate dinner together," said Denise.

On November 19, 2009, Lea and Denise traveled to Florence. Lea was due in court, accused of a minor assault from years earlier when she had slapped a teenage girl in the street after the girl accused Denise of trying to steal her boyfriend. The case was to be heard on November 20. Enza had agreed to represent Lea. The day before, Denise and Lea went window-shopping in the city. Denise spotted a sweatshirt she liked, but she knew Lea wouldn't have the money for it and worried she would sell the gold necklace and bracelet Carlo had given her to buy it. So Denise called her father. Carlo said new clothes were no problem and suggested that after the case, she and Lea come to Milan and they all go shopping together.

When Enza heard about the plan, she told Lea, "It's a bad idea.

Carlo's trying to kill you." But, said Enza, "Lea was a strong woman and she had decided." Lea told her lawyer, "It's Milan, not Calabria. A big city. People everywhere. I'll never be alone and Denise will be with me. Nothing's going to happen. He wouldn't be able to organize anything in time."

On the day of the court case, Enza managed to negotiate an official reprimand for her client. Hours later, Lea and Denise caught the evening train to Milan. Watching them leave, Enza decided she would try to stop them one last time. "Turn around," she texted her client. "Get off at Piacenza. Libera has a place for you where you can be safe."

As they neared Milan, Lea sent her reply. "Thank you, my lawyer, thank you. But Denise and I have to try to make a life for ourselves. God bless you. God bless us all."[2]

"And that was the last I heard from her," said Enza.

ACT TWO

❦

Rebellion in Rosarno

IX

TWO HOURS BEFORE dawn on the first Sunday of 2010, the rattle of a scooter could be heard curling up through the empty streets of Reggio Calabria. Two figures leaned into the windscreen to protect themselves from the January cold. In front was a slim man in a dark jacket and tight jeans, a dark helmet pushed down over his long hair. Behind him sat a plumper man in jeans and a striped jacket. Despite the speed at which the pair were racing across the icy cobbles, the second man declined to hold on to his companion. Instead in his arms he cradled a bulky canvas bag, almost as though it were a baby.

After following the shoreline for a few minutes, the pair turned away from the sea and climbed up steeply toward the center of the old town. They passed the floodlit walls of the Castello Aragonese, built by the Normans and expanded by the Spanish in the fifteenth century. When the pair reached the castle gardens, the driver executed a wide U-turn, eased off the throttle, and allowed the bike to coast gently over the cobbles back down the hill. After a few yards, he pulled up in front of an imposing metal gate, holding the bike on the slope with his legs and keeping his hand on the accelerator. Behind him the man bent over his bag and pulled his jacket around him as though he were lighting a cigarette. Suddenly there was a spark. Flames licked up out of the bag. The man jumped off the bike and ran toward the gate, swinging the burning bag high and wide like a lasso to avoid the flames. The driver revved the engine and let the bike roll slowly down the hill. The man dropped the bag, ran back to the moving bike, and jumped on, and the pair roared off. Seconds later, the bag exploded.[1]

In the predawn calm, the noise of the blast rolled out across the Strait of Messina like thunder. The noise woke the carabinieri barracks where Alessandra had her apartment. A few hours later at a press conference, a carabinieri commander described the bomb as the kind of crude device—a stick of dynamite attached to a ten-kilo gas cylinder—familiar to anyone with experience of southern Italy's protection rackets. Aside from some damage to a gate and a railing, and a few shattered windows, there was little physical harm done.

That didn't mean the attack wasn't serious. The mayor of Reggio, the chamber of commerce, the president and vice president of the Italian parliament, even Italy's head of state, President Giorgio Napolitano, sent the Reggio authorities messages of solidarity. Italy had declared war on the world's most powerful mafia. The mafiosi had started the New Year by signaling their intention to strike back.

The stakes in this new fight had escalated radically over the previous few months. Thanks to years of surveillance, for the first time the Italian state now had a comprehensive picture of the 'Ndrangheta's structure and its cocaine business. The prosecutors were now confronting the full scale of the mission they had undertaken. Their priority was also clear: Calabria's west coast, the heart of the cocaine business. That explained the bomb's target, detonated outside Reggio's courthouse, the seat of justice in Calabria for as long as the 'Ndrangheta had existed and, in 2010, the offices of Calabria's attorney general, who oversaw the confiscation of mafia assets. If the 'Ndrangheta liked to send messages, this was the group at its most unequivocal: Calabria's prosecutors should end their campaign or face violent consequences. But as Alessandra and her colleagues absorbed the implications of the warning, they drew a second conclusion, too. To provoke this kind of reaction, their crackdown must be having an effect.

There followed other signs that the west coast 'Ndrangheta was feeling the pressure. A week after the bomb, Rosarno erupted in three days of riots. The violence began when a group of 'Ndrangheta teenagers, apparently bored and looking for kicks, fired an air gun into the tented camp behind Gioia Tauro port where more than a thousand West African migrants lived. Hundreds of Africans marched into Rosarno, protesting, burning several cars, and fighting with the police. Rosarno hoodlums armed with iron bars set up roadblocks. At least two Rosarno men tried to run over migrants in the street. More than twenty Africans were injured, many of them beaten and three shot. Eventually, riot police descended. On the orders of the interior minister, they expelled every last African—a total of 1,200 people—from the town. Rosarno and its people, said Minister Roberto Maroni, were the unfortunate victims of "too much tolerance."

But if the Rosarno *picciotti* considered such unashamed racism a victory, they were mistaken. The violence drew condemnation and outrage from across Italy. Pope Benedict XVI urged pilgrims gathered in St. Peter's Square in Rome to remember that "an immigrant is a human being." One opposition leader, Luigi Manconi, said that by expelling the Africans, the authorities had been complicit in creating "the whitest town in the world." The media attention also exposed the wretched hypocrisy of the 'Ndrangheta—who, it turned out, were attacking the very people they had brought to Rosarno to work as fruit pickers for as little as three euros a day. The spotlight on Rosarno also gave Alessandra's office an opportunity to score a very public victory. A day after the violence died down, with the eyes of Italy still on Rosarno, her office arrested seventeen suspected members of the Bellocco clan, the Pesces' main rival in the city, and seized assets of several million euros.[2]

Almost straightaway, the 'Ndrangheta tripped up again. Nine days later in Reggio, hours before President Napolitano arrived to reinforce his support of Calabria's authorities in their new war, a telephone tip-off led carabinieri to a stolen car parked close to his route. The vehicle contained two bombs and two pistols. But what was intended to intimidate quickly managed to do precisely the opposite. The tipster was arrested almost immediately and charged with mafia association. Napolitano's visit went ahead, though now he was able to strike a courageous profile by defying the mafia's threat to his life and, on 'Ndrangheta turf, hailing a "turning point" in the fight against them. As a final insult, by the end of the month Reggio Calabria had been selected as the location for a new Italian agency tasked with seizing mafia businesses and transforming them into Libera shops or offices for policemen, magistrates, or the tax department. As fightbacks went, it felt uncomfortably like humiliation.[3]

But even if the 'Ndrangheta had lost the opening exchanges in its war with the state, the fight was far from over. Alessandra, in particular, was convinced that a crucial weakness in the state's strategy meant it could never win. Pignatone and Prestipino were freethinkers who had no trouble imagining a woman 'Ndranghetista could be as much use as a woman prosecutor. Cerreti described joining their team as finally finding "fertile territory" for her ideas. But among the rank and file, "Italian prosecutors were still not investigating women," said Alessandra. Many rejected outright the idea that women could serve justice in any way at all. ("I mean, *really*, women do have eyes and ears," said Alessandra.) They also refused to see as anything other than exceptional what Alessandra was observing in Rosarno: that by early 2010, 'Ndrangheta men had realized their women were being left alone by the authorities and were starting to give them power. Across the province, at least two women had become clan bosses. Nevertheless, said Alessandra, "it was still very hard for us to make our colleagues believe that women had a role."

Alessandra understood that if many prosecutors and carabinieri were barely able to conceive of a woman 'Ndranghetista, then they would dismiss out of hand the idea of an 'Ndrangheta woman with the strength to rebel against her men. "This was another form of the same prejudice," she said. "The belief that no one, and certainly not a woman, is going to talk about their own family, let alone testify and accuse their own family." She conceded that it would take unusual bravery. But to write it off as impossible was to guarantee it never happened. "When justice shows to people that it is strong and that the state is present and can help you if you want to collaborate," she said, "then you find collaborators appear."

At heart, thought Alessandra, this was a failure of perception. Whenever many of her male colleagues saw women and children, they saw family and nothing else. Most seemed incapable of identifying what a family might represent in a place like Rosarno or Pagliarelle: a living, breathing criminal organism. "The entire structure, the family nature of it, makes it hard for many people even to recognize it as a problem," she said. Once again, Alessandra was confronting the 'Ndrangheta's astute understanding of family. "The part played by family, and by women, makes them so difficult to track." Sometimes she felt that she, Pignatone, and Prestipino were the only ones who could see what was right in front of them: women who were simultaneously mothers, mafiosi, and potential state witnesses. That had been the problem with Lea Garofalo. The state had seen her too simplistically, as a battered wife, a troubled witness, a victim. Only one prosecutor, Sandro Dolce, had grasped everything that Lea was and everything that she offered the state. What Alessandra needed was another 'Ndrangheta mother to change her colleagues' minds.

As it happened, she would have two.

ACCORDING TO THE precepts of clan rivalry, Giuseppina Pesce, thirty-one, and Maria Concetta Cacciola, thirty, were unlikely friends.[4] The Pesces led the most powerful clan in Rosarno, which had ruled the town since the 1920s. The Cacciolas were muscle for their rivals, the Belloccos. The Pesces and the Belloccos sometimes cooperated in business and on occasion their children even married each other. But as the Pesces climbed ever higher up the 'Ndrangheta's new vertical hierarchy, the Bellocco name meant ever less— and the Belloccos hated the Pesces for that.

Giuseppina and Concetta also weren't alike. Giuseppina was tough, an 'Ndrangheta wife who had pushed the men in her family to let her become an 'Ndranghetista in her own right. There were limits on what a woman could do in the organization. Murder and violence were out, and any involvement in extortion, corruption, or drug smuggling was confined to bookkeeping and passing messages between the men. But Giuseppina was dismissive of any man who imagined her to be less than him and communicated her adamant equality in a tomboyish appearance. She wore bulky woolen V-necks over cheap and baggy worker's shirts. She had no time for makeup. Her dirt-brown hair was cut in a scruffy parting at whatever length kept it out of the way, and from under it her brown eyes would stare out at the world with a blankness that conveyed an intimidating intimacy with brutality.

Concetta could not have been more different. She took no part in the men's business, and her knowledge of it extended little beyond gossip about where the bunkers were and who had killed whom. Unlike the Pesces, the Cacciola men didn't accept even a hint of independence or assertion in their women, and they kept Concetta confined to the house for weeks at a time. On the rare occasions she was allowed out, Concetta's own private rebellion was to emerge immaculately dressed, as though she were a busy socialite. She favored tight jeans with unbuttoned blouses that hung loosely across her perfumed chest. Her jet-black hair was styled in a long undulating curl that swept across her forehead, nestled over her ears, and executed a jaunty ski jump on her shoulders. She plucked her eyebrows, waxed her legs, painted her fingernails and toes, and paired dark shades of plum and scarlet on her lips with heavy mascara and a brush of mauve over her eyes. If Giuseppina's appearance implied equivalence to any man, Concetta presented herself as nothing like them.

Despite their differences, Giuseppina and Concetta had been close friends since they were girls. When they were growing up in Rosarno in the 1980s, the town had been a cold, hard place of loveless lives where girls could be beaten just for stepping out of the house unaccompanied. Rosarno was also small, however, and as schoolgirls Giuseppina and Concetta would see each other every day in the playground or on the street. As they approached their teens, their lives also followed a near-identical prescribed course, which—since the town had no secondary school and 'Ndrangheta girls weren't allowed to leave it—meant marriage, quickly followed by motherhood.

Giuseppina finished her education at thirteen. By then, she had already met her future husband, Rocco Palaia, twenty, whose father managed weapons for the Pesce clan. At fourteen, Giuseppina eloped with Rocco, a common event in Rosarno, known as *fuitina*. At fifteen she gave birth to the first of the couple's three children, Angela. By then, Rocco was doing little more than smoking weed and lying around the house all day, so Giuseppina went to work in the family store. It wasn't long before Rocco was arrested and jailed for mafia association.

Concetta had always had it harder than her friend. When she was eleven, her brother Giuseppe caught her playing in the street with a few local boys. He beat her, dragged her home by her hair, and forbade her to leave the house alone again. After that, Concetta never went out for pizza or gelato. "You know my brother 'Peppe," she would say. "If he saw me, you know he'd kill me." When Concetta was thirteen, she met her twenty-one-year-old future husband, Salvatore Figliuzzi, and eloped with him. When she was just fifteen, Concetta gave birth to Alfonso, the first of the couple's three children. Salvatore was also soon hauled off to jail.

By the time of his arrest, Salvatore was already beating Concetta regularly. One day he held a gun to her head. When Concetta complained to her father, he replied, "It's your marriage and your life. You deal with it." Concetta might have expected things to improve with Salvatore in jail. Instead, her father took over the role of violent disciplinarian, slapping her to the ground in the street one day when she returned late from a shopping trip to Reggio. On conjugal visits to prison, Concetta conceived a second child, Tania, then a third, Rosalba, whom she named after her mother.

By their early twenties, Giuseppina and Concetta were alone, married to jailbird husbands, and mothers to three children each. They would meet at the school gates or the doctor's or in the Pesce family minimart where Giuseppina worked, across the street from the Cacciola family home. The two women negotiated their situations as best they could. Concetta had somehow remained "a sunny girl," said Giuseppina years later, through tears. "Strong. She was an optimist . . . She cared so much." As Lea had done growing up in Pagliarelle, Concetta sustained herself with a dream of true love that would take her away from it all. With Salvatore in jail, she began fantasizing that she was not the abused wife of a violent small-time gangster at all but, rather, a woman tragically separated from her love. On prison visits, she would wear scarlet lipstick with thick eyeshadow and frame her face with thick long curls. She wrote Salvatore wistful letters. "I go out in the morning to take the children to school but I have no contact with anyone," she wrote in 2007. "How can I live if I cannot even breathe? If I can't even speak to anyone? My father likes to see me miserable from dawn to dusk. If only I could have a little peace of mind. I'd pay anything, take anything, for a little peace. I don't know how long I can go on without you."

If Concetta survived by retreating into fantasy, Giuseppina endured through sheer will. Like Concetta, she was beaten by her husband. But Rocco would hit Giuseppina not because she was out on her own or because she was looking at other men, or even just because he could, but because Giuseppina insisted on speaking out of turn. "He beat me when I said what I thought," she said. "He attacked me to get me to shut up."

After Rocco went to jail, Giuseppina's father, Salvatore Pesce, told her to confine herself to the home like Concetta. He refused to let her go to college or divorce Rocco or continue her piano lessons. "You're not going anywhere," he shouted. "You'll stay locked up in the house." Giuseppina's way of conserving some autonomy was to join the family firm. Within a few years, she was running messages between bosses in jail, laundering money, and overseeing the collection of *pizzo*. No one had to tell her what to do, she said later. "I lived in this family. I breathed these things, the superiority and the power and the privilege. I knew because I was there. I have always known, since I was a child."

WITH EVERY YEAR that passed, Giuseppina's knowledge of the 'Ndrangheta grew. She knew its power structure intimately. The nominal head of the clan was Giuseppina's uncle Antonino. Since he was in jail, however, others handled day-to-day operations. By primogeniture, Giuseppina's father, Salvatore, should have been the first choice to replace Antonino. But Salvatore had never been leadership material: since he was a boy, his nickname had been U Babbu, the buffoon. The mantle instead fell to Antonino's son and Giuseppina's cousin, Francesco "Ciccio" Pesce, a hothead given to angry and violent outbursts who wielded absolute power in his father's stead.

The 'Ndrangheta was run as an autocracy. But Giuseppina would later insist it was one willingly accepted by its subjects. In the 'Ndrangheta, tyranny was what passed for effective leadership, and what it took to have and hold power. At its heart, however, Giuseppina said an *'ndrina* was a collective. "They decided together, as a family, who took state contracts, who handled extortion, who oversaw the drug trade. That's the strength of the clan—that we are all family members together."

Inside the *'ndrina*, *picciotti* like Giuseppina were expected to help out however they were needed. Her work gave Giuseppina a comprehensive view of the Pesce empire. The house of her seventy-eight-year-old grandmother, Giuseppa Bonarrigo, often served as a base for operations and a meeting place. There the family would discuss at length the delicate question of how much *pizzo* to charge. The younger men tended to squeeze as much as they could out of everyone, once even extorting tickets for the entire family from a visiting circus. The older men would warn against overdoing it, arguing that driving a business to ruin was in no one's interest. Another point of discussion was how to divide the take. Giuseppina saw many *picciotti* try to resist handing over their revenues to a common family pot, as required. What everyone agreed on, however, was that there could be no exceptions to paying *pizzo*. "An outsider can't say no, because he is afraid," said Giuseppina. "The men would go and ask for money like they were doing people a favor. But everyone knew they couldn't refuse."

Giuseppina got to know other sides of the business. Her father, Salvatore, her cousin Ciccio, and her husband, Rocco, all moved cocaine through Gioia Tauro port and stashed packages in the house, ready for onward transport. Negotiating the interminable roadworks on the A3 from Reggio Calabria to Salerno one day, her brother pointed out which sites belonged to the Pesces and which to other clans. 'Ndrangheta rules also required each clan to have a stash of automatic rifles, shotguns, and pistols. Rocco and his brother had buried the Pesce arsenal around town, wrapping the guns in sheets of plastic and duct tape. "We're prepared for a war," Rocco liked to say.

It was the Pesces' firepower that guaranteed the family was feared or, as they liked to see it, respected. Around town, people would make way for Giuseppina. In restaurants, bills never appeared. In grocery stores, the manager would come out to serve her personally. If she went to the doctor's, she walked straight to the head of the queue and "no one could ever say anything to me because I was part of the family." One time she went to an ear specialist in Gioia Tauro. On hearing her name, the man asked after the health of her niece and her daughter, then knocked his price down to bargain-basement level, saying he wanted to send "his greetings to my uncle and my family."

But if the family enjoyed their local fame, other kinds of attention made them paranoid. The ability of the police and the carabinieri to listen in was unreal. They tapped phone calls, filmed the interiors of houses from several kilometers away, mounted secret cameras outside homes and schools, and planted bugs almost anywhere—in cars, in walls and fireplaces, in orchards and schools, even under stones in Giuseppina's grandmother's garden. The Pesces bought bug detectors to sniff out these devices, as well as jammers to block their signals and scanners of their own to monitor the carabinieri's radios. Still, they were often reduced to whispering and using sign language in their own homes. Ciccio was always telling the others, "Don't talk too much." More than once, his paranoia led him to smash up his phone and television, unscrew every light bulb in his house, and throw everything into the street.

This mistrust forced many a boss into hiding. Most sought sanctuary in secret underground bunkers buried deep in the countryside. It wasn't as bad as it sounded. The bosses would trick out their bunkers with lights, televisions, kitchens, and comfortable beds. Some had their hideouts built into the cliffs to give them a sea view and a sunset. Others enjoyed bucolic locations in orchards or olive groves. Instinctively territorial, however, the Pesces built their bunkers in town, often under their own houses. Before he was arrested in 2005, Giuseppina's father had been hiding for years in a bunker that he'd spent thousands of euros renovating under the floor of Giuseppina's grandmother's house.

IF RESPECT WAS everything to the Pesces, shame was unacceptable for the same reason. The treacherous and unfaithful didn't just need to be killed. They had to vanish from the face of the earth and leave no reminders of the dishonor they had brought on the family.

By 2010, Michele Prestipino was looking into a number of deaths in Calabria, including some officially recorded as suicides, that he suspected were actually honor killings. In one of the most recent, a widow called Dominica Legato had jumped to her death from her balcony in Rosarno in 2007. At least, that was what her son told police. Giuseppina, Concetta, and every woman in Rosarno suspected another version of events, as did the coroner, who found knife wounds on Dominica's hands, suggesting she had been fending off an attack when she fell. A few months later the Rosarno man with whom Dominica was said to be having a relationship also disappeared.

The full fury of the Rosarno 'Ndrangheta's rage could be terrifying. What made it even more disturbing was how the 'Ndrangheta could sustain it. In 1979, when she was twenty-five, the husband of Concetta Teresa Galluci, a mason, died in an accident, falling from the fourth floor of a building he was helping build for the Pesces. Concetta and her husband had had three children. More than a decade later, she began a relationship with twenty-three-year-old Francesco Alcuri. One night in November 1993 in Rosarno, Alcuri was shot nine times in the groin, dying eleven days later in agony. Concetta, now forty, fled for Genoa in northern Italy, where her sister lived. One evening four months after arriving, she opened her sister's front door and was shot in the head. The gunmen then shot the dead woman's seventy-two-year-old mother as she ran into the living room in her nightdress, before killing her twenty-two-year-old niece while she slept in her bed.

The Pesces were deeply secretive about their own family embarrassments. Not for them the scrutiny that accompanied the discovery of a dead body. Long ago, the Pesces had calculated that since Rosarno's graveyard was the most obvious place to dump a body, it would be the last place anyone would look. Up there, buried under the floor in the family's chapel, was Giuseppina's grandfather, Angelo Ferraro, killed for having an affair. Alongside him was Annunziata Pesce, Giuseppina's cousin, who had betrayed her husband and the entire 'Ndrangheta by running off with a policeman. Kidnapped off the street in broad daylight in 1981, she was shot in the neck by the boss, Antonino Pesce, while her elder brother, Antonio, watched. Antonio's reward for his unflinching loyalty? Promotion to a dominant position inside the *'ndrina* for him and his immediate family.

Killings like these left no doubt about the price of betrayal. It was a measure of the desperation of many 'Ndrangheta women that the men kept finding it necessary to carry them out. Perhaps it was inevitable. 'Ndrangheta mothers knew their sons would grow up to be killers and drug dealers destined for prison and an early grave. They knew their daughters would be married off as they had been, barely pubescent, to an older, abusive, criminal husband. They expected to lose their own abusive, criminal husbands to death or jail. Faced with a life in which what Concetta called Rosarno's "stone-hearted men" extinguished all the light and joy in the world, it was hardly surprising that the town's women grabbed what little sweetness they could.

Many of the men seemed to understand this. Their response was not to ease off but to take preemptive action, particularly when, with a husband dead or in jail, an 'Ndrangheta wife found herself alone. Concetta's cousin Giuseppina Multari had been locked up at home as a virtual slave since the day in 2005 that the Cacciola men had killed her husband, their cousin, for being a junkie. When her brother tried to confront the Cacciolas about the way they were treating his sister, he also vanished.

When Concetta's husband, Salvatore, went to jail, her father and brother resolved to prevent her from almost ever leaving the house. But such blinkered conservatism blinded them to the fact that they were living in the twenty-first century, in which friendship—or more—was only ever a click away. "In the land of the 'Ndrangheta, the Internet is an open window in a closed world," said Alessandra. "It introduces women to a free world. It tends to provoke a kind of emotional explosion." A colleague, Roberto di Bella, said he had seen the same pattern repeat with many wives of jailbird 'Ndranghetisti. "They are very young and they are on their own," he said. "But they have the Internet and Facebook and that gives them the chance to communicate with a different world. There are cases of women falling in love with people who treat them like human beings. And with their new horizons opening up for them, they come to understand that they are prisoners in their families. The Internet has opened their lives and their minds."

So it proved with Concetta. "She began to explore the world through the web," said Giuseppe Creazzo, a prosecutor in Palmi who would later investigate the Cacciola family. Concetta found she liked celebrity news: charming people leading beautiful lives. She imagined the famous couples watching sunsets together and going out at night. Soon, said Creazzo, she was looking for friends for herself. She joined Facebook. Slowly, a feeling began to grow inside her. "Every day," said Creazzo, "Concetta felt more and more like rebelling."

By the middle of 2009, Concetta was chatting regularly to a Rosarno man who had moved to Germany. Giuseppina, more assertive, went further than her friend, beginning a clandestine affair with a man called Domenico Costantino, with whom she had worked at a family factory that made crystallized fruit. "He was the first man who ever seemed to care for my children," said Giuseppina. "He was the first man to respect me as a woman, the first who ever loved me."

Almost anywhere else in Europe, either of these liaisons would have merited condemnation or, perhaps, understanding. In Rosarno, Concetta and Giuseppina were risking death. It was a gauge of their loveless lives that both women courted that danger without hesitation.

X

I N PAGLIARELLE, THE carabinieri were watching another illicit
romance unfold.[1]

For Denise, a birthday without Lea had been followed by Christmas without Lea, then New Year's without Lea, all of them spent in
Lea's apartment, upstairs from Lea's mother. One night, a friend's
family took Denise to a restaurant on the coast for dinner—but
someone had brought Christmas presents from Milan. Another
time, when Carlo took his daughter to the dentist, Denise let herself
imagine that it would be the most natural thing in the world for a
daughter to ask her father if he had any news of her missing mother.
Carlo snapped that Denise needed to get it through her head that
her mother had left them. He knew nothing about where she was or
what she was doing.

Denise already had a difficult relationship with food. Now she
took to binge eating to relieve the stress, gaining twenty kilos in
months. If Carlo noticed, he didn't seem concerned. Denise's aunt
Marisa took her niece to a clinic but when that proved ineffective,
she also offered Denise little other help.

Desperate, Denise turned to the man her father had deputized
to keep an eye on her in Pagliarelle. Carlo had given thirty-one-
year-old Carmine Venturino orders to escort Denise wherever she
went and, above all, to keep her away from the authorities. Carmine
would drive Denise around all day. He gave her pocket money. He
worked with her in the Cosco family pizzeria in Petilia. When De-

nise started at a new high school in January, it was Carmine who helped settle her in. Watching all this, the surveillance teams began to feel uneasy. The officers knew Carlo had told Carmine to watch Denise. But this looked like something else.

What made the officers particularly uncomfortable was what they were learning about Carmine's movements on the night Lea vanished. Phone records showed that Carmine spoke to Carlo dozens of times in the hours after Lea disappeared and in the days that followed. Carmine said little of substance in his calls. But his tone had been panicky and his movements erratic. His GPS signal showed him driving outside the city several times in the days and nights after November 24. Recordings of his voice showed he'd been desperate to find the keys to a warehouse and that, once he located them, he kept going back to the place. Besides, thought the officers, Carmine was Carlo's sometime flatmate and one of his key lieutenants. He *had* to be involved.

ON FEBRUARY 3, the carabinieri in Campobasso announced they had enough evidence to arrest Carlo for ordering the attack on Lea in her apartment in May 2009. They detained Carlo just as Denise returned from school. Watching her father being led away in handcuffs, Denise recognized the look on his face as the same he'd had on the night Lea went missing. A newspaper report about Carlo's arrest the next day was accompanied by a picture of another man charged with the Campobasso attack: Massimo Sabatino. The paper said Sabatino was an associate of her father's and was already in prison on a drug charge.

Two months in, the officers investigating Lea's disappearance could be pleased with their progress. They had a prime suspect, for whom they had established motive and opportunity, and from Lea's case files, they had ample documentation to back up their allegations. Handily, Carlo was now also under arrest for another attack on Lea. But the murder case against Carlo also had a giant flaw: no body. Without it, a prosecutor couldn't even say for sure that Lea had died, let alone how.

Then the carabinieri got lucky. Massimo Sabatino, thirty-six, was a career criminal with a long list of convictions for robbery and drug dealing. When he was served his indictment for the Campobasso attack, he was already in San Vittore prison on a charge of dealing heroin after being arrested in December 2009. Slow and poorly educated, Sabatino handed the charge sheet to his friend and cellmate Salvatore Sorrentino, who had been picked up in Milan in January for absconding from house arrest at the end of a five-year sentence for robbery. While Sorrentino digested the document, Sabatino explained to his friend that for a few years he had been working for an 'Ndrangheta boss in Milan called Carlo Cosco. His connection to Carlo was through his sister Rosi, who was engaged to Rosario Curcio, one of Carlo's crew.

One day in April 2009, Sabatino said, Carlo had offered him €25,000 to drive to Campobasso and recover a drug debt from a woman living there. Carlo later refined the plan, saying Sabatino should go disguised as a washing-machine repairman and tie the woman up, drag her to his van, and take her to Bari on Puglia's east coast, where Carlo and his brothers would be waiting. Carlo had also given him fifty liters of sulfuric acid to carry in the back of the van. Sabatino said he had done as instructed but failed to kidnap the woman because her daughter, who wasn't supposed to be there, had appeared from nowhere and jumped him.

Sorrentino said that according to the charge sheet, Sabatino's fingerprints had been found on the washing machine in the apartment. Sabatino agreed that was possible: he'd worn latex gloves but torn them in the struggle with the women. Sorrentino continued that the woman Sabatino had been trying to abduct was a Garofalo,

a name familiar to anyone in the 'Ndrangheta. Sabatino claimed
he'd never known the identity of the woman. Sorrentino said that
according to the indictment, Lea had not only been Carlo's wife but
also a *pentita* who had testified against him.

It began to dawn on Sabatino that he was in real trouble. He told
Sorrentino that he knew of a second, successful attempt to kidnap
Lea in Milan on November 24. Though Sabatino stressed that he
had played no part, he assumed Lea was now dead. He added that
he had no alibi for either May or November.

Sorrentino agreed it looked bad. Sabatino had to be looking at
life. Sabatino swore. Carlo was a motherfucker, he said. He hadn't
paid him for the Campobasso job and had refused even to give him
money for a lawyer when he was arrested in December.

Sabatino didn't know what to do. But his cellmate Sorrentino
did. A day or so later, he sent a letter to the Milan prosecutor investigating Lea's disappearance, offering to relay everything his
friend had told him in return for a reduced sentence. The prosecutors, skeptical at first, were reassured when Sabatino was moved to
a different cell and his new cellmate made a statement confirming
many of the same details. When a prosecutor confronted Sabatino,
he lied so badly—initially claiming he was meant to recover a debt
from Lea, then claiming he was robbing her, then admitting he was
trying to kidnap her—that he managed to solidify the case against
himself and Carlo.

To the investigators, the case was beginning to look conclusive.
But Sabatino had given them something else, too. According to Sorrentino, Sabatino claimed that the Cosco brothers had also killed
two Garofalo men in the past. Sabatino even named Giuseppe Cosco
as the shooter in the first killing, which he added had taken place
in a Milan apartment block in 1995. Allowing for the distortion of
jailhouse hearsay, this seemed to be corroboration of Lea's allegation
that Giuseppe Cosco had shot dead Antonio Comberiati at No. 6 Vi-

ale Montello in May 1995. The allegation that the Coscos had killed a second Garofalo seemed to refer to the 2005 death of Lea's brother Floriano, a killing that was unsolved. Here, finally, was the evidence to substantiate Lea's allegations. Disbelieved in life, she was being vindicated in death.

THERE WAS STILL the mystery of what had happened to Lea, however. In Catanzaro, down on the coast below Pagliarelle, the prosecutor's office had informed Annalisa Pisano that her former client had disappeared. "They told me clearly that it had to be *lupara bianca*," she said. Though she and Lea hadn't spoken in a year and a half, Annalisa still felt a strong bond with her. That night, said Annalisa, "I dreamed of Lea. She was in a warehouse, surrounded by flames, and she was asking me for help. She was calling me by my name. 'Annalisa!' But everybody was telling her 'No!'" And every night from then on, to the day years later when Lea was found, Annalisa had the same recurring dream. "People would ask me: 'How do you know she has been burned?' And I'd reply: 'Because I see her. You can believe me or not.' And I am not the kind of person who believes in these things. But I saw her. Almost every night. She was on a chair, in a warehouse, surrounded by fire, calling for me. And at that point, I would wake up."

For Denise, Carlo's arrest only sharpened the questions over her mother's death. *How* had Carlo killed her? Did he shoot her? Suffocate her? Slit her throat? Did he have one of his men do it? Did she scream? Was it quick or did he draw it out? Did he torture her? At what point did Lea know she was going to die? Would Denise know when her own time came?

While Carlo's arrest should have come as some relief, in Pagliarelle it just made it harder for Denise to maintain the lie. In mid-February, on the eve of her first visit to see Carlo in jail, the surveillance team picked up a text message from Denise to Carmine. Denise was losing her mind. The situation was impossible, she said. How could she keep on pretending when her father was in jail accused of trying to kill her mother? How could she face him? "Carmine calmed me," Denise said. "He made me laugh. He made me feel good."

The respite was temporary. When Denise went to Catanzaro jail the next day with her uncle Vito, she wept throughout. Vito tried to be sympathetic but didn't seem to know how. "Crying when your father is in prison and your mother is missing is only natural," he said blankly.

Carmine was waiting for Denise when she returned. Once inside her aunt's house, she collapsed. "It was an hour of crying and eating at the same time," she said later. "I was so desperate. I wasn't thinking about who I trusted and who I didn't. I was desperate for some affection. I cried. I ate. I was shouting out: 'Leave me alone! I have to go to a place where I don't want to go, live in a place where I don't want to live, with people that I suspect? What do you want me to do? Laugh?' What I suffered, nobody can understand." In the end, Carmine just held Denise. They hugged for what seemed like forever. Then they kissed.

Over the next few weeks, the surveillance team watched as Denise and Carmine became inseparable. "She fell in love with this guy and he with her," said Enza. "She was able to open up to him, to speak with him and cry with him." But Denise was also mindful that Carmine was a member of Carlo's 'ndrina. She would ask him over and over again what he knew about what had happened to her mother. "He always said he didn't know and didn't want to know," said Denise. "I never had an answer." Adding to the pressure on Denise, her affair with Carmine was something else she had to keep secret. "Carmine told me to say absolutely nothing to anyone," she said. "If my father knew, he'd be furious. He'd given Carmine the job of accompanying me and controlling me, not dating me. No one could know we were seeing each other. We would meet at midnight in the meadows outside Pagliarelle so that no one would find out."

Unable to express almost any of her thoughts and on constant guard against letting her true feelings show, Denise took to staying silent for most of the day. "I couldn't shout [about] what they had done," she said. "I couldn't cry out: 'You are all killers!'" When the Coscos asked her to write to her father in jail in early March, she agreed, then found she had almost nothing to say.

To Dad
   Even if you are away from me, you are still close to me.

                                        I love you,
                                        Denise

PS Don't worry about me.
PPS I could get you some wild boar if you want. As you can see,
like you, I am someone of few words. But what I write here is what
I could never say to you. I just want you to be fine.

On February 25, in a public demonstration of her loyalty to the family, Denise signed a formal waiver giving up her right to witness protection. Secretly, however, she reestablished contact with Enza and other activists in Libera, asking if they could hide her if she left Pagliarelle. On March 5, she also clandestinely met the carabinieri a second time and gave a further statement. For the officers, Denise's new evidence filled in most of the remaining gaps in Lea's life, right up until the last few hours. But for Denise, reliving that night only increased her stress. She couldn't shake the thought that seemed to be getting ever louder in her head: that she should run away from Pagliarelle like her mother.

In early April 2010, when her aunt went away for a few days,

Denise seized her chance. She took the bus to Crotone, then jumped on a long-distance train to the north. After a day, she arrived at a Libera safe house near Turin. "I had to go," she told her hosts. "They wouldn't let me live." Initially, the Coscos didn't notice Denise was gone. But when one week became three, there was no hiding it any longer. On April 23, Vito Cosco drove down from Milan and confronted Marisa and her husband, demanding to know where Denise had gone.

That afternoon, the surveillance team tapped a series of calls between Marisa and Denise. "Vito's been here!" Marisa said. "Wherever you are, you have to be here tomorrow! They say they just want to talk to you. Afterward you can go off wherever you want." Failing to return would be sending a message to the 'Ndrangheta to go screw itself, said Marisa.

"I know I have to go back to talk to these assholes," replied Denise.

"Look, they just want to feel relaxed," said Marisa. "They want to know that you know what you have to do."

"What I have to do?! What I have to do?!" shouted Denise. "I have to keep quiet! I have to be stopped!"

"So fuck them all!" said Marisa. "But we're all so sick of this mess here. And I think once they know where you are and what you're doing, they'll calm down. Vito was going to see your father, but he didn't go because he didn't know what to tell him. Right now, they're afraid that you're back in the program."

"The program your sister was in!"

"They're just afraid, Denise," said Marisa. Denise shouldn't overthink what she had to do. She shouldn't imagine the worst. "They don't care where you are or how you are. They only care about themselves. They only care that no one speaks the truth."

Denise returned to Pagliarelle the next day. Vito, apparently reassured, flew back to Milan. Denise had to wait a week before visiting her father in jail. The prospect of speaking to Carlo once more terrified her as much as it had the last time. She turned to Carmine once again. "I have to wait a week," she texted him. "I know what you think—that I'm wrong—but I just want to have the chance of a different life."

"This is the week you can change things," Carmine wrote back. "No one's standing in the way of the life you want. Just do things right, and the others will relax."

The reality, as Enza discovered years later, was precisely the opposite. Carlo's brothers had kept him closely informed of Denise's behavior. She wasn't getting any better, they told him. When Denise had disappeared, Carlo told his brothers that he had made a decision. If and when she reappeared, she had to die. Carlo added it would be easiest if Carmine did it.

Carmine, ever more in love with Denise, had been half expecting the call. He had already decided to disobey. But now that it had come, the clock was ticking. The boss had given the order that his only daughter, whom he loved, was to be killed. It wasn't a decision he would have taken lightly. But it was one that, given Denise's erratic behavior, he would have concluded was unavoidable. Carlo had to protect the 'ndrina and the 'Ndrangheta. He had to enforce the code. Women were the organization's property and the repository of its honor, to be cherished or disposed of as duty required. Now that he had made the decision, he would want his orders carried out as swiftly as possible. As Carmine's betrayal became apparent to Carlo over the next few weeks and months, he knew Carlo would make him pay dearly for it.

XI

B ARELY A DAY after Denise returned to Calabria's east coast, Alessandra made her first strike against the Pesces on the west. In the early hours of April 26, 2010, in simultaneous raids in Rosarno, Reggio, Milan, and Bergamo, code-named Operation All Inside, hundreds of carabinieri moved in on the Pesce empire. They arrested a total of thirty people. Ten warrants were issued for *'ndrina* members on the run. Among those accused was clan boss Antonino Pesce, Giuseppina's uncle, who was already in jail. His son and protégé, Giuseppina's cousin Francesco Pesce, was arrested in Rosarno. Reflecting Alessandra's convictions, seven of the detained were women. They included Giuseppina's mother, sister, cousin, grandmother, and great-grandmother, as well as Giuseppina herself.

The charges against the Pesce family included extortion, money laundering, loan-sharking, drug smuggling, mafia association, and two counts of murder.[1] The range of accusations indicated how, inside their dominion of Gioia Tauro and Rosarno, the 'Ndrangheta's hegemony was total. "They completely control their territory and their government," said Michele Prestipino. "People who live there accept that to get something they have to knock on the door of the mafia and that there is no future other than what the mafia sees." The mafiosi's power in Rosarno was at its peak. In a town of fifteen thousand people, the authorities had identified five hundred 'Ndrangheta members and hundreds more associates. That crushing dominance meant a strange kind of peace prevailed. "There is not much need for a lot of violence," said Prestipino. "Everybody knows that if these people want to use violence, they can. They achieve consensus without firing a shot."

The range of assets seized during Operation All Inside was further evidence of the Pesces' reach. While the prosecutors promised heftier hauls to come, even on this first pass they confiscated vehicles, properties, and businesses worth €10 million from one of the poorest areas in Europe. Pesce businesses included a gas station, a car dealership, a food distribution company, and a chocolate distributor whose company documents named Rocco Palaia, Giuseppina's husband, as its owner. A Rosarno radio station, Radio Olimpia, was particularly interesting. The carabinieri had discovered that jailed bosses and *picciotti* were using Olimpia's request show to communicate with each other. Prisoners would ask their family a yes/no question—Is my appeal successful? Were my orders carried out?—and the families would reply by calling in and requesting one of two songs to relay the answer. Giuseppina's fugitive uncle Vincenzo would also call in from time to time and ask the presenter to use his nickname and describe him as a listener "at large." In other words: *I am still in the area; I am still free.*

GIUSEPPINA WAS CHARGED with mafia association, money laundering, extortion, and running messages. She faced more than a decade in jail. That wasn't what troubled her, however. The Calabrian newspapers had reported that she had been detained with a man. Three weeks earlier, she had been warned by her uncle Vincenzo that her family suspected she was having a relationship with Domenico Costantino. Her cousin Francesco had had her followed day and night. Now that she had been found with Domenico in the middle of the night, their suspicions would be confirmed. The family's punishment would far exceed the state's. "In my family, those who betray and dishonor the family must be punished by death," said

Giuseppina. "It is a law." "She was going to die and she knew it," said Alessandra. "She accepted it."

What Giuseppina could not accept was the sudden implosion of her three children's future. She had never been apart from Angela, fifteen; Gaetano, eight; and Elisea, three. Now they were with Rocco's family. With Giuseppina headed for a lengthy sentence, or execution, and probably both, one way or another her children were going to be raised by the 'Ndrangheta. Her son, Gaetano, was a gentle boy especially unsuited for the life now before him. Ahead were years of brutalization. Giuseppina's father, Salvatore, used to joke that when a cousin was giving birth, he'd send flowers for a girl and a .38 for a boy. A few years back, when an uncle had asked Gaetano what he wanted to be when he grew up and the boy, in all innocence, had replied "a policeman," his uncle beat him, then promised to get him a gun to remind him who he was. Giuseppina's fear, she wrote later, was that "they will put a gun in his hands anyway. When I get out of jail, my son could already be in a juvenile detention center. And my two daughters will have to marry two 'Ndrangheta men and be forced to follow them around."

Giuseppina vented her frustration by starting a hunger strike and refusing to talk to prosecutors. But at other times, her spirit seemed broken. She tried to hang herself in her cell a few days after she was arrested. Three months later, by which time she had been transferred to San Vittore prison in Milan, she slashed her wrists with a razor. "There were times when I wanted to die," she said later in court. "I couldn't stand the thought of my children without me. They'd always been with me. I wanted a way out. I was watching my world collapse in on me."[2]

THE PROSECUTORS WERE largely unsympathetic. If an 'Ndranghetista was feeling guilt or paying some other price for her crimes, then they had done their job. This was war. Prosecutors had begun finding gun cartridges leaning up against their windshields. One bullet sent to Pignatone in May 2010 was accompanied by a note that read simply: "You're a dead man." Two of his staff found their cars' wheels had been loosened. Nor could the prosecutors rely on much public support. The same day as the raids on the Pesce clan, police in Reggio arrested Giovanni Tegano, an 'Ndrangheta boss on the run for seventeen years. As he was led from the city's central police station to a squad car to take him to jail, Tegano was cheered by a crowd of hundreds. "Giovanni is a man of peace!" shouted one tearful seventy-year-old woman, to which Tegano smiled and waved back.[3]

The threats against them only reconfirmed prosecutors' determination to bring down the 'Ndrangheta. The pace was relentless. Alessandra and Giovanni Musarò had thirty separate investigations under way against the west coast 'Ndrangheta. "We weren't going to let them breathe," said Giovanni. "They were used to enduring one operation, then having a rest. But we just kept on. Someone would be arrested, they would be replaced, and then we arrested that person, too."

On July 13, in a follow-up from Operation All Inside, the carabinieri staged more raids across the country. This time they were more ambitious. Operation Infinity involved more than three thousand officers and resulted in three hundred arrests across the 'Ndrangheta hierarchy. The standout success was the arrest of *capo crimine* Domenico Oppedisano, now eighty, in Rosarno.

Oppedisano, his gray hair swept back across his head, arrested in the kind of dark gray, open-necked striped shirt you might expect to see on a market trader, conformed to the traditional image of a southern mafioso. But other arrests reflected the organization's more recent sophistication. Around half of the raids took place in and around Milan. Those detained included businessmen, lawyers, bankers, accountants, politicians, policemen, and public health care managers. Pignatone marveled at the range of figures now behind bars and what it revealed about the 'Ndrangheta's ability to "infiltrate such a wide variety of environments." A new cosmopolitan generation of 'Ndranghetisti was emerging, he said, who understood how globalization had opened up the world to illicit businesses as much as it had to legitimate ones. "They are graduates," he said. "They can count on a network of professionals, bureaucrats, and politicians. They can penetrate any part of Italy and anywhere overseas."

Pignatone's junior prosecutors were jubilant. Many had prepared for this moment for years. Alessandra had been waiting all her life. Now the 'Ndrangheta was being hit hard, its bosses arrested, and its precious secrets exposed. "That was the moment we revealed that we knew not only that the 'Ndrangheta existed as a hierarchy and a structure but that it could be proved," said Alessandra. The interior minister, Roberto Maroni, described the raids as a "blow to the heart of the 'Ndrangheta's organisational and financial structure." Oppedisano's arrest was greeted with a standing ovation in the Italian Senate.[4] It was going to be a long war. But the prosecutors had finally shown that they could make the world's mightiest mafia bleed.

THE 'NDRANGHETA WAS a secret criminal organization that oppressed people with inhuman violence. If the Italian state was to win its war with it, if the government was to lift the yoke the mafia had imposed on the people, it had to offer them transparency, legality, and humanity. But in the heat of battle and with the first flush of victory, the last of those, humanity, was being forgotten.

Giuseppina was useful to Alessandra. She represented further evidence to support her theory about women's influence in the

'Ndrangheta. But when Alessandra heard about Giuseppina's suicide attempts, she felt little compassion for a woman whose predic-
ament was entirely her own fault. "I didn't believe Giuseppina was
sincere," she said. "And in fact, she quickly admitted that she wasn't
really trying to kill herself but merely trying to persuade us to help
her reunite with her children."[5]

The same cold-bloodedness was on display in the state's indictment of Carlo Cosco and Massimo Sabatino for the murder
of Lea Garofalo on May 27, 2010. The charge sheet, confidential
at this stage in the Italian legal process, included a detailed reconstruction of Carlo's movements on the night Lea died. But
there was also an extensive account of Lea's relationship with
the witness protection program. To many inside the small group
of lawyers and officials allowed to read it, it made for damning reading. Lea had put her faith in the state, and the state
had abandoned her. It seemed minded to do the same to Denise.
How could Italy expect to beat the mafia if it couldn't even protect those who tried to help it? The state's lack of sympathy
had killed Lea almost as surely as Carlo had. Enza Rando, Lea's
lawyer, was especially critical. "Lea had to make her own way,"
she said. "The state just didn't understand how to make witness
protection work, especially for a woman. Lea had the strength
and weakness of a mother. Brave but at the same time afraid. She
never received the help she needed."[6]

Alessandra bristled at the criticism. She would have preferred
a faultless protection program that led seamlessly to the prosecution and conviction of mafiosi. But people died in war. Sometimes
mafiosi, sometimes carabinieri and prosecutors, and sometimes
witnesses. Lea's death was no reason to show weakness. It was every reason to show resolve. "Prosecutors always get blamed," she
said. "But the facts are that Lea applied for witness protection and

didn't have enough information to justify it. Protection costs a lot of money. If your information is not important or deep enough, you don't get it."[7]

Even if Alessandra was right about the limits on government finances, there was no disputing that the state had failed in one of its primary duties: the protection of its citizens. Lea had crossed the divide to fight on the side of the government, and had lost. As a result, according to the indictment, she had probably been tortured, killed, and dissolved in acid. Why? Because the 'Ndrangheta thought she was theirs to keep or discard as they chose—and because, in the end, the state had done the same. Alessandra might be right that this was a war. But if the state was fighting with the same ruthlessness as the 'Ndrangheta, would the people care who won?

It wasn't that Italy's anti-mafia prosecutors had been born peculiarly unfeeling. It was that they were trained to be. From law school through their training to their years on the job, they had been told that emotion had no place in the service. The mafia was heat and blood. Prosecutors were focus, discipline, and procedure.

But as long as they withheld their hearts from the fight, it was easy to confuse a prosecutor's professional detachment with indifference, or even disdain. The mafia's victims deserved sympathy. Often the best the prosecutors could muster was pity. Cut off from the world, on an endless shuttle between windowless office, bulletproof car, steel-doored court, and secure apartment, it was easy for a prosecutor to forget that war was ultimately played out in flesh and blood, and often won by capturing hearts and minds. Alessandra dismissed Giuseppina's suffering. She marveled at the emotional decision making that had led Lea Garofalo to her death. "Lea Garofalo went to Milan, where she knew her husband was, even after she had been threatened by him, almost like a form of protest," she

exclaimed. Lea had followed her heart, and that had doomed her.
Alessandra's considered response was heartlessness. "I study women
in the 'Ndrangheta," she said. "I go to conferences about it. It's a
subject I'm very passionate about." But no one should mistake in-
tellectual interest for personal attachment. "I don't get involved in
these women's lives," she said. "I can't."[8]

XII

THE WAR WAS heating up. In August, a bundle of industrial dynamite was detonated outside the Reggio home of Calabrian attorney general Salvatore di Landro. In early October, an anti-mafia magistrate in Sicily announced that he had intelligence on a secret summit between the leaders of Cosa Nostra, the Camorra, and the 'Ndrangheta at which Italy's three big mafias had drawn up a hit list of assassination targets. On that list was Giuseppe Pignatone. The next week, Pignatone received a phone call at work telling him there was a surprise waiting for him outside. That turned out to be an Eastern European rocket launcher hidden under a mattress. The Italian press began calling 2010 "the year of bombs and bazookas."

Pignatone professed he was encouraged by what he viewed as the actions of an organization in distress. While the threats had to be taken seriously, there was no question of easing off when the crackdown was so clearly being felt. There were more indications that the 'Ndrangheta was being shaken. Ordinary Calabrians were stepping forward to assist the state and that, said Pignatone, "had never happened before." When Justice Minister Angelino Alfano prematurely declared the 'Ndrangheta "fatally wounded," the Calabrian prosecutors winced at his haste. Still, said Pignatone, there was no doubt that "positive results are giving us even more positive results."[1] One development was almost unprecedented, he added. Inside jail, an 'Ndranghetista had begun talking.

AT THE BEGINNING of October 2010, the prosecutor's office in Palmi received a letter from San Vittore jail in the center of Milan. San Vittore is Italy's most notorious mafia prison. Thousands of mafiosi have served time there, and most pass through at some stage, including Carlo Cosco, Massimo Sabatino, and Salvatore Riina, the Cosa Nostra boss who ordered the executions of Giovanni Falcone and Paolo Borsellino. Even to write to an anti-mafia prosecutor from inside San Vittore and request a meeting was a risk. But to specify that the meeting must take place without a lawyer—indicating that the inmate was considering talking freely, since mafia lawyers worked for the organization rather than the individual—was so dangerous as to suggest the prisoner was beyond caring. Giuseppina Pesce was already a dead woman walking. Maybe she was thinking of becoming a dead woman talking, too. "If you can make her talk," said Pignatone as he handed the letter to Alessandra, "we'll have done in three years in Calabria what took us thirty years in Palermo."[2]

Alessandra was doubtful. Still, she agreed with Pignatone that Giuseppina was more likely to open up to another woman. And to Alessandra, even the smallest chance of a woman prosecutor unlocking the 'Ndrangheta through the evidence of a woman mafiosa was irresistible.

On October 14, 2010, Alessandra was driven by a security detail through the gates of San Vittore. She was escorted to a meeting room by a prison warden and a marshal. After a few minutes, Giuseppina was led into the room by a prison guard. She walked slowly and hesitantly. Giuseppina had the prison look: wan, with greasy hair, her shoulders hunched like a beaten animal. "She looked at me with such loathing," said Alessandra, "with pride, resentment, and hatred. I represented the state, which was ruining her life."[3]

After this inauspicious beginning, the atmosphere quickly de-

teriorated. Giuseppina blurted out that she wanted to be moved
to a state safe house and to see her children. In return, she would
help them catch some 'Ndrangheta bosses on the run. Alessandra
dismissed the offer out of hand. "She wanted to give us a couple
of names in exchange for her freedom," she said.[4] It was a pathetic
offer—and, in any case, it wasn't how the prosecutors worked. They
didn't negotiate with gangsters. That was how the mafia drew you
in. Alessandra closed her laptop and made to leave.

Giuseppina looked up at Alessandra with alarm. This wasn't
how the meeting was meant to go. Giuseppina's idea had been to
negotiate with Alessandra the 'Ndrangheta way, which was to say,
hard: reveal little of what you have, affect nonchalance about any
deal offered, and eventually extract as much as possible for as little as possible. What's more, Giuseppina was a Pesce. Her family
killed people. Her family was power. She had summoned the state
to see her. And yet here was this woman prosecutor—a woman!—
turning everything upside down and heading for the door.

Alessandra would later admit she was bluffing. Of course she
wanted to know about 'Ndrangheta fugitives. She wanted anything
Giuseppina could give her. But Alessandra was angling for *everything* Giuseppina could give her. The state had painstakingly built
its case against the Pesces and the 'Ndrangheta. The evidence was
good enough for trial. But it could always be stronger. It was all
but inevitable that several mafiosi, including a few kingpins, would
walk. There was so much the prosecutors didn't know or couldn't
prove. Who ran what? Who, precisely, moved how much cocaine?
Who laundered whose money? Who, exactly, pulled the triggers? In
Giuseppina Pesce's head was the evidence that could solve hundreds
of crimes stretching back decades. A full confession would split the
'Ndrangheta wide open, devastating an organization whose power
depended on secrecy. It would transform the fight against the mafia. Most crucially to Alessandra, it would also finally prove—to

the 'Ndrangheta, the judiciary, and all Italy—that chauvinism was toxic, witless, self-destructive folly.

Alessandra, then, was gambling. But as she reached the door, Giuseppina cleared her throat. "Everything I testify to now," she said, "I do it for my children, I do it to give them a different future."[5]

GIUSEPPINA WOULD EVENTUALLY tell Alessandra everything she knew. It took time. Alessandra and Giuseppina began talking inside San Vittore prison. Once the carabinieri retrieved Giuseppina's children from the Palaias, who had been looking after them, and took them to a safe house near Aprilia, south of Rome, where they were reunited with their mother, Giuseppina and Alessandra spoke for several more months. It wasn't just the size and scale of Giuseppina's knowledge. At the beginning, in those first few hours and days, she also delivered it slowly. Giuseppina was still torn between love for her own small family and loyalty to The Family. "She was desperate to be reunited with her kids," said Alessandra. "But it was really hard for her to betray her relatives."[6]

But gradually, as Alessandra offered reassurances about her safety and that of her children, the two women established a rapport. "She *knew* she was going to die," said Alessandra. "She *knew* it would be her brother who killed her. I had to explain to her over and over that it's not normal that if you cheat on your husband, then you have to die."[7] Giuseppina started to relax. There was even a moment on that first day in October when Alessandra saw her eyes shift from terror and confusion to courage and trust. As they talked, Giuseppina became calmer and more confident. Alessandra could feel an almost tangible sense of a beginning, like the first glow of a new era of collaboration opening up right in front of her.

Transcribed, Giuseppina's evidence would eventually run to 1,514 pages. It included diagrams she drew of the 'Ndrangheta hier-

archy, descriptions of rituals, evidence of several murders, and detailed accounts of cocaine smuggling rings, extortion rackets, money
laundering, credit card fraud, and public corruption. "No stone was
left unturned," said Alessandra. "She told me so many things."[8]
Giuseppina's evidence not only backed up the existing cases, it
prompted a raft of new ones. "The whole character of our investigations changed from that moment," said Alessandra. "It was a real
turning point." Based on what Giuseppina told her, over the next
year Alessandra would confiscate a total of €260 million in property
from the Pesces and the 'Ndrangheta, including forty businesses,
four villas, forty-four apartments, 164 cars, sixty plots of land, and
two soccer teams. The number of arrests skyrocketed. Eventually,
Alessandra would be able to bring charges against a total of sixty-
four 'Ndrangheta men and women from the Pesce *'ndrina*, including
two Palaias and fourteen Pesces. Giuseppina revealed the location
of three houses in Rosarno under which the Pesces had built bunkers and pinpointed five other underground hideouts. Even when
she didn't know a bunker's whereabouts, she offered other help. Her
cousin, acting clan head Francesco "Ciccio" Pesce, she said, "liked
women, a lot of women." After she gave Alessandra details of one
girlfriend, the carabinieri followed the woman until she led them to
Ciccio's hideout, which he had equipped with sixteen infrared cameras. Another boss was tracked to a bunker by tailing his friends,
whose names were also provided by Giuseppina.

More than the loss of money or personnel, it was the act of Giuseppina's betrayal that shook the 'Ndrangheta. "Pesce was a name
that creates terror in Calabria," said Alessandra. "This—breaking
the chain, making it possible for women and children to leave the
mafia and be free and safe—it was like a bomb."[9] When news of Giuseppina's betrayal reached Rosarno, their rivals the Belloccos held
a party to celebrate the Pesces' shame. In Reggio, Prestipino and
Pignatone were equally ecstatic. "A woman with the name of Pesce,

an organic member of this fearsome 'Ndrangheta family, a woman from a place where women don't have the same rights as men, she betrays them and moves to the side of the state," said Prestipino.[10] "Immediately, they lose prestige. They lose power. It's devastating. Ordinary people see it's not true that they will always go unpunished. It's not the case that they're invincible. People say: 'They're no longer capable of silencing even one of their own members.' People start having doubts about them."

Just as important, 'Ndrangheta members themselves would start to feel the old certainties erode. "Giuseppina showed everybody that there was an alternative to 'Ndrangheta—that the state could save you and save your family," said Alessandra. "She was living proof that you could leave the 'Ndrangheta. That you could survive it. That you could be free."[11] Prestipino concurred. "'Ndrangheta members start realizing that the 'Ndrangheta life is not irreversible. They have an alternative. Giuseppina is proof to all 'Ndrangheta members and women that a mafia member cannot just quit but can organize their life in a different way. Anyone can do it. This undermines and jeopardizes the consensus the mafia has built. It's an existential crisis."[12]

Giuseppina's motivation for her betrayal was rooted in her desire to give her three children a better life. "I want to change my ways now and take my children with me and try to create a different future for them," she wrote in a testimonial statement.[13] But there was something else, too. She and Alessandra had made a connection. In one sense, they were two women united against a world of violent men. When Alessandra felt Giuseppina was holding back on a sensitive matter—her marriage, her affair, how the Pesce men were—she would ask the male carabinieri officers in the room to leave, so Giuseppina would feel less liable to be judged and able to speak more freely.

Alessandra and Giuseppina were discovering they had more in

common than they initially thought. They were two women with a common enemy, living difficult, isolated, and sometimes terrifying lives. That made them natural allies. More than that, it ensured that both were starved of friendship. Giuseppina, in particular, had broken faith with her entire family and her whole life. "I am alone," she would often tell the prosecutors. Alessandra sensed that Giuseppina needed someone new to rely on. A state that kept its promises. A prosecutor whose word she could believe. A new life, not just security and survival but a full and meaningful existence, even a hope of joy and love.

Perhaps more than Giuseppina knew, Alessandra understood. Almost for the first time in her career, Alessandra began to allow herself to feel something, too. This was not just another case, Alessandra told herself. Departing from a creed she had held on to since law school, she began to see Giuseppina not just as a tool for getting the job done but as an individual with discrete strengths, flaws, and needs. Alessandra saw to it that Giuseppina was never alone and was always able to phone her or her lawyer, day or night. She began visiting Giuseppina even when they had nothing professional to discuss. She was aware she was breaking her own rules. Her relationship with Giuseppina was evolving into something beyond the technical or the objective. At times, Alessandra saw herself as a gondolier, ferrying Giuseppina from her old life to the new. In other moments, she spoke about how she and this young girl were establishing "an umbilical cord."

At the age of forty-two, in the most unlikely of circumstances, Alessandra was becoming a mother.

XIII

In Pagliarelle, Denise was unaware of the prosecutors' progress in the hunt for her mother's killers.[1] She had no idea that her father, Carlo Cosco, had ordered her own death, nor that Carmine was refusing to obey him. Still, pretending to live as a good 'Ndrangheta girl while secretly seeing Carmine and keeping contact with Libera, Enza Rando, and the carabinieri was an impossible balancing act. On September 28, 2010, she visited Carlo in jail. The conversation was awkward and stilted. Denise could sense her charade was wearing thin. "I had no wish to see my father," she said later. "I didn't feel sincere about seeing him."

A few weeks later, on the morning of October 18, 2010, the Milan prosecutor leading the investigation into Lea's disappearance, Giuseppe Gennari, finally released a public indictment for murder against Carlo. Describing Lea's death as an "execution" planned and ordered by Carlo, Gennari said Carlo had organized a van to transport Lea out of the city, secured a warehouse where she would be interrogated and tortured, procured a gun to kill her, and supplied fifty liters of sulfuric acid in which to dissolve her body. Erasing any trace of Lea would allow the conspirators to claim she had run off to Australia, he said. The motive for the killing, Gennari told reporters, was "the statements Lea made to the prosecutors, none of which, for unexplained reasons, were ever used in a trial." Specifically, said Gennari, Lea was killed for her testimony about the murder of Antonio Comberiati. Though Carlo never knew what Lea had told prosecutors, Gennari said he had not wanted to take any chances. In any case, he continued, Carlo believed Lea had to be punished for her disloyalty and the shame she had brought on him. From the moment Lea left witness protection in April 2009, Carlo had been working toward the chance to abduct, torture, and kill her. Gennari added that Carlo had had five accomplices, whom he named as Massimo Sabatino; Carlo's two brothers, Vito and Giuseppe; Rosario Curcio; and Carmine Venturino.

The morning of October 18 in Calabria was warm, one of the last days of summer. Denise and Carmine had driven to Crotone to buy supplies for the Cosco family pizzeria, where both of them still worked. Afterward, they took a ride along the coast to Botricello beach. Their plan was to swim, sunbathe, and perhaps grab a bite for lunch. Around midday, as prosecutor Gennari was speaking to reporters in Milan, the couple watched a line of carabinieri cars drive up along the seafront and pull to a stop. Several officers got out. They started walking across the sand. Denise and Carmine watched them come. Then Carmine sighed, tugged on his T-shirt, and stood with his head bowed, his arms by his sides.

As Denise watched the officers surround her boyfriend, cuff him, slap their hands on his shoulders, and start to lead him off across the beach, she felt the blood drain from her face. Her relationship with Carmine was still a secret. Something in their manner told Denise the officers knew all about it. But she had a sudden intuition about something else, too. She followed the officers as they walked Carmine to a waiting squad car. One man put his arm around her and led her to a different car, where he opened the door for her. "This is one of the men who killed your mother," said the officer. "This is the guy who dissolved your mother's body in acid."[2]

XIV

GIUSEPPINA PESCE AND her children were reunited at a safe house near Aprilia on November 5, 2010. Days later, her eldest daughter, Angela, received a package from Rosarno. The carabinieri had spirited away Angela and her brother and sister, Gaetano and Elisea, with such haste that the children had left with just the clothes they were wearing. Now the Palaias, Giuseppina's in-laws, were forwarding their belongings. The children were delighted. Unpacking her sweatshirts and favorite jeans, Angela found her mobile carefully wrapped up in her clothes. She didn't tell her mother.[1]

The calls from Rosarno started almost immediately. Angela's uncles and grandparents would ask her whether she was eating OK. How was she coping without her family? Was she keeping away from those others? For most of the seven months their mother had been in jail, the children had been living with their aunt, Angela Palaia, with whom Angela shared her first and last names. Aunt Angela called almost every day. She would tell her niece that her family missed her. She would promise Angela to buy her this jacket or those trainers once she returned to Rosarno. Sometimes she would say that Giuseppina had made her own decision for her own reasons but hadn't stopped to consider the consequences for her children, who were being ripped away from their family and friends. It was unfair, said Aunt Angela. Unfair, and bad parenting. Witness protection was no life for a teenage girl. Think of everything Angela was missing out on. The Palaias had everything she wanted. What could the state give her that her family could not? "Tell your mother you want to be with us," Aunt Angela would say. "If she wants to go on, she should go on alone. But you come back to us."

Angela was torn. She loved her mother. But she had also become close to her aunt in the time they had lived together. And while Giuseppina had promised her a better life once they were reunited, Angela found it was nothing like that, nor like any life she'd ever known. She was soon arguing with Giuseppina, calling her mother selfish for taking her, her brother, and her sister away from their school, friends, and family. Angela stopped eating. She refused to get out of bed. Her aunt would tell her that it was her mother who was making her ill. And it was all so unnecessary, said Aunt Angela. She promised the family would forgive Giuseppina. Everyone loved her. Everyone loved Angela, Gaetano, and Elisea, too. They were family, after all. The men had a lawyer standing by who would deal with whatever statements Giuseppina had made. Life could go back to normal. It would be as if nothing had happened. Why didn't they all come home? "My daughter started calling me her enemy," said Giuseppina. "She would tell me how good Aunt Angela was to her, how Aunt Angela loved her."

The Palaias' aim was true. Realizing that Giuseppina had started collaborating for the sake of her children, they guessed correctly that she would stop for them, too. At the time, Alessandra had no idea of the secret phone discussions taking place inside the safe house. When she found out later, she conceded that with its keen understanding of family, the 'Ndrangheta had found Giuseppina's weak spot. "Angela was only sixteen and didn't understand her mother's choice," she said. "And everyone knew that without her daughter, Giuseppina would not proceed."

For the 'Ndrangheta, forcing an end to Giuseppina's cooperation was becoming critical. On November 23, 2010, Alessandra staged Operation All Inside II, a series of further raids aimed at dismantling

the Pesce empire, this time guided largely by Giuseppina's information. Twenty-four more Pesce clan members were arrested. They
included two policemen, a prison guard, and two more women: the
twenty-eight-year-old wife of a low-level 'Ndranghetista said to be
passing messages between bosses; and Carmelina Capria, forty-
seven, wife of clan head Antonino Pesce and, allegedly, the family
accountant.

In response, the clan stepped up the pressure on Giuseppina.
As 2011 began, the calls to Angela became more frequent. In early
March, a second mobile somehow found its way to Giuseppina. She,
too, was soon speaking to Aunt Angela. Aunt Angela told Giuseppina that her husband, Rocco Palaia, still loved her, as did the whole
family. She tried to reassure her, saying she shouldn't worry about
retribution. Everyone made a mistake once in a while. Rocco was
prepared to forgive her. What was most important was her children's health. For a sixteen-year-old girl to be apart from her family wasn't natural. It was clearly distressing her. For her daughter's
sake, said Aunt Angela, Giuseppina had to stop collaborating, renounce the statements she had made, and come back to Rosarno.

Giuseppina said little in these conversations but neither did she
hang up. And as March 2011 passed into April and Aunt Angela
continued her emotional blackmail, Giuseppina's brother-in-law,
Gianluca Palaia, began relaying precise instructions as to how Giuseppina should end her collaboration. Once she left witness protection, Gianluca told her, the family would find her a lawyer, cover
her legal fees, and rent her a new apartment. He arranged for her to
receive €3,000, which he described as a gift from "a good man." Like
Aunt Angela, Gianluca tried to be reassuring. Don't worry, he said.
No one was going to do anything to her. Even Giuseppina's daughter, Angela, tried to persuade her. "You see? You see?" she would
say. "Now it's up to you."

Toward the end of March, Giuseppina was granted permission

to leave her safe house for a few hours to meet a lawyer. At a carabinieri station in Aprilia, she met Giuseppe Madia, a defense lawyer
from Rome who had represented mafiosi before and had now been
retained by the Palaias. Madia asked Giuseppina to read a letter to
the prosecutor's office that he had drafted on her behalf. It stated
that Giuseppina's health had suffered from her time in prison; that
the authorities had taken advantage of her fragile state of mind by
forcing her to cooperate; and that her evidence was false and she
was withdrawing it. Giuseppina objected to several claims but eventually agreed to sign. She also accepted Madia's proposal that she
refuse to sign off on the witness statements she had given Alessandra and exercise her right to silence in any further interviews.

Giuseppina copied into her own handwriting the typewritten
letter drafted by Madia, then signed it and dated it April 2. On
April 4, she consented to a carabinieri interview during which she
freely answered all questions. She was, she said later, "caught between two fires." When Madia told the Palaias that Giuseppina
was still cooperating, Aunt Angela, Giuseppina's brother-in-law
Gianluca Palaia, and a third clan member, Angelo Ietto, simply
turned up at her safe house, saying that they were there to give
their cousin "emotional support" at this difficult time. Giuseppina
realized that, once again, her destiny was being decided for her. "I
had made the choice to make my daughter's life better, but collaborating had ended up hurting my daughter," she said. Now she had
to do what her daughter wanted. The 'Ndrangheta were inside her
house, sitting with her children. If she refused to cooperate, they
would take them away forever. "I couldn't betray my children," said
Giuseppina. "I couldn't say no."

On April 11, Alessandra flew up from Reggio to Rome, then
drove down to Aprilia to see Giuseppina. Months of interviews had
been leading to this moment. It was 179 days since Giuseppina had
begun cooperating and one day before the legal deadline by which

Italian prosecutors in any investigation must present their evidence to court. Alessandra was bringing with her close to two thousand printed pages, transcripts of all Giuseppina's interviews over the past six months. Within those pages was the most detailed portrait of the 'Ndrangheta that had ever existed. It was enough to bring down one of Europe's most powerful crime families and blow open a secret, murderous, cocaine-smuggling cabal that had terrorized Italy for 150 years. It was also the fullest possible vindication of Alessandra's intuition about 'Ndrangheta women. She found it hard not to feel a moment of triumph as she set the stack of files down on the table in front of her star witness.

Alessandra explained to Giuseppina that her signature was just a legal formality. All she had to do was sign a covering letter, declaring that the statements that followed were her own words and a true representation of the facts as she knew them to be.

Giuseppina looked at the papers. She told Alessandra she couldn't sign.

"Are you refusing to sign because everything you've told us is lies?" asked Alessandra.[2]

Giuseppina, trying not to look Alessandra in the eye, started to cry. Sobbing, she invoked her right to silence. Stunned, Alessandra packed up her files and said she would leave Giuseppina with her lawyer for a few minutes to consider her options. She returned half an hour later.

"Is this really what you want?" she asked.

Giuseppina began to cry again. "It's not what I want," she said. "It's what I must do for my children." She refused to say any more.

ALESSANDRA TRIED TO carry on as before. On April 16, she arrested Giuseppina's mother, Angela Ferraro, and her sister Marina on charges of extortion and mafia association. The two had been detained a year earlier and released on bail, but with the new evidence from Giuseppina, their offenses were now serious enough for custody. Their detention brought to seventy-four the number of Pesce clan members that Alessandra had arrested in the year since she launched All Inside.

The next day, however, the Pesces hit back. A report appeared in the *Gazzetta del Sud*, the main southern daily, quoting Giuseppe Madia saying Giuseppina had recanted. Alessandra shrugged off the story as typical mafia lies. They just couldn't admit weakness, she thought. The state was winning this war.

On April 21, Alessandra struck again. Once more acting on Giuseppina's evidence, she launched Operation All Clean, this time aimed at the Pesces' finances. Forty-one companies were seized, most of them based in and around Rosarno, including trucking firms, orange and lemon traders, service stations, a sports complex, a sports fishing operation, a plastics firm, and a pizzeria. In addition, the prosecutors confiscated fifty properties—villas, apartments, houses, and garages—fifty-four plots of land, fifty-one cars and motorcycles, and 102 trucks. The total value was estimated at €190 million. "Today we can say with satisfaction that Rosarno is truly free," said Pignatone.

But barely had Alessandra had time to savor her new victory when, on April 26, 2011, she was handed a copy of the Reggio newspaper, *Calabria Ora*. On its front page, the paper had printed what it said was a letter from Giuseppina Pesce to Calabria's attorney general.[3]

> *Dear Mr. Judge,*
> *With this letter I want to withdraw all the allegations I made in my previous statements. I resolved to do this not out of fear but out of conscience because I said things that do not correspond to reality. I made those assertions at a time when I was seriously ill and suffering a great deal from being separated from my children.*

*The doctors who came to visit me when I was detained witnessed
the seriousness of my illness and how severely I was depressed in jail
where, out of desperation, I put my own life in danger. I was hoping
to see my three children, one of whom has serious health problems.
But my hopes did not last long because . . . I was sent on to Milan.
That was the moment I realized I would die if I did not make the
statements I was expected to make.*

*I will explain in court how my answers were born of questions
loaded with accusations. The more you accuse, the more you are
believed. The more you accuse your family, you will be believed even
more. I was so sick that I slandered my closest family members with
untruth. Fear and illness made me make those statements, which
now make me feel nothing but shame in my heart. I feel stripped
naked, exposed to everyone, with no thought for my dignity or my
loved ones. I feel like I have been used. Now that I feel better, I
have found the courage to retract my allegations, even as I fear the
monstrous process that I know awaits me. I ask everyone, even those
whom I have hurt unjustly, spare me a little understanding and
respect for the situation in which I am living.*

Sincerely,
Giuseppina Pesce

Calabria Ora added to its scoop with an interview with Madia, the lawyer, under the headline: "Forced to Repent: Pesce Said
Whatever the Prosecutors Wanted." The article began with a quote
from Madia: "Do you know how many times I have spoken with my
client? Once, in a carabinieri station, then nothing. Can you imagine? Today I don't even know where she is."

Madia alleged that Alessandra had "extracted" Giuseppina's testimony by using the "threat" that unless she cooperated, she would
never see her children again. "Read this medical report, read what it
says about Mrs. Pesce," he told the *Calabria Ora* journalist, handing

him a file that he said was signed by Nicola Pangallo, a psychiatrist who interviewed Giuseppina in prison. "The prisoner has particularly serious conditions that do not allow her custody in prison . . . The service agent reports that the prisoner had attempted suicide by hanging. The patient is completely detached from current reality and obsessed by the idea of leaving prison and seeing her children again. When she spoke to her daughter, her daughter replied: 'Is that my mom?' [The patient said]: 'I'm afraid my children no longer recognize me.'"

Dr. Pangallo went on to recommend that Giuseppina receive specialist care in a prison located close to her children, in order to allow more frequent contact. "And where do the prosecutors think the nearest prison to Reggio is located?" Madia asked the journalist. "Why, Milan, of course, a thousand kilometers away." It was after her transfer that Giuseppina had collapsed and begun collaborating, he added. "It's obvious Mrs. Pesce has not told the truth. She only said what the judges wanted her to say. That's why she made these statements."

In an editorial, *Calabria Ora*'s editor in chief, Piero Sansonetti, decried the prosecutors' conduct. "The fight against the mafia, like all exercises of justice, must be conducted within the rules, strictly within the rules, totally within the rules," he wrote. "Otherwise it might land a few blows on the mafia but inflict far greater damage to our legal system and society." Three days later, April 29, which happened to be Alessandra's forty-first birthday, Sansonetti gave a television interview in which he repeated Madia's allegations, demanded a parliamentary inquiry, and accused Alessandra of extortion and blackmail.

It was the start of a yearlong campaign by *Calabria Ora* against Alessandra and the other anti-mafia prosecutors. Throughout Giuseppina would be described not as an individual who had made her own choices but as a disturbed and weak woman who had been used by the prosecutors and manipulated into betraying her family. A week later, Sansonetti wrote another editorial in which he appeared to justify breaking the law and to characterize the 'Ndrangheta as victims of oppression. "To tell the truth, I actually don't care for lawfulness," he wrote. "To respect the law is not always, in my opinion, a merit. I have never sided with the law. Disobedience is a virtue. I tend to think it's right to stand for the weak whoever they are, and whether they're good or bad, guilty or innocent." Over the next few months, *Calabria Ora* published a string of stories castigating the prosecutors. One was an interview from prison with Salvatore Pesce, Giuseppina's father, who criticized the way his daughter had been treated. Giuseppina's uncle Giuseppe Ferraro also spoke to *Calabria Ora*, accusing Alessandra of blackmailing his niece by having the carabinieri kidnap her children and forcing her to make statements under the influence of psychotropic drugs.

It wasn't clear how much of this the Pesces actually believed. The intended audience seemed to be the citizens of Rosarno as much as Alessandra and the state. Still, the judiciary had to respond. The head of Italy's Anti-Mafia Directorate in Rome first denied any wrongdoing, then summoned Alessandra to the capital, where she was ordered to make out a report and explain her actions. A prosecutor in Catanzaro was even deputed to investigate Alessandra for extortion. "This slander campaign went on and on," said Alessandra.

Alessandra knew she was becoming a liability to the judiciary. Even to colleagues who backed her, she was in danger of becoming a cautionary tale: the spectacular rise and fall of the woman prosecutor who flew too high. She had the backing of Pignatone and Prestipino. But no prosecutor could tolerate criticism forever, least of all one on the front line of a war against the mafia.

Alessandra's only hope was to change Giuseppina's mind again. It seemed improbable. But in the months that followed, Alessandra began to fixate on the last conversation she had had with Giuseppina, going over it in her mind time and again. The letter in *Calabria Ora*, in which Giuseppina withdrew her statements, was clearly written for her. But when Alessandra had challenged Giuseppina to declare that her evidence was lies, Giuseppina had refused to speak. She became convinced Giuseppina was trying to tell her something. Refusing to sign wasn't recanting. Giuseppina might only be refusing to sign her statements *at that moment*. Who knew what kind of pressure the 'Ndrangheta was putting on her?

In early May, Alessandra was passed transcripts of bugged conversations between the Pesces. The contents seemed to support the idea that, contrary to Giuseppina's letter, she was far from reconciled with her family. In one exchange on May 5, caught on video, between her brother Francesco Pesce and her grandmother Giuseppa Bonarrigo, Francesco reassured the family matriarch that the Pesce family itself had "nothing to be ashamed of. If she [Giuseppina] screwed up, she did it alone, without anyone else from the family." Besides, Giuseppina's evidence wasn't all that damning, said Francesco. The family had found experts who would testify that she was mentally ill. "She's crazy, crazy," agreed Giuseppina's grandmother. "She did it for the children. Imagine!" Francesco added that Giuseppina's testimony was, in any case, mostly hearsay. Women weren't like men, he said. They just stayed in the home and listened to men talk. All Giuseppina had been able to pass on was what she had heard. It was a problem made in the home, said Francesco, "and we'll solve it. We just have to try to get her home. I'm trying to approach to tell her I have nothing against her, that I love her." At the words "solve it," Giuseppina's seventy-eight-year-old grandmother clasped her neck as though she were being choked.

That conversation would stay with Alessandra. Giuseppina's motivation for talking had always been to give her family a better life. That maternal compulsion meant all was not lost. Giuseppina would still want a new life for her children. She hadn't disavowed her statements, merely set them aside. If she was planning to take her children back to Rosarno, it would only be until she thought it was safe to leave again. Over the months they'd worked together, Alessandra had grown to trust Giuseppina, to care for her, and to respect her. Giuseppina was resilient and resourceful. The more Alessandra thought about it, the more she was convinced Giuseppina was executing a plan by invoking her right to silence. "She's being clever," she told her staff. To the 'Ndrangheta, Giuseppina was trying to appear as though she had been successfully brought to heel. But to Alessandra, Giuseppina was indicating she remained true to the cause. She was still planning to cooperate. She was just biding her time. "She's telling me that what she had said in all those months of interviews was true," said Alessandra.

Still, time was not on Giuseppina's side. As her grandmother's gesture indicated, her family would likely kill her as soon as they could. Since Giuseppina had stopped cooperating, the witness protection service would soon eject her, as they had done with Lea Garofalo—and if Lea's fate was any indication, Giuseppina's death would follow swiftly. However Alessandra was planning to save her star witness, she needed to act now.

XV

EVEN AS SHE struggled to find a way to rescue Giuseppina, Alessandra found her *pentita*'s example was inspiring another 'Ndrangheta woman to follow suit.[1]

In June 2010, anonymous letters began arriving at the yellow two-story house in Via Don Gregorio Varrà, Rosarno, that Maria Concetta Cacciola shared with her parents. The letters claimed that Concetta was having an affair with one of her Facebook friends. The accusation was absurd. Her friend had been in Germany all the time that Concetta had known him. But Concetta's father and brother, Michele and Giuseppe, didn't hesitate. Shouting, "You filthy animal!" they grabbed Concetta, punched her to the floor, and kicked her until they cracked one of her ribs. Desperate to avoid any public tarnishing of the family name, the two men then refused to let Concetta be treated at the hospital. Instead, they arranged private visits to the house by a doctor related to the Pesces. All this happened in front of Concetta's three children, Alfonso, fifteen, Tania, twelve, and Rosi, six.

It was three months before Concetta was well enough to step outside. Even then, one of her cousins followed her wherever she went. Finding herself alone in the house one day, Concetta called a women's refuge on the other side of Calabria but hung up before anyone answered. Then on May 11, 2011, the carabinieri summoned her to the station in Rosarno. Alfonso's scooter had been confiscated for a minor driving offense, and Concetta needed to pay his fine before it was returned. The twenty-minute walk to the station was the first occasion in months that Concetta had been allowed out of the house on her own.

Concetta entered the carabinieri station and asked to speak to an officer. From the moment Officer Carlo Carli led her into an interview room and closed the door, it all just tumbled out of her. Concetta first asked if Carli knew the reputation of the Cacciola family and her husband, Salvatore Figliuzzi. When Carli said he did, Concetta told him her family had kept her a virtual prisoner at home for the eight years since Salvatore had gone to jail. The situation had become intolerable in the last eleven months, she said. She told Carli the saga about her Facebook friendship with a man called Giuseppe in Germany, the poison-pen letters, and the beating. Her family now never let her out of their sight. As if to underline the point, Concetta's phone soon started ringing. It was her mother, Anna Rosalba Lazzaro, asking where she was. Concetta said she had to leave. At the door of the interview room, she predicted that one day her family would murder her. "If they find out I'm here saying these things, they'll kill me for sure," she said.

Officer Carli wanted to know more. Using Alfonso's scooter as an excuse, he summoned Concetta back to the station four days later. This time, she spoke to a female officer and, feeling less inhibited in front of a woman, told the officer she now wanted to escape her family and Rosarno. She had bought tickets to northern Italy several times but never had the nerve to go through with it. She'd even ripped up her ticket once when one of her cousins followed her into the travel agent's. The thing was, Concetta confided to the officer, her family was right. Calling herself "Nemi," she had begun a second online relationship with "Prince 484," a Reggio man called Pasquale Improta.[2] Initially, it had been innocent. But now it was starting to evolve into an affair. Pasquale was living a few hours away in Naples. When she'd told him about the beating, he'd urged her to go to the carabinieri to ask them to protect her. Concetta wanted to be with Pasquale. She had told her mother she wanted to divorce Salvatore. After all, he had never loved her and had only married her to assist his rise inside the 'Ndrangheta.

Concetta said her father would never let her divorce her husband. But it was her younger brother, thirty-year-old Giuseppe, who really scared her. He had been raised as a true believer, she said, and knew nothing outside the 'Ndrangheta. She had had to warn friends to stay away from her in case Giuseppe suspected they were helping her. The only time she could relax was when Giuseppe went away on business or once when he vanished for a few days immediately after a murder in Rosarno. Even then Giuseppe's wife had taken Concetta aside and whispered to her not to speak freely inside their house because Giuseppe had had the place bugged. "Giuseppe gets these rages," said Concetta. "He could do anything." He was just waiting for proof that she was having an affair, she said. "Sooner or later, he'll come to me and say, 'Come with me.' Then he'll make me disappear."

On May 23, Concetta returned to the station and spoke to Officer Carli again. With each successive visit, she seemed to be building up her courage. This time she gave more details about how her father and brother beat her. She added that she was thinking of leaving for Naples. On May 25, she went to the carabinieri station in Gioia Tauro. On this occasion she ended the conversation by saying she was prepared to make a statement about her family in return for witness protection. When she returned to Gioia Tauro station the next day, her fifth visit to the carabinieri in fifteen days, she found Alessandra and Giovanni Musarò waiting for her.

Concetta told the two prosecutors she could talk for a maximum of ninety minutes. "It was a complicated interrogation," said Alessandra. "We had to know who we had in front of us, why she was talking to us, what she was able to tell us, and whether she was lying. And she was very scared. She had told her family that she had to go to the carabinieri to pay a fine. That gave her more time than usual away from home. But she was worried. She kept looking at her watch."[3]

The prosecutors quickly concluded Concetta was credible. Her knowledge of the Rosarno clans was extensive. She told them details about the murder of Palmiro Macri, sixty-two, shot in a clan feud by a gunman using a Kalashnikov in July 2008 as he drove through Rosarno in his Fiat Panda. She described how a boss called Umberto Bellocco had killed Salvatore Messina, his wife's brother, then blamed the murder on Concetta's cousin, Gregorio Bellocco, something that caused a rift between the Belloccos and the Pesces for years. She told the story of how the Belloccos had extended their protection rackets to the nearby coastal town of San Ferdinando. She pinpointed the location of at least two bunkers, buried under an old factory in Rosarno, and explained how they were equipped with televisions and refrigerators stocked with food and champagne. The bosses' hypocrisy seemed to outrage Concetta. Hanging on the wall where "these men without honor shut themselves up like beasts," she said, would be an image of Saint Pio of Pietrelcina. "I'm speaking about murderers," she added, people who "butcher wretched people that thought they were friends, men they invited to dinner, not killed for honor or the family's sake but just for money and power."

The two prosecutors were struck by Concetta's resolve. "I was very impressed," said Giovanni. "Very often, people like her who go through pain and suffering—they are conflicted. Concetta was terrified but she was also very resolute."[4] When Alessandra asked her whether she would want to take her three children with her into witness protection, Concetta demurred. "I don't want my children to weaken my resolve," she said. "I need to find my strength in the choices I make, then you can go and find them, tell what I've done and why, and they can make their own decision whether to join me or not."[5]

But something about Concetta's story bothered the two prosecutors. Giovanni zeroed in on the reason her father and brother had beaten her. He asked her to explain the anonymous letters. They couldn't just have appeared from nowhere. "Giovanni was pressing her a bit," said Alessandra. "He could see she was lying. She was hiding something."

Concetta said nothing. But when the two prosecutors called a short break, Concetta waited until Giovanni and a male carabinieri officer were talking, then approached Alessandra. "If you wish, I can tell you about my relationship with Pasquale," she said, "but I'm too ashamed to talk in front of the men." Even inside a carabinieri station, negotiating her exit from the 'Ndrangheta, "Concetta was still a victim of the mafia system," said Alessandra.[6]

FOUR DAYS LATER, on the night of May 29, 2011, Concetta stole out of the family home in the middle of the night and ran to a waiting carabinieri car. In her room, she had left a letter for her mother.

Dear Mama,

I do not know where to start. I can't find the words to justify this action of mine. Mama, you're mama! Only you can understand a daughter. I know the pain that I'm causing you. By explaining everything to you, then at least you can explain to everyone else. I didn't want to leave you without saying anything. How many times have I wanted to talk to you? How much did I want to spare you pain? But I failed. And all this pain, I turned it into aggression, and I took it out on the person who, above all, I love the most.

That's why I'm entrusting my children to you. But one thing I beg of you. Don't make the mistakes that you made with me. Give them a better life than I had. Paired off at thirteen, I thought marriage would give me a little freedom. Instead, I ruined my life. Salvatore never loved me nor me him. You know that. So don't make the same mistakes with the children, I beg you. Give them space. If you shut them away, they'll start to behave badly because they'll feel trapped by everything. That's how you treated me.

I can't write much more. I just wanted to ask you to forgive me, Mother, for the shame I'm bringing you. In the end, I realized that I was alone—alone among everyone. I've never known luxury and I never wanted money. But now I have the peace and love and the satisfaction you feel when you make a sacrifice. This life has given me nothing but pain. The most beautiful thing in my life is my children. I keep them in my heart. Give your strength to them. Don't let their father have them; he's not worthy of them. Take care of Alfonso. He suffered as a boy and that's why he is how he is. He's not strong. You need to watch him closely.

I will live as long as God allows but I have to try to find some peace in my heart. Mama, forgive me. Please pray for forgiveness for all the harm that I'm causing. I'm going to a place where I can find some serenity. Don't look for me or you'll get into trouble. I can't speak to you anymore and I can't hug you, I can only write—but I couldn't leave without telling you I was going and wishing you well. I have only you and my children in my mind's eye. I love you, Mama. Hug my children as you always have and don't talk about them to anyone who's not worthy of them. Ma, farewell. And forgive me. Forgive me if you can. I know I'll never see you again. This is how it must be with a family of honor. That's why you have lost your daughter. Good-bye. I will always love you. Forgive me, as I, too, pray for forgiveness. Good-bye.

On the dashboard of the family car, Concetta also left a brief note for her father and her brother. "I'm going over to my friend Giusy's," she wrote.

———

FORMALLY ADMITTING A witness to the protection program took
months. But Concetta needed immediate protection. The carabinieri
took her to a secluded holiday resort, the Colle degli Ulivi, near
Cosenza, in the hills above the coastal town of Sibari, two hours'
drive north of Rosarno.

The Colle degli Ulivi was a safe, nondescript place, generally
used by northern Italian families on holiday. It had three restaurants, a bar, a solarium, a Jacuzzi, and a giant pool, and it offered its
guests horse riding, mountain biking, tennis, archery, karaoke, and
walks in the hills or down to the beach. At mealtimes, giant buffets
would be laid with fruit, salads, and cold meats, or you could order
à la carte, and there was every type of wine. Concetta's protection
officers stayed on-site but otherwise let her roam as she wanted.

Concetta loved it. She could walk into town or down to the shoreline whenever she chose. In the hotel, as the temperature rose with
the onset of summer, the rooms slowly filled with guests: young
families, old couples, foreigners. No one knew her. No one knew the
meaning of the name Cacciola. There was no shame and no punishment. And Concetta realized that at thirty-one, for the first time in
her life, she was truly free.

Pasquale came to visit for a couple of nights. Staff and guests
would later recall how Concetta seemed just as happy striking up
conversations with perfect strangers, arriving promptly at mealtimes in the hope of meeting someone new. She picked up several
lone men over the two months she was there. "In this new environment, she got to know a lot of men," said Giuseppe Creazzo, the
prosecutor who would later investigate her case. "She made love
with a lot of them. It was a way for her to be alive. It was the best
way she knew to communicate."

On June 16, Alessandra drove up to Sibari, and Concetta gave
her as much detail as she could on the bunkers. Two days later,
Giovanni arrived for a third interview to go over Concetta's ear-

lier evidence. Concetta identified various 'Ndranghetisti from mug shots that Giovanni brought with him and added details of the murders and protection rackets she had described. When Giovanni asked, Concetta reconfirmed in a written statement that she was willing to leave her three children with their grandmother. "I believe they're in no danger," she wrote. "I believe my children don't need the state to protect them."

Concetta struck Giovanni as "more serene and at peace" than when he had last seen her. Importantly, "she was also still determined." Unprompted, Concetta went into fine detail about how the Bellocco clan ran their loan-sharking operation. Two brothers of a friend of hers, Rita Stefania Secolo, had borrowed €600,000 from the Belloccos. Two years later, their debt was €1 million. "Stefania told me that the Belloccos had threatened to kill her brothers if the money was not repaid," said Concetta. "They told her they would take an apartment building owned by her family as part payment. They even shot up a shop on the ground floor and told Stefania they would have killed somebody if the gun hadn't jammed." Stefania ended up living on the top floor of the building, above her old apartment, paying rent to the Bellocco extortionists who had moved in below.

Every day Concetta stayed at Colle degli Ulivi was another small adventure. When the formal approval for her witness protection came through in late July, she was moved to Bolzano in the Alps. But when a new man she brought back to her hotel room turned out to be a former convict, her protection officers moved her again, this time to Genoa on Italy's northwest coast.

IF LEAVING GAVE Concetta a new sense of peace, it created uproar in Rosarno. "Your escape sparked off hell," her friend Emanuela Gentile told her, in a call tapped by the carabinieri. "Your father really freaked out. Your mother went around yelling 'They ruined us,' and was crying and tearing her hair out. Your brother grew a long beard and locked himself far away in a house by the sea out of shame. He never leaves. Now *he* is the prisoner."

Alessandra and Giovanni couldn't help enjoying the ruckus. "It was the fact that she was a woman called Cacciola," said Giovanni. "That was really unacceptable to them. The 'Ndrangheta's reaction to Giuseppina and Concetta was not proportional to the information they gave us—most of it was hearsay, not a murder confession or anything—but to the 'Ndrangheta it wasn't about the information. It was the symbolic value of them turning state's evidence."

Alessandra took particular pleasure in reading the transcripts from the Cacciola family. The carabinieri had tapped their phones and planted a bug in the family car. You could almost hear the 'Ndrangheta shattering. In one recording, Anna Rosalba Lazzaro, Concetta's mother, railed about the female carabiniere in Rosarno with whom Concetta had spoken. "That officer slut!" shouted Lazzaro. "She has a thing going with the judges! She's a whore!" Another time, Alessandra listened as Concetta's mother tried to wrap her mind around her daughter's actions. "She saw nothing in her life," said Lazzaro. "But she never saw the whole truth. She's always been like that. She eloped at thirteen! She's never seen anything in her life, poor devil. And they took advantage of that, those unworthy bastards! Bastards! It's so easy just to talk. You just say your brother told you this, your father told you that, your mother's cunt told you something else." Lazzaro suspected that one day Concetta would send for her children. She found the thought unbearable. "She wants to tear them away from their roots and take them where? How is she going to provide for them? She can't even sweep the floor! No! She must come back home. The carabinieri don't have any actual evidence. In a week nobody in Rosarno will ever speak about these things again."

Michele Cacciola, Concetta's father, was just as disturbed. At home, he would unleash tirades that could last an hour. "This unworthy piece of shit!" he shouted in one episode recorded on July 11, 2011. "I worked twenty years for her!" Michele seemed most upset at his loss of standing. "I had [such] a family that they [the people of Rosarno] were all jealous of me," he yelled. "I enjoyed watching my grandchildren grow. Nobody was happier than me!" Michele saw Concetta's departure not as her bid for a new life but as an attack on him by the state. "These contemptible people, these unworthy bastards, to take a daughter from her father! How is this the law to come at me and take my daughter? Did I start a fight with them? Do they even know who I am? If they have something on me, then arrest me! They are taking daughters away from their fathers!" Not that talking to a mere woman would serve the state's purpose, said Michele. "They wait for her to disgrace me. But what can she know about me? She knows nothing. What can a *woman* know in my house? You think I told my daughter about my fucking business? She knows nothing!"

These 'Ndrangheta men, thought Alessandra. Treat their women like dirt. But one walks away from them, and they fall all to pieces.

Lea Garofalo. The picture is undated but seems to capture Lea in her early twenties, just after she became a mother. The image became iconic. (*http://www.wikimafia.it*)

Lea, on the left, and Denise captured by CCTV in Milan in their last minutes together on the evening of November 24, 2009. (*Milan Carabinieri*)

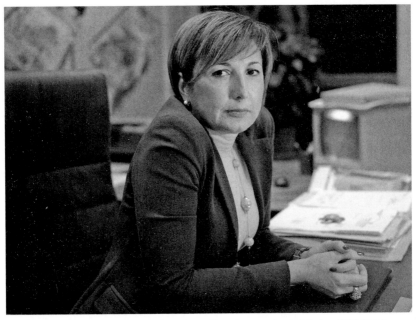

Alessandra Cerreti, pictured in her office in Reggio Calabria. (*FILIPPO MONTEFORTE/AFP/Getty Images*)

Reggio Calabria, as seen from the hills to the southeast of the city, looking northwest across the Strait to Messina. (*Anna Quaglia/Alamy Stock Photo*)

San Luca. For decades, the 'Ndrangheta have convened an annual meeting on September 2 in this Aspromonte hill village, using a religious festival as cover. (*ROPI/ Alamy Stock Photo*)

Carlo Cosco in a police mug shot taken after his arrest in February 2010. (*Lanese / Epa/REX/Shutterstock*)

Giuseppina Pesce the day after her arrest in April 2010. (*ANSA*)

Domenico Oppedisano being driven through the streets after his arrest in Rosarno in July 2010. (*Franco Cufari/Epa/REX/Shutterstock*)

Giuseppina Pesce in her mug shot after her arrest. (*ANSA*)

Maria Concetta Cacciola. Confined to the family home for weeks at a time, only one other picture of her has ever surfaced. (*ANSA*)

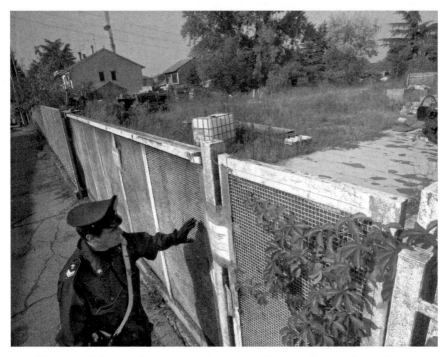

The gate of the warehouse in San Fruttuoso, Monza, where Lea's remains were discovered in October 2012, three years after her death. (*Fabrizio Radaelli/Epa/REX/Shutterstock*)

Breaking a lifetime of omertà, Carlo speaks in court on April 9, 2013. (*Corriere TV*)

Giuseppina's mother, Angela Ferraro, and sister, Marina Pesce. (*ANSA*)

Concetta's mother, Anna Rosalba Lazzaro, and father, Michele Cacciola. (*ANSA*)

Lea's funeral on October 19, 2013. Thousands from all over Italy turned out for a woman who, four years after her death, united the nation against the mafia under the slogan "I see, I hear, I speak." (*Marco Aprile / NurPhoto / Corbis via Getty Images*)

XVI

A S SOON AS Alessandra was sure Concetta was safe, she switched her focus back to Giuseppina. Since she had stopped cooperating with the judiciary, Giuseppina's options had steadily narrowed. The 'Ndrangheta plan to return her to Rosarno was well under way. Her family had rented her an apartment in Vibo Marina, a small seaside town north of Rosarno, and a judicial order transferring Giuseppina's house arrest there was being drawn up. Alessandra suspected the clan would kill her almost as soon as she arrived. In May, the witness protection service ordered Giuseppina's ejection from the program as an uncooperative witness. There would be a delay before the command was implemented. But as May turned to June, Alessandra reckoned she had days to save her witness.

The order for Giuseppina's transfer to Vibo Marina was issued in early June. On the morning it was due to be executed, June 10, Alessandra received a call from the protection officers at Giuseppina's safe house outside Aprilia. Giuseppina; her boyfriend, Domenico Costantino; and her daughter Angela had gone for a day in Lucca in Tuscany, four hours to the north, leaving her younger children, Gaetano and Elisea, with a babysitter. The officers added that Angela had been threatening for a while to sneak out of the house to go and see a friend in Lucca. When Domenico had driven up from Rosarno a few days earlier, Giuseppina had seized the chance to make her daughter happy one final time. "I was living those days as if they were the last I would ever spend with my children," she said later.

It was the opportunity Alessandra needed. As a collaborator, even one who had stopped talking, Giuseppina enjoyed a measure of freedom. But she still needed permission to travel long distance. By the letter of the law, a trip to Lucca violated the conditions of her house arrest. Alessandra raced to the carabinieri surveillance office in Reggio. En route, she called the Lazio carabinieri's mafia surveillance team. Alessandra told the officer on duty that she needed the carabinieri to intercept Giuseppina on the highway from Lucca back to Aprilia. If Giuseppina could be caught in the act of flouting the conditions of her detention, then Alessandra could have her summarily sent back to prison. A jail cell, explained Alessandra, was now the only place Giuseppina could be sure of staying alive. But they had to catch her first.

No problem, the carabinieri officer replied. What car were they looking for?

Alessandra said that she didn't know the make of the car, its color, or its license plate, or the route it was taking.

That wasn't much to go on, replied the officer.

Alessandra said that was precisely why she was asking for a hundred carabinieri to set up as many checkpoints as possible along the various routes from Lucca. Somewhere in the four hundred kilometers between Lucca and Aprilia would be a car of some description in which would be three people—Giuseppina, her boyfriend, and her fifteen-year-old daughter.

The officer said he would call her back. Minutes later the duty officer in charge of all Lazio's carabinieri, a captain, was on the line. "We wouldn't use a hundred men even for Osama bin Laden," he said.

Alessandra insisted. This one *pentita* could take down the entire Rosarno 'Ndrangheta, she said. "And unless we arrest her right now," Alessandra said, Giuseppina was going to be murdered. Alessandra told the captain she had something that would help: Giuseppina's mobile, whose GPS signal the carabinieri could use to track her. According to the screen Alessandra was watching at that moment in Reggio, Giuseppina had just left Lucca and was now heading to Florence. That meant she would likely be taking the main toll road all the way to Aprilia. The journey would take three and a half hours. That was how long the captain had to save the most important witness ever to testify against the 'Ndrangheta.

The captain said he would try. Within minutes, his men were setting up roadblocks and checkpoints. "We were following her mobile in real time on the screen," said Alessandra, "and I was in constant contact with the carabinieri captain and his officers on the ground." But as Alessandra watched, the dot on the screen approached the first roadblock, then sailed through. Half an hour later, it approached a second, then kept on going as before. Alessandra phoned the captain. "What is going on?!" she yelled. "How come they're getting through?"

The captain, unaccustomed to being shouted at by a southerner, and a woman, told Alessandra that his men were doing their best. She had given them almost nothing to go on. But his men would do what they could.

By now Alessandra was also phoning officers at individual checkpoints, asking them to keep the line open so she could listen to what was happening. One by one, they all reported seeing nothing. The dot on the screen kept moving south. As Giuseppina floated through roadblock after roadblock, the carabinieri captain's attitude changed from defensiveness to despair. When the screen showed Giuseppina approaching Aprilia, the captain told Alessandra it was over. "We've lost her," he said. "We've lost her."

"You have to block *all* the traffic on the highway!" shouted Alessandra. "All of it! Do it right now!"

The captain protested. The screen had Giuseppina at three kilometers away. Only one checkpoint lay between her and the safe house. Alessandra was suggesting that he block one of the main arterial roads in all of Italy when it was already too late. "She's gone, she's gone," he said.

"You do *not* give up, Captain!" shouted Alessandra. "You block the entire highway, you do it right now and you keep this line open! Do it, Captain!"

The officer reluctantly agreed. Alessandra went back to checking the screen. There were a few moments of silence. Then the captain's voice came back on the line.

"*Hold on!*" he shouted.

"Hold on . . ."

"There's a car . . ."

"With a *woman*!"

Alessandra heard a commotion. She guessed several squad cars had encircled the suspect vehicle and brought it to a stop.

There was a moment of silence.

Then a woman's voice shouted: "Don't shoot! Don't shoot! My name is Giuseppina Pesce!"[1]

REGULATIONS REQUIRED GIUSEPPINA be kept in isolation for three weeks. Alessandra wasn't unhappy that Giuseppina would have to stew for a while. She had been desperate to save Giuseppina but that didn't mean she was pleased with her. She had put her faith in this 'Ndranghetista, and the 'Ndranghetista had reverted to type: shutting down, submitting to The Family, resuming omertà. Giuseppina had ground to make up with Alessandra. She needed to know it.

Of course, it was also possible that Giuseppina wouldn't see her rescue as anything of the sort. There was the manner of her capture: men with guns drawn, screaming at her to lie on the ground. And since Giuseppina was back in jail, the authorities had had no choice

but to separate her from her children once more and send them back
to the Palaias in Rosarno. After all the risks she had taken and the
torment she had endured, precisely nothing had changed for Giuseppina. She could be forgiven for questioning the point of it all.

Alessandra was counting on the transformation she thought she
had discerned in Giuseppina. When she had first arrested Giuseppina in Rosarno a year earlier, the 'Ndranghetista had been defined
by the men in her life: daughter to a criminal father, wife to a violent
husband, obedient servant to violent and criminal men of honor.
Even Giuseppina's identity as a mother had been defined by the
men. Though she loved Angela, Gaetano, and Elisea, she had also
accepted that her role, however repugnant, was to prepare them for
the 'Ndrangheta.

But in the last year, Giuseppina had broken with all of that. She
had become the director of her own life. She had reclaimed her freedom. She had retrieved her children. She had even chosen her own
lover. Above all, she had recovered herself—and there was no giving herself away again. She had not, as the Pesce men told reporters,
acted as a sick, weak woman. She had not been used by Alessandra.
Just the opposite. The first time she went to prison, she had been
cowed and terrified and had tried to kill herself within days. Now,
back in a cell and away from her children once more, she was calm
and in control. A jail cell had a way of stripping everything away.
Being reunited with her children was the only thing that mattered,
and Giuseppina knew what she had to do to achieve that.

As Alessandra bided her time, she monitored Giuseppina's correspondence. Dispatches arrived every day from Aunt Angela; Giuseppina's mother, Angela Ferraro; her sister Marina; her father,
Salvatore; even her husband, Rocco Palaia. Mostly her family congratulated her on ending her cooperation and described the new life
that they had prepared for her in Calabria. But by now, Alessandra
thought she knew Giuseppina well enough to hope that she wouldn't

believe a word. Not that her husband forgave her, not that the Palaias would take good care of her son, not that anything could ever go back to how it was. The likelihood was that the 'Ndrangheta would try to turn her children against her and even persuade her son to kill her. Alessandra felt that by insisting on the pretense, the clan was overplaying its hand. Moreover, as Alessandra saw it, by attempting to give Giuseppina no choice, they were offering her no alternative but to reject them. The only way for Giuseppina to save her children was to stay alive and look after them—and the only way to do that was to reenter witness protection and take her children with her. There was every chance, thought Alessandra, that her family's letters would have the opposite effect from what was intended.

The letters Giuseppina received from Rocco, laced with sarcasm and suppressed fury, were especially useful. "My dear tourist," he began in a letter dated June 15:

> *I hope you are in as good health as I. I thought you were allergic to jail but I see I was wrong. I told you many times to stay in your own place, in your own shoes. But you walked off alone for a holiday in Lucca. Who are these relatives in Lucca that I do not know? I'm not angry with you so much, but with that bastard Mimmo [Costantino] who took you there. What was he doing there? Tell me.*

Rocco wrote that he feared his children were suffering. He couldn't understand why his wife was in Lucca when she was meant to be in Vibo Marina. So much of what had happened was confusing to him, he wrote. "If [only] you were in your place at this time. But you are out." Still, he had advice for Giuseppina on how to set things right:

> *The first thing you need to do is to write to your father and explain the situation. How come you were with Mimmo? I want to know*

as well. After that, if you leave protection, good. If not, I'll see
you on July 12th. We can still return to being a normal family,
as we were before. I hug you and urgently await your news and
explanations. I have forgiven you many times. I hope this is the last.

On June 24, Rocco wrote again. "My dearest love (if I can call
you that)," he began. He then described a prison visit from his
brother, Gianluca Palaia, and their daughters, Angela ("my princess
who fell from the clouds") and Elisea. He assured Giuseppina that,
as a responsible parent, he would make sure the children had money
for clothes. "It doesn't matter that you abandoned me like you did.
Let's leave our arguments until we're both out. Even then, we can
pretend it never happened."

He added that he had to tell her about her friend Maria Concetta
Cacciola:

Do you remember 'Cetta? Who lives near the minimarket? Her
husband is also in prison and she had an affair, possibly with a
cop—something she should rightly be killed for. Anyway, when
she realized her family had found out, what did she do? She called
the police and entered witness protection—and in the family car
she left a note saying she was "going with her friend, Giusy."
They say she's making statements to the authorities now. She
really did it all.

Your situation, of course, is very different. Everyone's forgiven
you for what you did. Me most of all. But, still, I wondered if this
put you in mind of anyone?

"It was typical mafia style, disguising a threat," said Alessandra
after she read the letter. "'Don't worry. You didn't do what Maria
Concetta Cacciola did, so nothing can happen to you.' Which is exactly the opposite of what he meant."[2] Alessandra sent the letter on

its way. When she received a letter from Giuseppina dated the same day, she knew Rocco's letter had hit its mark.

> *I am writing to tell you a few things that I feel I have to tell you, and I really hope from the bottom of my heart that you can hear me. After the last time we met, a lot has happened. All that publicity in the media, and all the accusations, and everything that came after. I would love to have the opportunity to explain what happened to you, especially to you, but also to the entire prosecutors' office. This morning I fired the lawyer, Giuseppe Madia, and am currently represented by the lawyer Valeria Maffei. It is my intention, if you are still interested, to resume the path of collaboration. I hope I can regain your trust. Sorry, again, for what happened. I hope I have a chance to apologize in person.[3]*

The next day, June 25, Giuseppina wrote again:

> *I urgently renew my invitation to be heard by you. I want to resume the collaboration that was under way and that I interrupted for the reasons you know. I am willing to finish what I started. I beg you to make it happen before my transfer hearing on July 12—for obvious reasons concerning my personal safety and the safety of those closest to me. I repeat my apologies for my hesitancy. I am keenly aware that I caused great difficulties and wasted so much time.*

The turnaround was amazing, thought Alessandra. The prosecutors had done nothing but let the 'Ndrangheta's internal dynamics play out. The clan's threats alone had been enough to propel Giuseppina back to the state. Alessandra's instinct was to give it longer. But Giuseppina was right to be afraid of the July 12 hearing. After it, she would likely be returned to the general prison population, and that would be all the opportunity the Pesces needed.

Alessandra waited a few more days, then sent word that she and Prestipino would see Giuseppina again on July 7.

At the meeting Alessandra was initially defensive. She adopted the same manner she had affected when she first met Giuseppina nine months before: cold and analytical, betraying little empathy or warmth. After all she had done for Giuseppina, she demanded to know how Giuseppina could accuse her of threatening her children. And how could she say that Alessandra had forced her to collaborate?

Giuseppina explained that her "retraction," published in *Calabria Ora*, had been written for her by the Palaias' lawyer. "I was opposed to this letter," she said. "They said this thing had to come out, had to be made public. Everyone had to know that I was not an informant. This would be proof that I wasn't collaborating anymore. They pressured me again and again to write this letter."

It sounded convincing, but Alessandra wasn't done. How could the state trust Giuseppina again, she asked. How could it know if she was genuine this time? The interview went on for hours, with Alessandra demanding Giuseppina explain herself and Giuseppina begging for Alessandra to trust her again. In addition to repairing her credibility as a witness, it seemed just as important to Giuseppina that she mend her friendship with Alessandra. "You have to trust me again," said Giuseppina.

"You have to earn it," replied Alessandra.

After several hours of talking, however, Alessandra was satisfied. She'd had to make sure, but she was now certain that Giuseppina's intention to collaborate once more was authentic. Trust between *pentita* and prosecutor was restored.

GIUSEPPE MADIA, THE Palaias' lawyer, passed word of his dismissal back to Rosarno. To the family, that could only mean one thing: Giuseppina was planning to testify again. Even when the clan had tried to appear gentle and understanding, Alessandra had always felt it straining to contain its crueler instincts. Now it unleashed them. Leading the campaign against Giuseppina was her own mother, Angela Ferraro.

Reading transcripts of bugs placed in the jail where Giuseppina's mother and sister were being held, Alessandra realized Ferraro had stopped referring to her daughter by name. Now Giuseppina was simply "the collaborator" or "the traitor" or "that whore." Like Concetta's father, Ferraro seemed most infuriated by her loss of prestige among other inmates. She set about revenging herself by trying to turn Giuseppina's children against her. On July 13, the day after Giuseppina's resumption of cooperation was confirmed in open court, Ferraro and Marina were visited together in jail by Sara, the third daughter in the family, who was mentally disabled, and Giuseppina's two daughters, Angela and Elisea.

Ferraro quickly told them all to cut all ties with Giuseppina. "She's dead to the family," she said. "If she calls, you don't answer. If you happen to pick up the phone, you have to tell her: 'You're dead to me. You don't exist anymore. For not doing your time in prison, you are the most contemptible, the most despicable.'" Ferraro was working herself into a fury, taking out all her frustration and rage on her grandchildren. "Tell her!" she shouted. "Tell her that her mother told you to pretend that she had died! She doesn't give a fuck about who's now in jail! She doesn't care about anything! When the phone rings, you tell her that her mother told you to forget you even have a mother! Your mother is gone!"

Sara began to cry. "Don't cry, love, don't cry, beautiful," said Ferraro, softening and gently kissing her daughter. "This is just how it is. This is the truth." She produced a letter from Giuseppina and began reading from it. "Forgive me if I am not the daughter you wanted," Giuseppina had written. "I know I've disappointed you.

I know my sister is very angry with me." See? asked Ferraro. Even Giuseppina knew she had done wrong.

Angela said she, too, had received a letter from her mother, asking for her forgiveness and saying that she wanted her children to join her but that they should "do what their heart tells them." Ferraro looked at her granddaughter. Five-year-old Elisea was crying, too. "From now on, it's you, me, and the family. Don't think that I'm not suffering in here. But I'm in here because of my love of family. You know what that means, love of family? It means loving you, loving my grandchildren, loving my children. My other daughter does not want to be in my heart. But that was her choice, not mine. I could never do what she did. Such a disappointment. But you should all go to the beach. Have fun. Mama is just fine here. It's just that I miss you. I miss you all. I miss my home. Let's all hug. We are a nice family. We love each other, no?"

Sara, crying once more, started hitting her hand on the table between them. "She is my sister," she said. "You're bad, and I don't care [what you say]. She is still my sister. She is still my sister."

Marina interrupted angrily. "You have to think of the rest of the family," she told Sara. "We've all cut her off. You have to turn your back on her. You have to be strong. Show me that strength in you that I love so much. Turn away from her."

Reading the transcripts, Alessandra was astonished by the two women's will. "They were ferocious. Brutal. The way they gave orders to the others. 'You must separate from your mother, your sister. You must forget her. She has betrayed the family.'" Among the adults, she said, only Giuseppina's disabled sister seemed to have a soul.

BACK IN ROSARNO, the clan began tormenting Giuseppina's children in earnest. Angela, Gaetano, and Elisea were forced to break all contact with their mother. Their aunt Angela threw them out. Forced to live with Giuseppina's father-in-law, Gaetano Palaia, they found that the family that had once offered their mother thousands of euros for lawyers and rent now claimed there was no money to feed them. They often went without. Elisea began to lose weight and developed leg cramps and insomnia. Gaetano regularly beat the grandson named after him with a belt. One day an uncle took the boy to a games arcade where he was hustled into a back room and set upon by four other older kids, including a seventeen-year-old cousin, as his uncle watched.

Angela was forced to play a part in torturing her mother. On July 18, a bundle of letters arrived for Giuseppina. In them her father-in-law accused her of being too cowardly for prison. Her husband, Rocco, told her, "The road you're taking will not be as easy as you think . . ." Aunt Angela wrote that "after everything we talked about, you were just lying. How happy we would all be if you'd only known your place." Finally, there was a letter from her eldest daughter:

> Hello, dear mother. How are you? I hope you're fine, though I believe you're not . . . Don't think that I'm not angry with you. You're wrong. I've got it in for you, Mama. I am mad at you for what you're doing. I know you're missing us and we're missing you, but does it make any sense to make the same mistake twice? . . . And now you can't change back again. This is your choice, and I respect it, but you need to know that you are doing this only for you, not for us. You are just hurting us by taking us away from everyone else, as well you know . . . You know that I will not come [to live with you]. You gave me the chance to choose and I did. I don't want to live that life again. I would have liked to be with you because I love you, and because you are my mom, yet I cannot do this. Making this choice twice . . . you're spitting in the pot you

eat from. I'm not telling this to be mean. I'm telling you this so you understand this is wrong. I don't know what they promised you and honestly I don't care. I wish to ask you a question, and for you to think it through. Is what they promised you more important? Or is your family, and our happiness, more important to you? If it is our happiness, and your family, then don't take this step. If you are more interested in what they promised, then it means that you are thinking only of yourself. I can't take it anymore, believe me. You ruined my life and I am only 16. Instead of having fun, I have to have this shitty life, only because of you, and you know it, Mama . . . Just leave me alone, please. I'm leaving you mom. Sorry for these words but this is what I think and what I want. I love you mom, but you should know that what you are doing is wrong.

The letter nearly broke Giuseppina's heart. It might have shattered it entirely but for one phrase: "spitting in the pot you eat from." That didn't sound like Angela or any sixteen-year-old Giuseppina knew. It was too old-fashioned. Too 'Ndrangheta.

The following week, a second letter came from Aunt Angela, urging Giuseppina to acknowledge that her son, Gaetano, was lost to her. From now on, he would be brought up by her in-laws. "He's terrified," she said. "I asked him about visiting you and he says he doesn't want to. He wants to stay here. I think moving him away again would just be more trauma. He would suffer even more. Try to think of your boy's happiness."

Four days later, on July 27, 2011, there was a second, short note from Angela. She was writing in secret, she said. Her mother should forget her earlier letter. The words had been dictated by her uncles.

It was not my doing. It wasn't what was in my heart.
Mom, I want to be with you.

I do not want to live with anyone else.
You're my mom, and without you, I am nothing.
Whatever choice you make, I will follow.

It was what Giuseppina desperately needed to hear. It was all she needed, too.[4]

M AFIA PROSECUTORS ARE realists, not optimists.[1] Still, there
was no doubt that the spring and summer of 2011 were a
heady few months for Calabria's Anti-Mafia Directorate. Giuseppina Pesce's testimony had dealt the 'Ndrangheta a devastating
blow, and though the clan had fought back, Alessandra's intervention had saved both Giuseppina's life and the case. Hundreds of
'Ndranghetisti were in jail. Hundreds of millions of euros in assets
had been confiscated. Giuseppina's example had then inspired a second 'Ndrangheta mother, Maria Concetta Cacciola. The panicked
reaction in Rosarno seemed to indicate that the clans feared being
undone by an avalanche of feminine assertion.

Moreover, any west coast 'Ndranghetista tempted to dismiss Giuseppina and Concetta as anomalies only had to look over the mountains to the east to see how women were humbling the 'Ndrangheta
there as well. After Carmine's arrest, Denise Cosco had left Pagliarelle, moved to a safe house in Turin run by Libera, reunited with
Libera lawyer Enza Rando, and formally reentered state witness
protection. Initially, said Enza, Denise was "destroyed" by the
knowledge that she had fallen in love with one of her mother's
killers. But in protection, Denise slowly began to remake herself.
She held on to the memory of what Carmine and she once shared.
"Fake love can still be true love," she insisted. But a memory was
all it would ever be. "It doesn't matter now," she said. "The arrest
brought things to an end."

Denise found new purpose helping prosecutors prepare the case against the Pagliarelle clan. "I have no pity," she said of Lea's accused killers in a statement released by Enza on the eve of Carlo Cosco's trial. "I don't care who is my father or who is my boyfriend. I don't even know what I feel more: hatred or anger. These people should get life. Or maybe just killed in the street. Until I hear in court that these people will pay for what they did, I have no life."[2] Denise elaborated on her state of mind in an interview with Libera's information service. "I want to live like any other normal twenty-year-old in the town where I was born, with my friends. I am a young woman and I want to be free to study and get a degree in Oriental languages. I don't want to hide. Only the men and women of the 'Ndrangheta should have to hide away, not justice witnesses. We did our duty. I want to live. I want to love. I want to be free to be happy, for my mother's sake if nothing else."[3]

Denise's defiance, continuing her mother's fight even after Lea had been murdered by her father, and giving hours of sworn testimony against the man she loved, attracted the attention of the national press. The city of Milan decided to join Denise in a parallel civil action against her father's *'ndrina*, symbolically uniting Italy's most progressive city with Italy's women against Italy's mafia. When Carlo, his brothers Giuseppe and Vito, and Massimo Sabatino, Rosario Curcio, and Carmine Venturino went on trial in Milan on July 6, 2011, the hearing was attended by hundreds of students. They filled the public gallery and held vigils for Lea in the street outside. In opening remarks that resonated with almost every woman in Italy, Enza described Denise as a "proud witness," once forced by the men of her family to live in silence, now reclaiming her "freedom to choose her own life." The case against her father and the other men of the 'Ndrangheta, said Enza, was the "start of new hope, and a new life."

These were giddy times to be an Italian prosecutor, and even an Italian woman. Looking back years later, Alessandra could even remember thinking that they might last.

AFTER HER TRANSFER to Bolzano on July 22, 2011, Concetta found herself in another strange town, free but alone. It was seven weeks since she had seen or spoken to her three children. Overwhelmed, suddenly, by an almost physical maternal need, Concetta e-mailed her twelve-year-old daughter, Tania. "And of course, the girl tells her grandmother," said Giuseppe Creazzo, the anti-mafia prosecutor who would later investigate the case. "And the family uses the girl to reestablish contact with Concetta and try to persuade her to come home."

The carabinieri missed the first call between Concetta and her mother, Anna Rosalba Lazzaro. By the time of the second, on August 2, Concetta was in Genoa, and the Cacciolas' plans were well advanced. Concetta had followed Giuseppina's example when she walked into a carabinieri station. The Cacciolas duly decided to copy the Pesces' methods to blackmail her into returning to them.

In that call of August 2, her mother told Concetta that she and her father, Michele Cacciola, would be arriving in Genoa that evening to pick her up. As a witness, rather than a *pentita*, Concetta was not bound by any restrictions on her movements. Within hours, the carabinieri were listening to a conversation inside the family car as the Cacciolas headed south for Calabria with Concetta in the back seat. Like the Pesces, Concetta's parents pursued two avenues of persuasion: promising their daughter everything would return to normal if she came home, and insinuating harm to her children if she did not. Unfortunately, Concetta did not have Giuseppina's steel. Confronted by parental authority, she was soon telling her mother and father everything that she had told the prosecutors.

"You told them about murders?!" exclaimed Lazzaro at one point. "Oh, the disgrace!"

"The sacrifices I've had to make for you, 'Cetta!" shouted Michele. "How you have dishonored me!"

Then Michele seemed to remember the plan. "Don't worry. I forgive you," he said, trying to sound calm. "You can't wrong family. You're blood. You're safe. You'll see. You'll say you know nothing. You'll say everything you said is not true. And in ten days, you'll be safe and quiet in Rosarno and no one will talk about you anymore."

After a lifetime of abuse from her father, Michele's uncharacteristic attempt at paternal understanding spooked Concetta. Then Michele revealed he had somehow obtained her phone records. He said he knew about her calls to her boyfriend, Pasquale Improta. That was even more worrying, thought Concetta. How could he possibly forgive that?

When the Cacciolas broke the journey for the night at Lazzaro's family home in Reggio Emilia, Concetta announced she would go no further and called the carabinieri. The following morning a pair of officers arrived to pick her up and drive her back to Genoa. Michele Cacciola and Rosalba Lazzaro continued on to Calabria. But now that they had found a way to reach their daughter, they weren't about to give up. En route they kept up the pressure in a series of phone calls.

"'Cetta, listen to me!" said her mother. "You must tell the truth. You must say you knew nothing about what was going on. You have to drop everything."

Between calls, the carabinieri could hear Concetta's mother and father discuss a plan to deliver their daughter to an 'Ndrangheta lawyer who would hand her a prepared statement to sign, as the Pesces had done with Giuseppina. It was her mother who, in another call to Concetta, hit on her daughter's weak spot. "Tomorrow morning, you call the lawyer," she said. "This is how you get what you want. This is how you get me to send you your children."

Concetta went quiet, and the line went dead. The carabinieri were stunned. Whatever her differences with the 'Ndrangheta, Concetta had always respected family. She was a dutiful daughter and a good mother, and it was her faith in the maternal bond that had persuaded her that she could safely entrust her children to her mother. She had paid dearly for her trust over the years. Now her mother was using it against her, in all likelihood to try to send her to her death. What kind of person would do such a thing? What kind of mother?

Concetta called her mother back a few minutes later. She sounded broken.

"Wait, Mom, just let me talk, and then you talk," she said. After her mother assented, Concetta continued.

"I get it," she said. "I get it already. Already I can't do anything else. I just couldn't talk right then because I was near those people who want to arrest you. Understand?"

Concetta's mother moved quickly to reinforce her position. "I don't care about them," she replied. "*O cu nui, o cu iddi.*" (You're with us, or you're with them.)

"Yes, I know," answered Concetta.

"You have to do this, 'Cetta! Tonight, I spoke with the lawyer. You understand? Tomorrow you go to the same lawyer. We've already paid him."

"I know, I know."

"Tomorrow! The same lawyer. Vittorio Pisani."

"OK."

"Swear to me, 'Cetta! You'll do this tomorrow!"

"Yes, I'll call him. I'll call him tomorrow."

"If you don't call him tomorrow, you can forget about me, 'Cetta. I'm destroyed here."

"Stop it, Mother. Enough. Leave me alone."

"Swear to me! Tomorrow morning! You don't understand, 'Cetta. The ones you are with. You're making the men crazy! You call the lawyer tomorrow morning!"

"All right, Mom. All right. Please stop."

"If you do everything the lawyer says, then the children will be with you again. You don't want to come home? Fine. You go to your aunt Angela's or your aunt Santina's or wherever you want. But you make the choice. Us, or them. And you shut up!"

Three days later, on August 6, Concetta called her friend Emanuela Gentile. To the surveillance team, the change in Concetta's tone was dramatic. A few days earlier, she had sounded free and confident. Now she was in pieces. "You know, Emanuela, the one mistake I made was to call home that one time," she said. "If I hadn't called, I would have continued on the same path. But I called, and I weakened."

Concetta told Emanuela about her talk with her mother and father. "They know everything I've been doing," she said. "They even have printouts of my phone calls."

Emanuela said she'd heard that Concetta's father and brother had visited Pasquale Improta at his home in Reggio. "Your brother's sick in the head," she said. "He's relentless."

"My father told me he wouldn't let Giuseppe lay a finger on me," replied Concetta. "He even started to cry. He told me: 'I forgive you.' But I'm afraid, Emanuela, I tell you. I'm scared. Even if they're telling me, 'Come back, daughter, come back,' you know how these families are, especially my family, especially the men. They don't forgive. They don't forgive injuries to their honor. My father has two hearts. One for his daughter and one for his honor."

Something was sure to happen to her if she went home, Concetta said. It had to, though probably not immediately, she thought. "They'll wait," she said. "If they already have you there, in their place, they don't need to hurry. But does it make sense for me to go home and live just a year, maybe a year and a half?" She couldn't make up her mind. "In one way, I'm thinking I should just do it, you know? Go home. Take the risk. Because I *have* to go back, Emanuela. I have to. They won't send my children to me."

"*Mamma mia!*" exclaimed Emanuela. "They're keeping your children from you?"

"I asked for them but they haven't sent them. And they won't. Because they know that if they send my children to me, their daughter is lost to them forever."

In another call, to Pasquale Improta, Concetta tried to prepare her boyfriend for what lay ahead. "If I go home, I'm finished," she said. "I understand that. I know how it will end. They don't forgive offenses to honor or dignity—and I injured both."

"Concetta," Pasquale replied, "can I tell you something? You're too good. Too good."

"Too stupid," joked Concetta.

"Too good. They broke your ribs. Other women wouldn't even call them."

"It scares me to go home, I tell you."

"If it scares you, Concetta, then don't go. If you go, you'll pay."

"Well, that's for sure."

Maybe because he wasn't 'Ndrangheta himself, or maybe because he wasn't a father, Pasquale didn't seem to get it. He imagined Concetta still had choices. Concetta couldn't make him understand. Before she hung up, however, she made sure to take time over her good-byes. "Pa," she said, "until my last breath, I will love you. Good night, my love. Good night. I love you."

ON AUGUST 8, Concetta wrote a note to her protection officers, saying that she had spoken to her mother, who was on her way to Genoa with her uncle Gregorio and her eldest daughter, Tania. Concetta explained that she couldn't bear not to see Tania.

In fact, Concetta had initially tried to resist. Her surveillance officers heard her on the phone trying to stall Lazzaro, saying she needed to check with the carabinieri before she agreed to meet. "Who do you need to call, 'Cetta?" her mother shouted back. "Why do you need to ask anyone? Do you hear your daughter?"

On the line came the sound of a small child crying and screaming. Lazzaro was holding the phone toward Concetta's youngest daughter, Rosalba, seven, named after her grandmother. The girl was in tears. "She's dying without you, 'Cetta!" she said.

"Tell her not to worry," said Concetta softly.

"Tell her to be quiet?" replied Lazzaro. "'Cetta, she's dying here."

"OK, OK. Tell her I'm close by. Tell her I'm coming."

"You meet us on the other side of town!" Lazzaro ordered, and hung up.

The following morning, when Concetta's protection officers went to her hotel room, they found the door open with the keys in the lock. Inside, her suitcase was gone.

THE SURVEILLANCE TEAM wouldn't hear Concetta's voice again for more than a week. That wasn't because she hadn't been talking, however. Three days after arriving back in Rosarno, Concetta secretly recorded a statement at the Cacciola family lawyer's office in town. The recording, including one brief interruption, lasted eleven minutes and seven seconds:

> My name is Maria Concetta Cacciola, today is August twelfth, 2011, and I want to clarify what happened to me this May.
>
> During a visit to the carabinieri barracks, I told them I had some problems with my family. My family had received some anonymous letters. At the time, I was in a bad way. I

was jealous. My husband was in prison. Then these letters came and I held up my hands to what they said, and my family shut me in my home, telling me I couldn't go out or have friends. I was angry at my family. I wanted to make them pay. So I told the carabinieri: "Maybe I can help you. I have problems with my parents and my family. I'm afraid that my father and my brother are going to do something to me."

Initially, they did not take me away. But a few days later, they told me that I should talk to their superiors and the carabinieri commander came to see me. And that's how it happened. I said whatever I needed to say in order to get away from home. I was confused. But my reasoning was to make them pay. I was so angry.

Two days later, they told me they had agreed to take me into custody and they met me again at the barracks. There was a car ready, and two magistrates were there to talk to me. At first, I was confused. But then, because I wanted to leave, I said things that weren't true and which hadn't happened. Because I just wanted to go away and make them pay for my suffering. Finally, one magistrate said to me: "It's Friday. Get ready to leave here on Monday."

In fact, they came to get me on Saturday. They took me to Cosenza. Three days later, the two magistrates came back and began pressuring me about my family. And I, because I was still furious with them, I again accused my father and my brother.

I was a month and a half in Cosenza. From there they took me to Bolzano. But by the time I got to Bolzano, I wanted to retract because I realized that out of anger I had said things that weren't true. It was all just things that I had read in newspapers or heard people talking about, and just because I was so enraged I accused my father and brother of being involved even when they were not. I realized I was in the wrong. I realized that because I was so angry, I was accusing people who had nothing to do with anything. It wasn't right. I wanted a lawyer. But they told me I couldn't have one because witnesses weren't allowed lawyers under the law. I told them I wanted to return to my family. But they told me: "Don't go back to your family. We are your family now. Your family won't forgive you if you go back now. If you thought they wanted to kill you before, imagine what they'll do now they think you have a relationship with us." And I was afraid, knowing what I had done and how gross an injury I had inflicted.

In Bolzano, I talked to my daughter by e-mail. After that, I spoke to my mother. I wanted to know what my mother thought of what I had done. In Bolzano, I also met people who might have recognized me. At that point, I was moved immediately to Genoa. They told me: "You can't have any contact with people you know."

From Genoa, I called my mother again and told her I missed her and wanted to see her. I spoke to my mother and my father, too. And now I really knew what I had done! My mother came to Genoa but the state told me I couldn't have any contact with my family. When I got into the car with my dad, however, I realized he had already forgiven me for the mistakes I had made. We reached Reggio Emilia. I was scared of going back to Calabria, though not of my father, and of my own free will I left again with the carabinieri for Genoa. They asked me: "Are you sure you haven't told your family that you're staying in Genoa?" I said I hadn't, even though I had told my mother.

I had also told my mother that I wanted to talk to a lawyer. From Genoa I called a lawyer, Vittorio Pisani, telling him

I was confused because the state had told me that if I hadn't been represented already in the process then I couldn't start now. Anyway, the state told me to stop calling the lawyer, and added that I was stubborn, that I shouldn't call my family, that I should turn off my phone and everything else. I didn't agree. And I called my mother again, asked her to come back up to Genoa, and she came with her brother and my daughter and I left Genoa of my own free will. Now I have decided to appoint the lawyers Gregorio Cacciola and Vittorio Pisani to represent me . . .

At that point the recording cut, then resumed:

I've now been back at home for three days with my father, my mother, my brother, and my children. Finally, I have found the peace . . .

"—that I have been looking for," prompted a female voice in the background.

. . . that I have been looking for. I should add that I have written a letter to go with this recording. In the future, I hope to be left alone, out of contact with anyone and with no one contacting me.[4]

On August 13 and 14, Concetta's surveillance officers picked up two text messages she sent to Pasquale Improta using a phone she had managed to hide from her family. In them, she told a different story. She said she was a prisoner of her family in the yellow house on Via Don Gregorio Varrà once more. This time, however, "they brought lawyers to make me retract," she wrote. "They made me say that I was using drugs, that I was angry. My brother won't speak to me. Their coldness is terrifying. I don't want to stay here, Pa. I don't see how any good will come of this."

Concetta asked Pasquale to pass a message to Chief Marshal Salvatore Esposito at the carabinieri headquarters in Reggio Calabria. She wanted to return to witness protection, she said. This time, she had to take her children with her. "I feel caged here," she wrote. "What can I do?"

Pasquale passed on the message. On August 17, Concetta spoke to the carabinieri several times to confirm she wanted to reenter witness protection. Just before 11 P.M. she called Marshal Esposito in Reggio. After confirming for himself that Concetta wanted to return to the program, Esposito asked how best to extract her and her three children. "Can you leave the house?" he asked. "Even later tonight?"

Concetta said no. She asked if Esposito could send officers to arrest her to make it look as though she were being taken against her will. "It's so difficult here, with my father and my brother," she said. Even outside the family, she explained, "there are also those around them, people know what happened. Word that I've been speaking to the carabinieri is spreading."

"Are you afraid of moving or of the repercussions?" asked Esposito.

"Both!" replied Concetta.

Eventually, Esposito and Concetta agreed that she would call when the time felt right—that night or the following morning—and that Esposito would dispatch a car immediately. It would be with her fifteen minutes after her call, Esposito said. "Call any time," he added. "We'll be waiting."

In Reggio's Palace of Justice, Alessandra was also waiting. It was August, the daytime temperature was breaching 100°F, and the entire country was on holiday. Pignatone, Prestipino, and Giovanni Musarò were all away. Only Alessandra remained. "The situation appeared to be calm with Cacciola," said Giovanni later. "There was a wiretap of her talking to a friend in which she said that she knew she would be killed—but not soon. She was talking about a year, a year and a half, because it would be stupid to kill her immediately. And anyway, Concetta was going to be back in protection soon. So we felt safe."

The next day, August 18, in a conversation recorded by a bug inside the Cacciola car, Concetta told her mother she had spoken to Chief Marshal Esposito. She added she intended to return to witness protection.

"'Cetta, no!" screamed Lazzaro. "No! Absolutely not!"

"You told me everything would be different!" shouted Concetta.

"I was resigned to you leaving us," replied Lazzaro. "But now I'm not. No! I won't accept this!"

"Mom, I have to finish what I started," said Concetta.

Half an hour later, Concetta phoned the carabinieri once more and told them she was in a dilemma. It was impossible to leave the house without being accompanied by her mother. On the other hand, if she left with her and her mother returned home without her, then her mother would face dire consequences. Eventually Concetta agreed with the carabinieri that the solution was to wait for everyone in the Cacciola house to fall asleep that night, then usher her children out into the street and into a waiting carabinieri car. They would do it around 1:30 A.M. Four hours later, Concetta called back to say her youngest, Rosalba, had a fever and everything had to be put off for a day or so.

Reading the transcripts, Alessandra was exasperated. "We were all waiting for her call to come and pick her up. She had called and said: 'I want to come back.' The barracks were all ready for her and her children. I'd even asked the carabinieri to come back from their holidays. So we were just waiting. And then this back-and-forth. Honestly, at that point, we thought that she was playing with us.

We discovered that the part about her daughter being sick was a lie. Her children were at the beach. Concetta just did not have a clear mind. She was changing it constantly. Some days she reached out to us. Some days she didn't. There was such indecision. We really wanted her to make up her mind and make a final decision, a choice. But we thought that at least she had the situation under control. And I think perhaps she herself thought she had more time."

THE NEXT DAY, August 19, Alessandra and the carabinieri waited by the phone in case Concetta changed her mind once again. No call came.

On August 20, Alessandra and the carabinieri gathered again to resume their vigil. "The whole team was there on alert, waiting for her to give the word and we'd go in and get her. But we couldn't do anything until she gave us the go-ahead. By law, since she was a witness, we weren't allowed to charge in and break down the door. She had to open the door for us. And she just couldn't open that door."[5]

At 6:40 P.M. on August 20, 2011, Concetta's father, Michele, arrived at Santa Maria Hospital in the town of Polistena, twenty minutes from Rosarno. Concetta was immobile in the back seat of the family Mercedes. She had burns around her mouth and foam spilling from her lips.

In emergency admissions, Dr. Fortunato Lucia confirmed that Concetta had no pulse. As staff at the hospital called the police, Dr. Lucia attempted to resuscitate her using CPR. The paramedics handed the doctor a red, one-liter plastic bottle of hydrochloric acid, which they said Concetta's family had found next to her in the family basement. Dr. Lucia tried to put Concetta on an intravenous drip, but without a pulse it wouldn't take. By the time a police patrol arrived at 7 P.M., Dr. Lucia had pronounced Concetta dead.

ACT THREE

Italy Awakes

XVIII

MARIA CONCETTA CACCIOLA's death certificate identified her as having been born three decades earlier, a few miles south of the hospital in which she died.[1] It listed her as living ten miles to the west in Rosarno. Born in Calabria. Lived in Calabria. Died in Calabria. As her family had promised her, it was as though the past four months had never happened.

Word of Concetta's death reached Alessandra and the carabinieri in a call in the early evening from the local police. The officer said the indications were that Concetta had drunk a liter of hydrochloric acid in the basement of the Cacciola family home. For the second time that year, Alessandra found herself momentarily overwhelmed. "It was terrible for everyone," she said. "No one had imagined it would end so finally, so completely. We were all ready to pick her up. It was very hard to come to terms with."[2]

Giovanni took Alessandra's call on holiday. He was speechless. Years later, he would say, "You can't let the work become personal. But the story of Maria Concetta Cacciola was terrible, really hard to bear. She hadn't even been arrested and had no convictions. She was just a witness."[3] It was the tragedy of Concetta's death, the way it seemed almost mythically predestined, that most disturbed Giovanni. "Maria Concetta Cacciola was a character from a Greek play," he said. "She went back even though she was aware she would be murdered. She went back out of love for her children. This almost symbiotic relationship that she had with her mother, the love letter she wrote to her—there is something beautiful about it. Beautiful, and unacceptable."

Giovanni and Alessandra knew only too well the effect Concetta's story would have on the small towns and hill villages of Calabria. "It was what had to happen," said Concetta's father, Michele, in an aside recorded by the carabinieri two days later—and the prosecutors knew every Calabrian would be thinking the same. Lea Garofalo was dead. Giuseppina Pesce had been forced to retract in public. Now Maria Concetta Cacciola was gone, too. This was what happened to women who betrayed the 'Ndrangheta. There was no escaping fate. The 'Ndrangheta *was* invincible. "If this phenomenon of women testifying had gathered momentum with Giuseppina, it was going to come to a sudden stop with Maria Concetta Cacciola's death," said Alessandra. "By contrast with Giuseppina, Concetta was a symbol that the 'Ndrangheta *could* get to you."

The evening Concetta died, the carabinieri sealed off the basement at 26 Via Don Gregorio Varrà in Rosarno where she was found. They seized mobile phones, a computer, Concetta's diary, and several letters addressed to her husband, Salvatore. When they questioned Michele, he told them he had returned home after 5:30 P.M. and had called for Concetta but couldn't find her. He eventually discovered her lying on the floor of a bathroom in the basement. Next to her body was an empty plastic bottle. Asked why his daughter might have killed herself, Michele exploded and refused to answer. Concetta's mother, Anna Rosalba Lazzaro, was more forthcoming. Concetta, she said, had taken her own life out of shame. "She felt bad. She said things that she had no knowledge of. She couldn't face those she had accused." Concetta's family had "fully supported her" after she returned home, added Lazzaro. They knew she had been unwell. After all, she had a history of it. She had pined for her absent husband for many years. She had also taken diet drugs obsessively. These things had affected her mind.

Giovanni dismissed Lazzaro's interview out of hand. "It was clear that something had happened that we didn't know about," he said. The prosecutors knew Concetta was at long-term risk from her family. Like Concetta, they had calculated the family wouldn't harm her so quickly after her return, since suspicion would immediately fall on them. On the other hand, they also knew Concetta had told her mother that she would shortly be returning to the protection program. Maybe the family decided they had to kill her while they could.

Because there was no doubt that Concetta had been murdered. Every gastroenterologist said drinking a liter of hydrochloric acid was impossible to do voluntarily. The human reflex was to choke and vomit after just a sip. The pain was unbearable. The acid would eat through the stomach wall. Unconsciousness would be swift. The coroner would later report that Concetta had died of a heart attack and respiratory failure but only after the acid had burned her throat, stomach, pancreas, and lungs. "It's simply not something you can do by yourself," said Giovanni.

The method of Concetta's death also had the 'Ndrangheta written all over it. Acid was a favorite 'Ndrangheta tool for traitors. They used it on the dead, to erase every shameful trace of a collaborator's body, and they used it on the living. In December 2010, Reggio council's budget manager, Orsola Fallara, had given a press conference in a downtown restaurant at which she admitted making suspicious payments and keeping irregular accounts—and, hours later, was found dying in her car after drinking acid.[4] In March 2011, another 'Ndrangheta wife, thirty-eight-year-old Tita Buccafusca, had run into a police station near Rosarno clutching her young son and offering to testify—and a month later her husband, an 'Ndrangheta boss called Pantaleone Mancuso, reported that she had committed suicide by drinking acid.[5] Mouths that spoke out of turn were rubbed out. Concetta's death was part of a pattern.

For the prosecutors, there was one anomaly in the case, however. Concetta had told them that her family never left her alone, especially since her return to Rosarno. But on the day she died, her father, mother, and brother had all been out of the house. "That seemed quite strange," said Giovanni. It suggested not just careful planning but also the involvement of a third party.

ON AUGUST 23, three days after Concetta died, the Cacciola family delivered a formal written complaint to the prosecutor's office in Palmi. Following the script established by the Pesces, Concetta's parents accused Alessandra and Giovanni of taking advantage of a woman in a frail mental state. Concetta had walked into the carabinieri station in May 2010 "depressed" and in "pathological distress," they said. The carabinieri had seen her weakness as an opportunity. They had promised her a new life, "which turned out to be a living hell, taking her away from her family."

By this view, Concetta, like her friend Giuseppina before her, was a pathetic creature. The complaint claimed that none of what she had done was by conscious choice. She had not elected to create a new life for herself and her children. She had not rejected her family and the 'Ndrangheta. She had not, above all, asserted her free will and reclaimed her independence from her parents and her husband. Rather, according to the Cacciolas, she had been pitiably weak and easily led. This daughter, this woman, had been dazzled by the state's perfidious offers of a better life. In return, her feeble mind had conjured up the kinds of stories about her family's criminality that she imagined the prosecutors wanted to hear. Concetta had soon come to her senses, realized her mistake, made contact with her family again, and eventually succeeded in escaping the authorities' clutches. Once back in the bosom of her "loving and attentive" family, she had confessed to everything, especially the "invented allegations" she had made against her kin to "ingratiate herself with the prosecutors." Happily, she had finally found the peace of mind that she had sought in her family's loving forgiveness and acceptance. Understandably, however, the shame had proved too much. The whole sorry saga could be heard in Concetta's own words by listening to the attached tape cassette or reading the attached transcript. The Cacciolas expected a reply forthwith from the prosecutors and the carabinieri, explaining their disgraceful conduct.

Even then, the Cacciolas weren't done. The same day they filed their complaint, Anna Rosalba Lazzaro wrote a letter to the *Gazzetta del Sud*, the main southern Italian newspaper, complaining that in their report on Concetta's death, the *Gazzetta* journalists had described her as having grown up in "an environment pregnant with the negative values of the 'Ndrangheta." "That's simply not true," wrote Lazzaro. "On this particular issue, I challenge anyone to show that my house has ever held discussions about criminal matters that have affected or involved the members of my family. I want to add that my husband and I dedicated our lives to giving our children the best civic education possible."[6] The next day, *Calabria Ora* splashed on an exclusive interview with Lazzaro, which it headlined: "You Drove My Daughter to Suicide!"[7] On its inside pages, *Calabria Ora* hammered home the message that Concetta's death was inevitable. "Chronicle of a Suicide Foretold" was the paper's banner headline.

It was unbelievable, thought Alessandra. The Cacciolas had blackmailed their daughter into returning to them, then stood by as she was executed. Now they were painting her killing as a tragedy for which the state was to blame, while using her death to mend their criminal reputation. At no point had they expressed sorrow or love or any feeling other than outrage at the wrongs done to them. They hadn't even buried Concetta. Had there ever been a family so unspeakable as the Cacciolas of Rosarno?

XIX

THE 'NDRANGHETA HAD reasserted itself in spectacular fashion.[1] Once more their challengers were dead or in disgrace. Just as Alessandra and Giovanni had been required to answer questions about the Giuseppina Pesce case, now they had to account for their handling of Maria Concetta Cacciola. The editor of *Calabria Ora*, Piero Sansonetti, celebrated the state's humiliation in a series of editorials. "The season of cooperation is over," he wrote.

In Milan, the six defendants on trial for the murder of Lea Garofalo seemed emboldened by events to the south. Their lawyers argued that the case against their clients should be dismissed outright. No body, no murder. Lea, they said, was actually living by the beach in Australia. "I hope she gets tired of Australia and does us the honor of appearing in this court," said one.[2] Their clients were innocent not just of killing Lea, they claimed, but of any criminality. Carlo's brother Giuseppe said he was a shoemaker. Vito said he was a builder. Rosario Curcio said he ran a solarium. Carmine Venturino asked to be excused from answering questions in court because he only spoke Grecanico, not Italian. Carlo had somehow managed to convince the legal aid authorities that his income was a mere €10,000 a year, thereby qualifying him for state assistance. He said he was mystified by the entire process. "It's not fair that I'm sitting here," he said. "I'm an honest person. My mother taught me to respect and love the family. My daughter wrote me letters in prison saying she loved me and missed me and wanted to be with me again. I had nothing to do with Lea's disappearance. I, too, want to know the truth about what happened."[3]

The defense paraded a succession of villagers from Pagliarelle through court to testify to Carlo's decency. Most claimed to have barely known Lea. When one prosecution witness, a friend of Carlo's and resident at Viale Montello, repeatedly failed to show up at court, the defendants laughed and whooped. "Maybe he's in the attic," came one shouted suggestion. A lawyer for Giuseppe further muddied the waters by declaring that his client had not spoken to his brother Vito in years, making a nonsense of any conspiracy between them.

There were, however, signs of tension between the defendants. From the start, Massimo Sabatino sat apart from the other men in the caged dock. "Shame on you!" Venturino hissed at him one day as they were being led away for the night. "Shame on me?!" Sabatino yelled back. "It's your fault I'm doing six years! If I get my hands on you, I'll rip your head off, you piece of shit!"

The defendants also seemed to lose some of their initial confidence as the weeks progressed and prosecutor Marcello Tatangelo painstakingly took apart their denials. Traces from their phones showed all of them had been busy moving around Milan and its outskirts and in each other's company for the three hours after 6:30 P.M. when Lea Garofalo was last seen alive. The carabinieri had unearthed a friend of Carlo's who said he had lent Carlo the keys to his grandmother's apartment. It was here, said Tatangelo, that Lea had been taken to be tortured, then shot with a bullet to the neck, before her body was disposed of outside the city. When Salvatore Cortese, Carlo's old cellmate, testified about Carlo's burning desire for revenge on Lea, Carlo couldn't contain himself. "What are you saying?!" he shouted. "What's this about getting permission from the bosses to kill Lea? He's making it up! I had nothing to do with anything!" When Sabatino's confession to his cellmate, Salvatore Sorrentino, was read out, it was Sabatino's turn to shout. "I never said those things about Carlo!" he said. "It's not true that I said they were bastards and I wanted to kill them! You're making it up! I agree with everything these men say."

Finally, Denise was called on to testify. A screen was erected in court so her father could not see her. Denise wore a hooded top to further conceal her face. Sensing his daughter a few yards away, Carlo stood, walked to the front of his cage, and placed his arms through the bars. In a clear voice and without hesitation, and in testimony that lasted two full days—September 20 and October 13, 2011—Denise told the story of her mother's early life and their years on the run and in the protection program. "We were like sisters," she said. "It was almost like we grew up together. We swapped clothes. We liked the same music." For seven years, she added, she had no contact with Carlo.

"That's a fact," said Carlo audibly.

Denise frowned. "Can you request that person to keep quiet?" she coolly asked the judge. "It's disturbing."

Denise went on to recount her mother's attempts to make peace with Carlo. She described the attack in Campobasso in May 2009, prompting Sabatino to stand and pace up and down inside the cage. Only once did Denise break down. When one lawyer rebuked her for accusing the defendants of murder when there was no body and no murder weapon, she cried: "She can't be allowed to say that! It's been two years since I saw my mother!"

In the face of such raw emotion, the defense lawyers tried to conjure up some sympathy for the defendants. "I know in my heart that my client is innocent," said Maira Cacucci, Carlo's lawyer. "Just one look in his eyes and you'll understand." Francesco Garofalo, a Calabrian lawyer representing Carmine Venturino and Vito Cosco, fell back on a familiar defense: the unstable nature of women. "Why all these attempts to sanctify Lea, who was born and raised by the 'Ndrangheta?" he asked. "She was a crazy woman, as her own daughter has described. Lea Garofalo wanted to go to Australia. What better time than after leaving her daughter with her father? That is what happened here!"

Nevertheless, the defense's histrionics did little to deflect what was starting to feel increasingly certain: that all six men would eventually be found guilty of murder. But as the trial wound toward its conclusion, on November 23, the eve of the second anniversary of Lea's disappearance, disaster struck. Out of the blue, the presiding judge, Filippo Grisolia, was appointed chief of staff at the Ministry of Justice. The trial would have to be abandoned, then restarted. What was more, the statutory limit on detention in custody meant any new trial would have to finish by July 28, 2012, eight months away. The trial had already taken five months. It wouldn't be hard for the defense to spin out a new trial past the deadline. At that point, Carlo and his entire 'ndrina would walk free.

XX

THE 'NDRANGHETA HAD always relied on fictions.[1] One of the biggest was that it could not be challenged, and never by a woman. Lea Garofalo, Giuseppina Pesce, Maria Concetta Cacciola, and now Denise Cosco had all exposed that lie. The 'Ndrangheta's response was uncompromising. The women had to die. And their stories had to be rewritten.

Alessandra and Giovanni were now confronting the possibility that after their early triumphs, the clans were succeeding, at least in public perception. The Lea Garofalo investigation might have revived several old cases and injected new life into the fight against the east coast 'Ndrangheta, but there was no resuscitating Lea. Likewise, despite Giuseppina's decision to start cooperating again, the last public memory of her was that she had recanted. As for Concetta, she had died and then, in a mafia masterstroke, had retracted from beyond the grave. Now, with the very public collapse of the trial against Carlo Cosco and his men, it seemed the clans had gotten lucky with Denise, too. "The truth is that there is no more important or fundamental investigative tool than the *pentiti*," said Giovanni Musarò. The prosecutors had had four women *pentiti*. None had emerged unscathed. The 'Ndrangheta had used Concetta's death, in particular, as a warning. "When the Cacciolas wrote their denunciation of the prosecutors, they weren't thinking of their daughter," said Giovanni. "They were ensuring that this never happened again. It went beyond Cacciola. It was a message to all Calabria. So, yes, at that time, you can say things were not in our favor."

On reflection, however, it was possible to view the 'Ndrangheta's vehement crushing of any opposition as a sign of weakness. Its absolutist intolerance of freedom seemed to stem from an appreciation of how, once released, it was almost impossible to contain again. And, despite the clans' efforts, Giuseppina and Denise were still breathing. Both also seemed strengthened by the resolve they had discovered in the gale of the 'Ndrangheta's oppression. In Milan, Denise had already faced her father once in court and was telling prosecutors she could do it again. As for Giuseppina, the death of her friend appeared to have had the exact opposite effect from that intended. Giuseppina told Alessandra she had no doubt that the 'Ndrangheta had forced Concetta to drink acid. Her friend's killing made her realize how close she had come to the same fate herself: she had been mere hours from her own return to Calabria when Alessandra arrested her. "You saved my life," she told Alessandra. "If you hadn't stopped me, my children would now be taking flowers to the cemetery, like 'Cetta's."

The realization seemed to release Giuseppina from any last doubts. On August 23, three days after Concetta's death, a letter from Giuseppina arrived at the Palace of Justice in Reggio Calabria, addressed to Alessandra, Pignatone, and Roberto di Bella, head of Reggio's juvenile court. "I know you already know my story," Giuseppina wrote, "but here I wish to start from the beginning."

After six months of imprisonment, on October 14, 2010, I expressed my desire to the prosecutor Dr. Cerreti to pursue this course of action, driven by my love as a mother and my desire to lead a better life, far away from the environment where I was born and lived. I never thought about doing that to obtain reductions to my sentence. It was also never my intention to tease anyone. I only did this because I was, and remain, convinced that this is the right choice, since because of our husbands' and relatives' life choices, we have endured a life full of pain and, above all, cowardice and fear of consequences. In reality, each of us should have the power . . . to choose between right and wrong.

Maybe I should have done this earlier, before being dragged into [this situation] . . . My hope is that we still have time and that I can act so my children can have a better life—a life of principle and freedom of choice. I also hope that many people like me who are in situations like mine will find the courage to rebel. I have found the strength to take this important decision and defy a fearsome, powerful, and unforgiving family, in the full knowledge of the risk to me and those I love. Finally, I am doing it.

There were times when I thought my choice had been hasty and not properly thought through. I have been fragile. The courage that I had back on October 14, 2010, deserted me. The bond between my children and their family also bewildered me. I began to think I had no right to deprive them of their father. I told myself neither I nor they could escape that life. It all weighed heavily on me. And after discussing with my partner, who disagreed, I decided I would arrange for [my children] to go back to Calabria. I would have my own battle in court, with a good lawyer to defend me. In my mind, giving back their freedom to my children was the fairer solution. But I was dying inside. It wasn't what I wanted. It was just what I imagined was right for them.

And, of course, there were the newspapers. What was written, day after day, made me look like a victim instead of someone in command of their own decisions. The letter I had to send to the judge . . . that made me feel even worse: all those lies, this impression of me that was created that was not me. I had to swallow that as well, not because anyone was forcing me to but because I felt that, like in the movies, there was a story I had to maintain—and that if I wasn't going to be a collaborator anymore but was one day

*going to be returning to Calabria, then maybe [those stories] would
be a shield protecting my children and myself from the prejudices of
my family and my people.*

*Driving back from Lucca with Domenico, I realized the
importance of my motivation to cooperate. My children's future.
My love of a man who loves me for who I am and not for my last
name. Today, while I may have lost credibility as a collaborator,
all these experiences have strengthened me as a woman. Even more
important, they have restored my confidence in myself. I feel now
that maybe I wasn't so selfish, after all. Perhaps if I had been more
courageous, today I would already be at the beach with Domenico
and my children. I gave them the freedom to choose. It is true that
I have always prioritized my love for my children, their health and
peace. And my children and Domenico chose me. They are the ones
who really love me. However many times I change my mind, they are
there for me, thank God.*

*That's why I believe my collaboration will make a real change,
for many people. I wish to tell you that I'm not crazy, like they
said. I tell you all these things so you can really see the person in
whom you placed your trust. I never told any lies. I just had a
moment of confusion. I patiently await your reply, aware of my
mistakes.*[2]

As her staff and colleagues read the letter, Alessandra was
pleased to note that they lingered, silently reading every line. Man
or woman, they were moved. Though she'd never show it, Alessandra was, too. In a world of deception, here was clarity. Instead of
hate, here was love. Gone was fear. Here was strength.

AFTER GIUSEPPINA'S LETTER, events moved fast. In early September, she gave Alessandra a comprehensive account of how her former

lawyer, Giuseppe Madia, and the editor of *Calabria Ora*, Piero Sansonetti, had coordinated the drafting and release of her retraction letter. (Madia told Giuseppina he had had to approach Sansonetti because the editor of Calabria's small, local daily "was the only one willing to publish it and adopt our cause.")

On September 15, Giuseppina received another letter from her husband, Rocco. At first, he admonished her. "I know you've started making *coccòdeo*," he said, using the Italian for "cock-a-doodle-do." "I do wonder why you've ruined all our lives, including your own, just to be with the children?" Perhaps sensing Giuseppina's renewed determination, however, he soon switched to a plaintive tone. "Please, don't make me look bad," he wrote. "I don't think I'm asking for the moon. There is no morning that I don't wake up and think of you. Sadly, this is how things have turned out. My family is broken. But I leave you with an embrace, and the hope that God will enlighten you."[3] A year earlier, Rocco's meekness might have swayed Giuseppina. Now it merely confirmed that she had emerged from their marriage the steelier of the two, and it further hardened her purpose.

She was unmoved, too, five days later on September 20, when the first trial to result from Operation All Inside concluded in the sentencing of eleven members of the Pesce *'ndrina*. Giuseppina's uncle Vincenzo and her cousin Francesco Pesce, who had been found hiding in a bunker on August 9, received the heaviest sentences: twenty years each for mafia association and other crimes; and a total fine of €70 million, of which €50 million was to compensate the citizens of Rosarno for decades of murderous oppression and €10 million each was to go to the Ministry of Interior and Calabria's regional authority.[4]

The sentencing began a bewildering few days of public humiliation for the Pesces. The next day, September 21, the carabinieri took Angela, now sixteen, Gaetano, nine, and Elisea, five, from their grandparents' home and delivered them to the protective custody of the juvenile court.[5] On September 22, Alessandra formally announced in court that Giuseppina was once more cooperating with the authorities.[6] On September 23, at her own request, Giuseppina appeared in court in Palmi by video link to hear charges put to clan head Antonino; her husband, Rocco; her mother, Angela Ferraro; and her sister Marina.[7] On September 27, Giuseppa Bonarrigo, the family grandmother, chained herself to the gates of Rosarno town hall, where she was photographed by journalists protesting the innocence of her sons.

The public dishonoring of the Pesces was far from over. On October 4, Giuseppina's in-laws, Gaetano, Gianluca, and Giovanni Palaia, were arrested, quickly followed by aunt Angela Palaia and Angela Ietto. On October 13, Alessandra seized another eight Rosarno companies worth a further €18 million, bringing the total value of confiscations from the Pesce empire to €228 million.[8] A week later, on October 21, Alessandra announced that besides Giuseppina, she had a second 'Ndrangheta woman ready to testify: Rosa Ferraro, a cousin from Genoa taken in by the Pesces as a domestic helper after she was thrown out by her husband.[9] The following day, 110 'Ndranghetisti who had been arrested during the mass raids of July 2010 were sentenced to terms of between two and sixteen years.[10]

The climactic disgrace came on November 25, the day the Pesce clan maxi-trial formally opened. Sixty-three 'ndrina members were accused. More than fifty were present in court, including several Pesces, Palaias, and Ferraros, along with fifty defense lawyers. Those already serving sentences in jail, like clan head Antonino and Giuseppina's husband, Rocco, attended by video link. A handful of Pesces remained on the run. They would be tried in their absence.

Procedure demanded that Alessandra read out the charges to the accused and submit the evidence gathered from years of investigation, including Operations All Inside, All Inside II, All Clean, and

Crimine. The evidence ran to 65,000 words, the length of a book. Running through it all would take several weeks, and a full trial was not expected to start until May 2012.

That first day did not go as expected, however. The defendants already knew they were being tried by a woman prosecutor on a woman's evidence. The news that Giuseppina would be joined by a second woman from the Pesce household had come as a shock. As they were led in, the men were surprised to see that, in addition, an unusually large proportion of the court officials, carabinieri, and even lawyers and reporters on duty that day were also women. When the judges entered, one president and two assistants, the 'Ndranghetisti were astonished to see three more women: Maria Laura Ciollaro, Antonella Create, and, taking the president's seat, Concettina Epifanio.

To the 'Ndrangheta men, it must have felt like a conspiracy. "No! No!" they shouted. Pointing at Alessandra and taking the name of another male prosecutor in the case, they yelled: "We want di Palma! We want di Palma! Not that! Not *that*!"

State and court officials would later insist there was no plot to unsettle the Pesces. The selection of staff and judges was a matter of neutral procedure. In particular, the three women judges had presided over the case since its inception. Nor was there any question that Alessandra had to lead the prosecution in court since she had led the investigation that preceded it. That didn't mean that the officials couldn't enjoy the defendants' discomfort. "When they saw us all in the court, they began screaming and shouting at me and my colleagues," said a smiling Alessandra. "They were humiliated to be in front of so many women—to be judged by women, to them something less than a man." To Alessandra and Giuseppina, listening by video link, there was something in the men's outraged reaction that suggested they knew, perhaps for the first time, that the tables were being turned. Alessandra described their shouts of indignation as something close to music. "A symphony of women's liberation!" she laughed. "Divine justice for these men!" Prestipino, who also denied any hand in the unusual number of women in court, was similarly jubilant. "Think of how many women in Calabria live the same lives as Giuseppina Pesce and Maria Concetta Cacciola," he said. "Now they have something, an example, some symbolism, to hold on to." Alessandra noted how across court Giuseppina's mother and sister, Angela Ferraro and Marina Pesce, remained seated and silent throughout. There was perhaps no better representation of the injustice in their own lives than watching their men howl at the sight of an assembly of modern, professional women sitting in judgment over them.[11]

XXI

G IUSEPPINA PESCE WASN'T the only one spurred to action by the death of Maria Concetta Cacciola.[1]

In Reggio Calabria, the youth courts had long been the poor cousin of their adult equivalents. The juvenile justice chief, Roberto di Bella, felt that was shortsighted. Like Alessandra, di Bella reasoned that the 'Ndrangheta was, above all, a family operation. "Since World War II, the same families have controlled the territory," he said. "Whether it's smuggling heroin or cocaine or business or politics, this culture, this phenomenon, is born of family and goes from father to son. It's hereditary. It's dynastic." Somehow, the Italian judiciary had contrived to focus on the fathers but forget their wives—and their children. This was despite di Bella's own experience in Calabria. In two decades in Reggio, he had dealt with more than a hundred serious crimes committed by 'Ndrangheta children. "We had extortion, robbery, kidnapping, and more than fifty cases of homicide or assisted homicide!" he said. "Kids who used Kalashnikovs. Kids who took part in clan feuds. Kids who were assassins. Kids who killed carabinieri."

Di Bella's experience also taught him that sending 'Ndrangheta children to detention mostly confirmed them on a path to more crime and incarceration. Once inside, they were fated to become killers and bosses, and before long wind up back in jail or dead. "These children start to breathe this 'Ndrangheta culture from the moment they are born," he said. The brainwashing was constant, and effective. By the age of twelve, an 'Ndrangheta child would spit whenever they saw a policeman. As teenagers, they would learn to exercise power "not just over children but over adults, too." By eighteen, they were beyond rescue. Sometimes hatred for the state was literally ingrained in them. Di Bella had found some children with tattoos of individual carabinieri officers on their feet "so they can tread on them twenty-four hours a day."

Di Bella had a gentle manner, and his neatly parted dark hair and gold-framed glasses suggested a small-town doctor or provincial academic or even a priest. And his work, it was clear, was a calling. One case in particular had stayed with him. In 2002, a sixteen-year-old scion of a Calabrian clan had been detained for possessing a gun and resisting arrest. "The serial numbers had been filed off the gun and there was a bullet in it," said di Bella. He surmised that the boy was preparing for his first murder. He knew the family well. The boy's father had been murdered when he was eleven. Di Bella had already sent three of his older brothers to jail. They were, he said, "one of the most violent and bloody 'Ndrangheta clans."

Throughout his trial, the boy made a show of appearing tough, said di Bella. "His eyes were like steel. He did not betray his emotions." In the end, di Bella felt he had no option but to send him to join his brothers for several years in juvenile detention. Several months into the boy's sentence, however, di Bella received a phone call from the director of the youth prison. The boy was unwell. "He was suffering from sleeplessness," said di Bella. "He had stomach disorders that were stress related. He needed to speak to a male role model but he had none."

Di Bella had the boy brought back to court for reassessment. He found him a shadow of his former self. "He no longer had eyes like ice," he said. "He was bewildered. He had a lot of fear. He was distressed—strongly distressed—because of the murders and the mafia wars and the people he had lost, including his father." Di Bella realized the boy's defenses were down and he could talk to him directly. "So I told him clearly that he had to leave his 'Ndrangheta family. I said he would be murdered or be put in prison, like his father and brothers. And this boy said to me, for the first time: 'I want to leave.' He did not hide that his family was 'Ndrangheta. He asked me to help him leave them at the end of his sentence."

Di Bella promised that he would do what he could. A few months later, however, he was transferred away from Calabria. Several years after that, the court registrar in Reggio got in touch to tell him that the boy, now out of prison, had come looking for him at the court in Reggio. "He had been waiting for me for over a year until someone told him I was no longer there," said di Bella. The magistrate was consumed by guilt. There was no question that he and the state had failed this boy, a child after all, with the simple misfortune to be born into circumstances beyond his control but who, from the depths of his turmoil, had reached out for their help.

When di Bella returned to Calabria in 2011, he discovered the boy, now a man, was back in prison, convicted of mafia association. "He sent me a greeting from the psychological clinic where he was being treated," he said. "A few months later, I heard his elder brother had been arrested once again. This all sat with me."

On his return to Calabria, however, di Bella was heartened to discover that the fight against the 'Ndrangheta had been transformed. Pignatone, Prestipino, Alessandra, and the other prosecutors had brought new energy and new ideas to the struggle. They had forged a new consensus. In Alessandra's words, "The 'Ndrangheta is a very complicated phenomenon that defies a single solution. We need to take action on several different levels at the same time." Alessandra, particularly, had been instrumental in refocusing minds on the internal family dynamics of the 'Ndrangheta. That, too, made sense to di Bella. The youth courts, he felt, had much to contribute to this new direction.

If di Bella had any remaining doubts about the need for change in his own court, they vanished when, one day in Reggio, he found himself judging the children of the children he had judged a generation earlier. Here was undeniable proof that the 'Ndrangheta and the justice system were locked in never-ending conflict. The 'Ndrangheta would keep thieving, maiming, and killing. The carabinieri and the judges would keep throwing them in jail. It was systemic, perpetual failure. "We were all *inheriting* the 'Ndrangheta," said di Bella. And if targeting an 'Ndranghetista when he was young was one of the ways to end this eternal battle, and all the blood and prison and death it wrought, then di Bella felt it was his duty to seize the moment.

WHEN HE READ the files on Maria Concetta Cacciola's death in August 2011, di Bella sensed his chance had arrived. "Concetta's children were used as a tool to make her come back and retract," he said. "Her parents made Concetta listen to her six-year-old crying 'I miss Mommy' on the phone." It was an unambiguous case of child abuse in the service of criminality. A few weeks later, di Bella read the transcripts of a bugged conversation between Concetta's sixteen-year-old son, Alfonso, and his father, Salvatore Figliuzzi. In the transcripts, Alfonso accused his grandparents—Concetta's parents—of treating his mother so badly that "they practically killed her. You lost a wife. I lost a mother. Nothing would have fucking happened if it hadn't been for Grandpa and his jealous rage." Here was another 'Ndrangheta boy crying out to be rescued from his family. One way or another, the state had failed Concetta. Di Bella couldn't allow it to fail her children. "After Concetta's death, we decided to try a very different approach," he said.

Di Bella's first move was to have the carabinieri remove Giuseppina's and Concetta's children from their grandparents. This twin seizure from two of the most prominent 'Ndrangheta families in Rosarno sparked immediate fury. Di Bella received threatening letters. The Calabrian newspapers ran interviews with fathers and mothers from Rosarno accusing him of breaking up families and stealing children out of sheer vindictiveness. Apparently in all seriousness, some accused him of trying to brainwash their children in the same way the Nazis abducted and indoctrinated their enemies' children during World War II.

Di Bella was unmoved. He had found legal justification for the seizures in international law, particularly the United Nations Convention on the Rights of the Child. "It says that a child's family has to respect their freedom, their rights, and their peace," he said. "None of that is respected by the mafia." The convention became di Bella's basis for a new policy for handling the children of *pentiti* so they could no longer be used to blackmail their mothers. "Now, whenever there is a woman who collaborates, the officers inform the court about the children so we can intervene and get the children to the woman. This avoids the dangerous vacancy of authority over the children, which the 'Ndrangheta tries to exploit."

Di Bella realized the convention had far wider applications, too. What he had been fighting all these years was not, as his colleagues sometimes excused it, the simple bad luck of being born into a southern mafia family or even some traditional version of *patria potestas*, the customary power of a father. The convention was unequivocal. What was happening inside almost every 'Ndrangheta family was illegal child abuse. "When we are talking about a child of twelve and his father is taking him to the beach to learn how to shoot a gun, the convention says it's our duty to intervene," said di Bella. "A father under house arrest teaching his twelve-year-old how to strip a gun or move a Kalashnikov from one house to another—we have an obligation to intervene there, too. A man who is a fugitive for twenty years with his children, forcing them to miss their education—we have the same obligation. All the cases where crimes are committed by children or parents relying on children, or if we have children extorting on behalf of their parents, or when a child is taken somewhere to shoot traffickers and witness a drug fight, or when they use their children as killers during clan feuds—in all these cases, when there is tangible and concrete detriment to the child, the convention says we have an obligation."

The same duty of care applied to 'Ndrangheta mothers schooling their children in mafia life, the very life force of the 'Ndrangheta. The convention recognized a parent's right to educate their child. But that was subordinate to the child's right to be protected from prejudice and abuse, physical or psychological; and to their right to a responsible education aimed at preparing the child for a tolerant, peaceful, legal life. 'Ndrangheta children didn't have any of that. They didn't have much of a childhood, full stop. "You take a seventeen-year-old 'Ndrangheta boy and ask him what music he listens to and he'll reply 'the tarantella,'" said di Bella. "He doesn't know Lady Gaga or Madonna. It's such a strict, narrow upbringing. They can't see further than their own family and their own little town."

Di Bella began to believe that the greatest problem with an 'Ndrangheta upbringing was the way it stunted a child emotionally. At an early age, children learned to hide and control their feelings, lest they betray themselves or others. They internalized the code, which forbade almost any individual expression or identity. And while they formed almost no relationships outside the 'Ndrangheta, inside it, as their friends and relatives were steadily murdered or were put in prison or went on the run, they became ever more lonely. "There is no one to tell the child the right road to take and no individual will to choose a different road," said di Bella. "The young man doesn't even contemplate it because he doesn't know a different reality exists. For children growing up in these little mafia towns, the cult of the 'Ndrangheta oppresses everything and every-one." No surprise, said di Bella, that court reports on 'Ndrangheta children showed psychological devastation. "Their symptoms are similar to Vietnam veterans," he said. "They are inhibited. They all have this strong sense of anguish and anxiety. Their dreams are full of nightmares. And they are alone."

Taken together, di Bella concluded, the "mafia family system" was itself "prejudiced against the welfare of children." "A mafia education, mafia indoctrination by the parents, the perpetration of crimes by the child, the physical danger to children," said di Bella, "all these are detrimental to the mental and physical integrity of the children and contravene the fundamental rights, liberties, and principles of the UN charter. The primary victims of the 'Ndrangheta are their own children."

The Family had always been an immoral perversion. Now it seemed it was illegal, too.

DI BELLA WAS proposing deprogramming 'Ndrangheta children, a matter in which the judiciary had no expertise. When he raised the subject with social workers and psychologists, they recommended not just taking the children away from their parents but trying to offer them a normal adolescence. Growing up was, at heart, about discovering freedom. Freedom was what the 'Ndrangheta denied its children, and that was why they turned out the way they did. If the state wanted to change them, said the psychologists, it should place younger children with families far outside Calabria who would let them attend school and hang out with friends and make the conventional choices of any child growing up. Once they were old enough, the children could stay in a hostel where they would be required to attend school. They should be allowed contact with their parents but, crucially, the power to direct their lives should rest with the children themselves. The advice made sense to di Bella. "These children come from small worlds where everything is 'Ndrangheta," he said. "Their inexorable destiny is to be killed or end up in jail. A desire to choose a different path is never contemplated because they don't know the alternatives. You can't desire another world if you don't know it exists."

The hope, said di Bella, was that if children were allowed to experience a conventional upbringing, a new idea would take hold in their minds: self-determination. "Our idea was to let them know there is a better world out there with different rules," he said. This was "a place where you can be free. Where there is love and affection. Where there is no need for violence or killing in order to let other people understand what you're thinking. Where there are equal rights for men and women. Where prison is not a medal you get on your chest. And where you can try out your personality free from the surname you have." What the authorities would be attempting, said di Bella, was a kind of "cultural infiltration." They would insert the children into everyday Italian life and let it gently subvert them. "The 'Ndrangheta infiltrated us," he said. "Now we were going to infiltrate them right back."

In court, instead of custodial sentences, di Bella began ordering 'Ndrangheta children to be separated from their families in another fashion. He sent many of the older teenagers across the Strait, to a hostel attached to a church high up in the hills above Messina. The program was run by a young Sicilian psychologist, Enrico Interdonato, who had made a specialty of the mafia. Interdonato would take his charges out for pizza and to nightclubs. When he took one boy to a bookshop, he was astonished to learn it was the first time the boy had ever visited one.

Initial results were mixed. One boy, Francesco, arrived with a propensity for violence and a set of rock-hard prejudices against women, immigrants, the police, and the state, which were only slightly softened by the time he left. But another boy, Riccardo Cordì, from the 'Ndrangheta stronghold of Locri, was transformed. Riccardo's father, an 'Ndranghetista, had been killed when he was a boy. His brothers were all in jail. Riccardo himself had been headed the same way, appearing in di Bella's court after being arrested for stealing a police car, and then again for fighting.

After a year at the hostel in Messina, that destiny no longer appeared certain. After he turned eighteen and left the hostel, Riccardo wrote a letter that was published in several newspapers.

> *Dear Editor,*
>
> *I am a boy of Calabria, I come from Locri and my name is Riccardo Cordì. On March 7, 2011, I was arrested by the police in Locri for the theft and damage to a car owned by the railway police. In July 2011, I was charged with another instance of assault. But the court in Reggio decided to send me away from Locri to see if I could leave behind these experiences. It was the start of my journey.*
>
> *When I arrived in Sicily, at first it was not easy to be alone and away from home. But everything changed when I began to see a psychologist in Messina who guided me toward the discovery of a new life. I did things, met people, and visited Rome, Milan, and other places that I had never seen. One morning, I went to see the sea with the psychologist. We could see Calabria, my land. But for the first time, I could see it from another perspective.*
>
> *I decided then and there that my life would be different. I want to return to Locri, but I do not want any more problems with the law. Not because I can't handle it but because I want to live in peace. I want to be clean. Before this experience, I believed the state did not care about the people. The state was just this thing that took you away from home, without you ever knowing when or if you would return. But in recent months, I have met a different state.*

This state didn't seem to want me to change. Rather, it tried to understand who I was.

And who am I, really? A boy of eighteen. A boy like any other. I was very small when my father was killed and I saw my brothers go to jail. I want a different future for myself. That doesn't mean that I renounce my family. My brothers will always be my brothers and Calabria will always be my land. But now a new road lies before me and I choose it for myself with my own free will. The state has given me this chance. I can choose what I do when I grow up. I can choose what job I do to get by in the city. I can stand tall. I have no idea if I'll succeed but I'm going to try—because something has changed for me. I changed. And I can change further. Others, too. There are so many guys like me who need the state to support them as it supported me. Right now, they don't believe this state exists. But I know, and I write this letter so that others can know, too. The road is still steep. But a happy ending, I now know, is not just a dream. It can be real life.[2]

Interdonato, Riccardo's psychologist, said even Riccardo's family, who were 'Ndrangheta through and through, seemed to accept that the state wasn't harming their boy and might even be opening up some new horizons to him. Interdonato and Riccardo still talked every day months after Riccardo had left the hostel. One morning, Interdonato turned on his phone to find Riccardo had sent a picture of himself with a small baby. "He married his girlfriend this year and they had a son," said Enrico. "Family is at the center of Italy's history. The mafia took those values and *extremized* them until it became a kind of psychological abuse. But Riccardo is beginning a new family. He's writing a new history."

XXII

ALESSANDRA AND GIOVANNI were still haunted by their inability to prove that Maria Concetta Cacciola's death was murder.

They had plenty of circumstantial evidence. For one, Concetta had never seemed suicidal. On the contrary, said Giovanni, "Concetta was organizing to leave her family again. She had her love affair. The wiretaps showed she and her lover were planning their future together."

There was also the physical impossibility of drinking a liter of hydrochloric acid by choice. Though initial forensics suggested Concetta had killed herself, a pathologist later found bruises on her neck and other marks on her arms consistent with someone holding her down while a second person held her mouth open, possibly with a funnel, and poured acid down her throat. In addition, the autopsy revealed Concetta had taken no sedatives to dull the pain. She'd felt everything. Presumably, surmised the prosecutors, because she was meant to.

Alessandra and Giovanni were also sure Concetta's family was behind her killing. That was the 'Ndrangheta code. Every family cleaned up its own mess. Alessandra still thought Concetta's indecision, and her belief that it would be months before the family acted, had given the Cacciolas the opportunity they needed. "This lack of determination, taking too much time," she said. "Maybe this was fatal to her."

There was a further possibility, however. Maybe the Cacciolas *had* planned to wait but had stepped up their plans after Concetta told her mother she was returning to the protection program. In that scenario, Concetta's mother, Anna Rosalba Lazzaro, would have been key. "Maria Concetta Cacciola still felt love for her mother," said Giovanni. "That's why she told her she was going back into witness protection. But Lazzaro was a classic mafia woman, tasked with preserving the clan. She was the one who said: 'You're either with us, or with them.'"

Precisely who killed Concetta, however, remained a mystery. "We can say she was murdered," said Giovanni. "The question remains: by who? Her mother and father left the house that afternoon. It wasn't them. Something else happened but we still don't know what."

If the two prosecutors couldn't say who killed Concetta, they couldn't charge anyone with her murder. They decided that even as they would continue trying to prove a case of homicide, they would prosecute the Cacciolas on a lesser charge. Article 110 of the Italian criminal code specified that "when more than one person participates in the same offence, each shall be subject to the penalty prescribed for such offence."[1] Article 580 made it illegal to help or instigate suicide, an offense punishable by between five and twelve years in prison.

Charging the family with pressuring Concetta into suicide would still show that in twenty-first-century Italy no one could expect to assist their daughter's death, to conspire in it, and get away with it. And it was a case Alessandra and Giovanni could readily prove. Concetta had told them how the family had beaten and threatened her. From wiretaps, they had the Cacciola family on tape discussing how to force Concetta to retract. They also had them using her children to blackmail her into returning to Rosarno. In the recording of her retraction, a second woman's voice could be heard coaching her.

Two months after Concetta's murder, they had her sixteen-year-old son, Alfonso, blaming Concetta's parents for his mother's death. Finally, the Cacciolas themselves were saying that their daughter had died of shame. There was some poetic justice here, thought Alessandra. The Cacciolas were so blinded by the cult of the 'Ndrangheta and their loyalty to the code that they hadn't realized they were effectively admitting an offense. Concetta had felt no shame on her own. Whether she had killed herself or been murdered, it was the shame poured on her by the family that had made her death inevitable.

During the last few months of 2011, Alessandra and Giovanni steadily built their case against the Cacciolas. By February 9, 2012, they were ready. That morning, as the prosecutors released their indictment to the public, the carabinieri arrested Concetta's parents, Michele Cacciola and Anna Rosalba Lazzaro, in Rosarno and issued a warrant for Concetta's brother Giuseppe, who was detained two months later in Milan. All three were charged with conspiracy to force Concetta to perjure herself and to commit suicide. The carabinieri called the arrests Operazione Onta, or Operation Shame.

The arrests made the press the next day. "Driven to Suicide by Her Own Family" read a front-page headline in *Il Quotidiano della Calabria*, the province's main paper.[2] What caught Alessandra's eye, however, was a lengthy accompanying editorial by the paper's editor, Matteo Cosenza. For the first time in an Italian newspaper, Cosenza linked the cases of Concetta, Lea, and Giuseppina as elements of the same essential story. "Giuseppina Pesce, Maria Concetta Cacciola, and Lea Garofalo had the misfortune to be born into a terrible world," he wrote. "Despite tremendous suffering, these women decided to break with their families and to choose the path of legality and justice." All three women had paid dearly for their courage, wrote Cosenza. All had plunged their lives and the lives of their children into dark turmoil. Two of the women had died. Cosenza continued:

*Some say we exaggerate when we talk about the 'Ndrangheta
and its penetration of Calabria's society and institutions. They
say it doesn't exist. These cases remind us of the truth. All honest
Calabrians must follow these women's example in their daily lives
and stand up to the 'Ndrangheta. Do it for yourself! Do it for
the young, who deserve a different future in this wonderful land!
It's almost impossible to imagine how someone can make a change
after being born into an 'Ndrangheta family—someone who sucks
arrogance and lawlessness from their mother's breast and who can't
even conceive of a world of civil coexistence, tolerance, respect, and
happiness. That's why we must bow before Giuseppina, Concetta,
and Lea. Despite everything, they were able to grasp that they were
living among evil and find the courage to say: "Enough! Stop! We
and our children must live in peace, not in perpetual war!"*

*They paid a high price. They will pay a higher one if we forget
them. Calabrians, don't turn away! Let's become the beautiful,
strong Calabria we all want! We know the evil among us. Step
by step, we will rid Calabria of this great malevolence and redeem
ourselves in the eyes of our children, and of the world.*

Alessandra could scarcely believe what she was reading. Her
big idea had always been to crush the 'Ndrangheta by freeing its
women. For years, it had been a private obsession. Over the last
two years, month by month, man by man, she had slowly persuaded
her colleagues. With the backing of Pignatone and Prestipino, and
each successive case—first Lea, then Giuseppina, then Concetta—
the strength of her argument had grown. Concetta's death, in particular, had given Giuseppina renewed determination and spurred
Roberto di Bella to rethink everything he was doing at Reggio's
juvenile court.

But Alessandra could never have predicted a newspaper campaign against the 'Ndrangheta, calling on all Calabrians to take the

three women as their standard-bearers. Two years earlier, crowds had blocked the road in Reggio to cheer 'Ndrangheta boss Giovanni Tegano as he was led away to jail. Only a year earlier, *Calabria Ora* had launched its campaign against Alessandra. Now, suddenly, here was everything she had been working toward, all her intuition from growing up during *la mattanza* in Sicily, the summation of her years of study and research, the mountain of evidence she had amassed detailing how 'Ndrangheta women were oppressed and how a tiny few had fought back—all of it, on a newspaper front page, in an article calling for something close to revolution. It felt miraculous. "*Il Quotidiano* created, for the first time, a public debate about the women in the 'Ndrangheta," she said. "And suddenly people all around us were talking about how the 'Ndrangheta had been corrupting our lives all these years. It was a real, immediate change."

It occurred to Alessandra that what she had resisted for so many years—sentiment, empathy, emotion—was precisely what *Il Quotidiano* was using to stir up its readers. To a prosecutor, the 'Ndrangheta's women were a technical tool with which to unlock Europe's biggest criminal conspiracy. To a newspaper editor, the story of the three good mothers was an epic tragedy to rouse a people. And *Il Quotidiano*'s reporters had been industrious. Across the inside pages, they laid out every element of the story for their fellow Calabrians to read. A report on the arrest of Concetta's parents was accompanied by articles on the Pesce investigation ("Pesce Clan Hit with 11 More Arrests") and the Garofalo case ("Garofalo Trial: One Defendant Threatened"). The letter Concetta left for her mother when she went into witness protection was reprinted in full, as was her recorded "retraction." There were backgrounders on the clans of Rosarno and eulogies to the two dead women from members of parliament. There were even descriptions of the three bunkers about which Concetta had testified.

The common thread that ran through the coverage was the her-

oism of Lea, Giuseppina, and Concetta and the imperative for all
Calabrians to follow their example. At heart, wrote Cosenza, this
was a tale about three mothers who had understood their families
were a curse on Calabria and who had defied centuries of violent
misogyny—whether mafioso, Calabrian, or Italian—to save their
children and their homeland. This was about sacrifice and pain,
abuse and terror, blood and acid—and a dream of a new future.
And now, said Cosenza, it had to be about the millions of Calabrians, men and women, who would join the rebellion the women had
started. Cosenza even set a date for Calabria's revolt: March 8, the
Festa della Donna, International Women's Day. On that day, he
demanded that all true Calabrians celebrate Lea, Giuseppina, and
Concetta. By doing so, he wrote, they would finally reclaim their
freedom.

BY COINCIDENCE, MARCH 8, 2012, was a date already looming
large on Alessandra's calendar.

That spring Thursday was sentencing day in the last of the maxi-
trials resulting from the 2010 raids against the 'Ndrangheta. More
than two hundred men and women from across Italy had already
been convicted and sentenced to a total of several thousand years in
jail. Hundreds of millions of euros in property and assets had been
seized. Entire crime families had been taken down and whole criminal empires dismantled. Now, in a caged dock inside a bulletproof
and bombproof court in Reggio Calabria, a final 127 'Ndranghetisti
would be judged and sentenced, among them bosses from every significant 'ndrina as well as Domenico Oppedisano, the capo crimine.

Alessandra knew that whatever happened, the 'Ndrangheta
would endure. Despite the convictions and confiscations, the organization retained thousands of men in its employ and hundreds of
billions of euros in assets. The bosses could still rule their businesses

from jail, even commanding clan feuds and overseeing international expansion. Every prosecutor knew that however hard they worked to bring the 'Ndrangheta to account, tens of thousands of crimes, including hundreds of murders, would remain unsolved.

But there was no doubt that Calabria's prosecutors had shaken the 'Ndrangheta in a historic manner. The organization's most precious weapon, its secrecy, had been shattered. The century-old myth about a band of southern Italian Robin Hoods was in pieces. No longer would anyone nurse the illusion that the Calabrian mafia was a bunch of brigands with blunderbusses and trousers held up by baling twine who rustled goats and kidnapped provincial grocers. At last, the 'Ndrangheta had been exposed for what it was: a violent, unified, modern criminal conspiracy based in Calabria that threatened every country in the world.

This day had been decades coming, since long before Falcone and Borsellino or *The Godfather* or the night in July 1973 that the sixteen-year-old grandson of a billionaire stayed out late in Rome. The investigation that led to the maxi-trials had taken years and involved tens of thousands of policemen, carabinieri, prosecutors, and judges. It had necessitated the biggest surveillance operation ever mounted in Italy, amounting to a total of 25,000 hours of tapped phone calls and 83,000 hours of video and audio. The result of all this work was a prosecutors' picture of the 'Ndrangheta that was comprehensive and, to most of Italy, Europe, and the rest of the world, nothing less than dumbfounding. Whether measured by the tens of billions of euros it earned every year, or the grip it exerted over the illicit global markets for narcotics and weapons, or the political corruption it fomented from Melbourne to Montreal, or even the way it subverted financial markets and national sovereignty around the globe, Calabria's prosecutors had exposed the 'Ndrangheta as the world's most powerful and dangerous mafia.

What especially pleased Alessandra was that the greatest injury to the 'Ndrangheta had been performed by the investigations into Lea, Giuseppina, and Concetta. Their cases revealed the organization not as some fairy tale about wandering knights and righteous honor but a grotesque, illiterate, make-believe murder cult that practiced merciless and bloody cruelty, twisted family in the service of greed, and delighted in crushing freedom, love, and hope. "More than just the arrests, it was the loss of image and the injury to their legend," said Alessandra. "It really wounded them."

EACH MORNING FROM February 10 until March 8, *Il Quotidiano* ran a front-page banner featuring pictures of Lea, Giuseppina, and Concetta. Each day, it sent reporters to cover how ordinary Calabrians were joining the fight against the 'Ndrangheta. The prosecutors and women's groups were among the first to pledge support. They were followed by companies and trade unions, schoolchildren and university students, political parties and town mayors. After that came youth groups and pensioners' associations, trattoria owners and farmers' cooperatives, the Rotary Club, the swimmers' club, ferry operators, fishing captains, theater companies, artists' collectives, social workers, olive farmers, gelato sellers, winemakers, dockworkers, folksingers, and long-distance truckers. By the time March 8 arrived, even the northern-focused national press had begun to take notice of the scores of anti-'Ndrangheta marches involving tens of thousands of people taking place across Calabria.[3] The story of Lea, Giuseppina, and Concetta was becoming big news. A slogan had emerged: "La Calabria Non Ci Sta!!!" ("Calabria Won't Take It Anymore!!!") And as the women's stories were repeated over and over, their faces printed and reprinted on placards and posters, T-shirts and banners, broadcast on television, and published in international magazines, Alessandra realized that, slowly but steadily, Lea, Giuseppina, and Concetta were becoming the new legends of the 'Ndrangheta.

To the clans, this was catastrophic. Their invincibility was cracking. "These women had rebelled against the 'Ndrangheta's machismo and that act, and the stories of what happened to them, had cost the 'Ndrangheta their control and their system of consensus," said Alessandra. "That was the 'Ndrangheta's whole foundation and its whole essence. This was a huge crisis for them."

On the morning of March 8, it took a full hour in Reggio Calabria's main court to assemble all 127 'Ndranghetisti and their lawyers, as well as the prosecutors, officials, reporters, and three judges. It took another two hours for the presiding judge to read the list of convictions. By the time he had finished, ninety-three 'Ndranghetisti had been convicted. Sentences ranged from eight months to fourteen years. *Capo crimine* Domenico Oppedisano got ten years, probably enough to ensure he would die in prison.

Most important to the prosecutors, in its judgment the court formally acknowledged the 'Ndrangheta as a cohesive global entity with a presence in 120 locations around the world. Once and for all, the true nature of the world's biggest mafia had been established in irrefutable case law. "Today's ruling recognizes the accuracy of our reconstruction of the structure of the 'Ndrangheta as a unified organization, arranged in a complex hierarchy, governed by a top council, rooted in Calabria with branches overseas," Pignatone told reporters. "This represents a crucial step in fighting the 'Ndrangheta in Calabria and wherever it has taken root."

As Pignatone and his team congratulated each other quietly inside the Palace of Justice, Calabrians were dancing in the streets outside. As *Il Quotidiano* had demanded, almost every town in Calabria was holding an anti-mafia parade. In Reggio itself, there were conferences, plays, rallies, workshops, exhibitions, and speeches. As a show of public defiance, it was unique in Calabrian history. The icons of this new movement were Lea, Giuseppina, and Concetta, their faces almost ubiquitous.

None of the women could be present to see their triumph. That morning, however, Alessandra had arranged for a letter from the students of Mattia Preti girls' high school in Reggio Calabria to be delivered to Giuseppina in prison. The girls' words, thought Alessandra, would at least give Giuseppina a flavor of what was happening. "Dear Giusy," it began,

> We wouldn't have had the strength. We wouldn't have had the strength and courage as women. We wouldn't have had the strength and courage as daughters or sisters. We wouldn't have had the strength and courage in this city and in this country, where so often everything is silenced by fear and shame. But when someone finds the strength and courage to speak, especially as a mother, that fear disappears, and we want to redeem ourselves and remain silent no more.
>
> We listened to your story in silence. And these seemingly distant events suddenly became real. You opened our eyes. You opened the eyes of so many young men and women who will not forget your strength and courage. With everything you've gone through, and are still enduring, with these words we wanted to give you back a little of the strength you've given us. You're a beacon for women's emancipation. Your freedom makes possible our own. Your freedom makes possible the freedom of this land.[4]

Giuseppina was overjoyed. Once, she had dreamed she and Concetta might be the start of something. Now it was happening. Everywhere, it seemed, people were hailing Lea and Giuseppina and Concetta and coming out against the 'Ndrangheta.

In Reggio, Alessandra was equally touched by *Il Quotidiano*'s front page. Above a child's drawing of the three women, the paper had printed a headline that encapsulated what, for more years than Alessandra cared to remember, had been her personal creed: "With

Women, We Will All Break Free." Below it, editor Matteo Cosenza had written an open letter to Denise Cosco:

Dear Denise,

I do not know you but you should know the affection and admiration I have for you. I don't know if you'll be able to read these thoughts in the secret place where, at this time of liberty and warmth and celebration, you are forced to live. Your choice, to testify twice against your father about the death of your mother, Lea Garofalo, reflects how your mother lived. You had to choose between your living father and your dead mother and you chose the triumph of truth, legality, and justice. You've even had to testify against a man who was your partner.

You should know that your mother is proud. She made her sacrifice for your future, which she dared to imagine as one of dignity and free of the oppression she was born into. It would be so easy to give in to hatred. But nothing can be built on hate. Nobody, either, is born a criminal. These people are part of our family, our neighborhoods, our schools, our traditions, and our homeland. Many 'Ndrangheta men did not decide to be as they are. They never had a choice. Our collective action, if it is serious and profound, can prick their consciences. It can make new men of them.

My dear Denise, this disease has spread so wide that as long as the fever doesn't heal, it will continue to infect us. We must remember the example of the women who broke this so-called code of honor to proclaim their own right to freedom, respect, and dignity. The road ahead is long and hard. We know this struggle will take more than a little festival. But we have your example. Your testimony gives us confidence that even in the darkest night, even amid the torment that you, your mother, and the other women have experienced, there is light ahead. We must build a different future.

Nothing about the present suffering and violence is either natural or inevitable. This task will take all our commitment. We will have won when you are once again free to stroll the streets of Calabria, enjoying the sun and the sea breeze in peace. It is your right. It will be our failure if you are denied it.[5]

XXIII

THE MAXI-TRIALS, THE marches, *Il Quotidiano*—something was stirring in Calabria. Alessandra and the other prosecutors sensed a moment of possibility, even hope. It was exhilarating, but also disquieting. The state had fought for generations to change Sicily, and that war still wasn't won. The campaign against the Calabrian mafia now had its first convictions but, really, had just begun. Even the cases against the Coscos, the Cacciolas, and the Pesces had years to run through the various appeals and procedural tiers of the Italian justice system. Lea, Giuseppina, and Concetta might be the icons of this new movement, but if Carlo Cosco or the Pesces or the Cacciolas somehow walked free, then the spring of 2012 would be remembered as a brief, bright instant that vanished as quickly as it appeared.

By now, Alessandra knew that the best way to ensure a result in the Pesce case was to end all contact between the family and Giuseppina. Roberto di Bella's juvenile court had already taken care of the children, Angela, Gaetano, and Elisea. Now Alessandra had Giuseppina moved to Paliano prison outside Rome, a penitentiary set aside for mafia collaborators.

Housed in an old fifteenth-century palace on a natural rock fortress with idyllic views of the town and the Apennine mountains, Paliano housed around fifty *pentiti*, men and women. Prison facilities included a library, a theater, a church, a sports field, three workshops, four kitchens, four laboratories, five gyms, and a playroom

for children. Inmates were taught primary and secondary education
in its five classrooms. For the better educated, there were courses in
accounting and business studies as well as vocational training. All
the inmates were encouraged to work: in the prison pizzeria, growing tomatoes and cherries and cavolo nero in the organic garden,
making clothes, or embroidering cushions. There was a choir. There
was Internet. There were private bathrooms with bidets.

The idea, said Paliano's head warden, Nadia Cersosimo, was to
show how life in the mafia was a pale, negative image of reality.
Inside a clan, respect was synonymous with fear, and family with
crime. Paliano taught its prisoners that true respect was about
voluntary admiration, not involuntary deference, and true family
was about love, not mutual defense. Mafia families coached their
children to despise the law and hate the state. Cersosimo said her
own parents had taught her respect for the law and loyalty to the
state—and at Paliano, she attempted to raise her inmates afresh as
she herself had been brought up. It didn't always work. But when it
did, it could change lives. One prisoner gained a degree in econom-
ics. Two inmates, a man and a woman, married in the prison chapel.
"We all share in these new paths," said Cersosimo. "It's a family."
Alessandra was among many prosecutors who were impressed. "She
runs that prison as if it were her home," she said.

At Paliano, Giuseppina was allowed regular visits from her children. She watched the Lea Garofalo trial and the Cacciola arrests on
television. She followed the proceedings against her own family in
Palmi by video link from an underground security bunker set up for
the purpose at Rebibbia prison in Rome. When she turned thirty-
two on September 24, 2011, she was allowed a small party.

As Giuseppina and Alessandra resumed their collaboration,
they also revived their friendship. Between trial days during late
2011 and early 2012, Alessandra would fly up to meet Giuseppina
at Rebibbia and finesse her testimony. Sometimes during the hour-

long drive from Paliano, Giuseppina's protection officers would report being shadowed by cars with blacked-out windows. But Alessandra had insisted on a new team of bodyguards for Giuseppina, and their evident professionalism convinced Giuseppina she was in no danger. Alessandra was pleased to note the tight bond of trust that was quickly developing between Giuseppina and her protection squad. When, in December 2011, Giuseppina began giving detailed evidence for the first time against her father and brother—the two 'Ndrangheta men to whom she was most loyal—Alessandra credited the confidence she now felt able to place in the state.

Giuseppina's main concern remained the happiness of her children. A year earlier, Angela's despondency had derailed Giuseppina's cooperation. Now Angela seemed resolved to support her mother. Gaetano and Elisea, too, appeared happy in the care of Roberto di Bella's youth program. Still, abandoning family and everything you'd been taught from birth was never going to be easy.

In December 2011, realizing that the three children would be apart from Giuseppina for Christmas, Alessandra decided to make sure all three received presents. Out shopping, she spotted a cuddly toy that inspired her to try an experiment with the youngest, six-year-old Elisea. "When these children think of carabinieri, they think of hooded people in black balaclavas who seize their father or uncle in the middle of the night," said Alessandra. Alessandra decided to give Elisea a bear dressed in a carabinieri uniform. "I thought she could see this bear as a more friendly figure and, through my gift, the girl could get used to the idea of the state."

When Alessandra saw Giuseppina in January 2012, she asked if Elisea had liked her present.

"Yes, yes, she liked it," replied Giuseppina. But Alessandra could see she was embarrassed. "I'm afraid she took the carabinieri uniform off," said Giuseppina eventually.

Alessandra told Giuseppina not to worry. "Slowly, slowly," she said. "Let's see if things change."

And slowly, slowly, they did. Each time they met, Alessandra would ask Giuseppina for an update on the bear. In February, Giuseppina smiled and said the bear was now wearing its shoes. "Then she told me it was wearing its trousers," said Alessandra. "Then it was wearing its hat. Very gradually the bear began to wear more and more of its uniform. It took from January to September. But, finally, the bear was completely dressed and Elisea placed it right by the front door. She told her mother it was 'so that the carabinieri can protect us.'"

Alessandra saw the bear's transformation as an extraordinary metaphor for how, with their mother's encouragement, Giuseppina's children were altering their outlook on the world. "It was something amazing, what Giuseppina was managing to do," she said. "Slowly and progressively, she was setting out with her very fragile young children on a new path to something else. It was small steps on a long path. But slowly and surely, she was making them understand that the state can help them."

ALL ALESSANDRA'S EFFORTS with Giuseppina were to prepare her for the trial ahead. The first hurdle came on New Year's Eve, 2011, when a new 180-day deadline for Giuseppina to sign her witness statements fell due. The day before, Alessandra flew in to see Giuseppina, bringing with her several thousand pages of documentation. Eight months earlier, Giuseppina had refused to sign. Now, even on the phone, Alessandra could tell she was nervous again. The prosecutor arrived at Rebibbia fearing a repeat performance. She relaxed when she realized that what she had understood as anxiety was actually excitement. Giuseppina signed then slumped in her chair. She had now officially replaced her family with the state.

A bigger ordeal for Giuseppina would be facing her family in court. The hearings in Palmi weren't scheduled to begin until May 2012, giving Giuseppina and Alessandra months to ready themselves. Once proceedings were under way, however, they would be a marathon. The trial was expected to last a year. Giuseppina's evidence was so detailed that her testimony and cross-examination alone would take a week, Monday to Friday, eight to ten hours a day.

Alessandra arranged for Giuseppina to speak via video link from Rebibbia. When a number of Pesce relatives were given permission to attend the trial in Rebibbia, Alessandra requested a screen in court to block their view. But Alessandra knew her star witness and her family would still be aware of each other's presence and would be feeling each other out, testing each other's will. She decided to train Giuseppina like an athlete. She stressed physical fitness, encouraging Giuseppina to exercise for her stamina and advising her to take chocolate and fruit juice into the hearings to sustain herself. She told her to ask for a break any time she needed it. To prepare Giuseppina's mind, Michele Prestipino began joining Alessandra on her visits to Rebibbia. The prosecutors would put Giuseppina through her paces, spending days going over questions and evidence and likely questions from the defense, so that Giuseppina knew the case and the judicial procedure back to front.

Alessandra had also long understood that if Giuseppina was to betray her family, she would need a substitute to hold on to. Alessandra had given up the habit of a lifetime to become something approaching a mother to her. As Giuseppina's day in court drew nearer, Alessandra was heartened to see their relationship deepening. Once they finished the formal work of taking statements and verifying evidence, the two women found that what remained was warmth and closeness, an acceptance and appreciation of each other. One day, when Alessandra was setting up her tape recorder in their usual room at Rebibbia, Giuseppina entered carrying a gift. Alessandra unwrapped it to find a small hand-embroidered cushion. On it, Giuseppina had stitched the words: "Thank you for everything. With love, Giusy." "I was touched," said Alessandra. "After all, I was the one who had arrested her. Twice. In prison, she couldn't make much but she had done what she could. And the care she took in making this cushion! The tiny stitching. She'd scented it with a flowery fragrance, and the smell filled my apartment for a week. It was a symbol, a token of her gratitude that she was still alive, thanks to my stubbornness. And a very feminine one, which seemed to indicate a particular warmth and regard for me."

WHEN THE FIRST day of Giuseppina's testimony finally arrived on May 22, Alessandra judged that she and Michele Prestipino had done all they could.[1] Giuseppina was determined and confident. In a remarkable reversal of roles, she even tried to soothe Alessandra's nerves. A year earlier, when Giuseppina had suspended her cooperation, Alessandra had told her in parting that she would hold on to the dream that Giuseppina would one day restart her collaboration and face her family in court. Now Giuseppina winked at Alessandra. "Don't worry," she said. "Dreams can come true."

Still, as Alessandra stood in Palmi's main court, watching the video monitor while Giuseppina took her seat in Rebibbia, she was tense. Bringing a collaborator to testify against the mafia in court was a high point in any Italian prosecutor's career. Bringing Giuseppina to testify against her family, perhaps the only time that such a knowledgeable witness would give evidence against so powerful a clan, was the judicial event of the decade. The next few days would be a procedural and bloodless war, but a war nonetheless. On one side, truth and justice. On the other, murderous criminality and intense blackmail. Alessandra found herself simultaneously in thrall to the proceedings and terrified by them. How would Giuseppina cope?

Alessandra began by asking Giuseppina to describe her life as a mafiosa. Giuseppina explained her duties, which included passing messages between the men and managing the Pesce extortion rackets. She gave an overview of the other businesses: trucking, drugs, weapons, and corruption. She laid out the organization's structure, specifying which of her uncles and cousins were its bosses and lieutenants, and the line of succession. She spoke about how the men maintained a legal fund for family members on trial or in jail. She explained how her grandmother Giuseppa Bonarrigo's house served as a meeting place where the men believed they could talk without fear of being bugged.

Giuseppina spoke in detail about the men's fear of surveillance, and how they used detectors to find listening devices in their cars or under the paving at her grandmother's house, even the secret cameras hidden in the walls of a nearby school and hospital. She described how her father, Salvatore Pesce, had lived in a bunker under her grandmother's house, linked to the surface by a passage hidden inside a barrel, before he was arrested in 2005. She talked about the family's links to judges, carabinieri, and government officials. She told the story of how her cousin Francesco would stay outside the polling station on election day, telling voters: "Vote for so-and-so, he's a friend." She ran through Rosarno's history of killings and clan wars, especially between the Pesces and their rivals, the Belloccos. The rules were straightforward, she said. "You killed one of ours, we killed one of yours." The same went for traitors. When a cousin, Rosa Ferraro, discovered that Salvatore had put the Pesce family supermarket in her name, and was using it to launder money and defraud a salami maker, Ferraro had denounced him in the street. To the Pesces, said Giuseppina, such disgrace could only be answered with death. Rosa's imminent murder had only been narrowly avoided by her surrender to the authorities.

Alessandra then led Giuseppina through her own decision to testify against her family. Giuseppina began by saying that her marriage to Rocco Palaia had been loveless. "He never worked and he was never at home if one of the babies was ill," she said. "He wasn't home for a Sunday walk with his family. He didn't even give me money for medicine." She cried when she talked about Domenico Costantino, and how she had finally met a man who loved and respected her for who she was. Still, once her affair was discovered, Giuseppina knew she was dead. Asked who would administer her punishment, Giuseppina replied that her husband, Rocco, had told her that the family had "a pit ready for me" but that it would be her brother, Francesco, who would pull the trigger. "It has to be the eldest son in the family," she said.

This attachment to primogeniture typified the backwardness of mafia life, said Giuseppina. So did the violent misogyny. It had been standard mafia behavior for her family to blackmail her into signing a retraction by holding her children hostage. So was beating and starving her children when she defied the clan and resumed her cooperation. Giuseppina had been able to give the culture of the mafia some thought during her months at Paliano. She now delivered her conclusions to the court. The 'Ndrangheta men turned love and sanctuary into hate, intimidation, and fear, she said. "In a sense, whatever problems we have as a family, it came from that, the whole environment in which we were living," she said. "*That*'s the evil I see." That was the reason that she, her sister, her mother, and others were in jail. For the women, the mafia was evil in the way it made them complicit in their men's crimes ". . . in the sense that this chain doesn't break—this willingness to go on committing crimes." It was the mafia's perversion of family that meant "women are always going to meet with prisoners and now are prisoners ourselves." But that corruption of family love was also "why I couldn't stand the idea of my children without me and why I made this choice: so my children might avoid my fate and have a better life, where they are their own masters and can choose what they want to do. That's also why I cut all contact with my brother. Because as a man, he'll never accept my choice."

As she spoke, Giuseppina could hear coughing from the defendants' dock. It happened whenever she mentioned her brother. Even from hundreds of miles away down a video line, she recognized the voice and understood the message. "Her brother was saying: 'I hear you,'" said Alessandra. "'I hear what you're saying about me.'" To Alessandra's relief, Giuseppina was unperturbed. Turning to Alessandra during a break, she joked, "Does my brother have a sore throat?"

It was the first of several attempts by the Pesces to throw Giuseppina off balance during the trial. Her mother still refused to use her daughter's name, referring to her only as "the collaborator." Through a prison guard, her sister Marina sent her a photograph of the two of them together with their children. "That was very destabilizing for Giuseppina," said Alessandra. "She loved her sister a lot. That was very strong pressure on her, and she just had to find a way to handle it."

Giuseppina found the presence of her father, Salvatore, hardest to bear. She had often told Alessandra that among her family, she was closest to her father. She would cry when she spoke of him, saying he was the only one who ever understood her and that if he hadn't been in jail, he would have protected her from Rocco.

In court, as Giuseppina finished her final day of evidence, her father asked to make a statement. Alessandra sat motionless. As Salvatore walked from the dock to the witness stand, Giuseppina could see him for the first time. He was wearing a white shirt with blue stripes. "Giuseppina started crying as soon as she saw him," said Alessandra. "The shirt was the last present she had ever given him. It was her father's way of reminding her of her blood ties, of telling her who she was. On the screen, I could see Giuseppina's tears streaming down her cheeks."

Quickly and quietly, Alessandra suggested Giuseppina take a break. With Giuseppina safely out of earshot, Salvatore Pesce then began to speak. Initially, he turned his anger on Alessandra, accusing her of abusing her office and forcing Giuseppina to lie by threatening to take her children away and giving her drugs. He said Alessandra had exceeded her powers by arresting Giuseppina's mother and sister, Angela Ferraro and Marina Pesce, in Milan. "You have acted unlawfully," he shouted at Alessandra. "And why? You want to die?"

Alessandra interrupted to request the court transcript be forwarded to the director of public prosecutions in Rome to decide whether Salvatore's threat to her constituted an offense. Salvatore was then allowed to continue. "I want to tell my daughter that everybody loves her," he said. "After this is all over, when all the lights have been turned out and all these careers have been improved and when you're all by yourself, you will find us here waiting for you. We'll be here."

Alessandra marveled at how, in open court, Giuseppina's father could tug at his daughter's heart while threatening her in the same breath. Was there no end to these men's malice?

WEIGHING HERSELF DURING the week of Giuseppina's testimony, Alessandra calculated that she lost two or three kilograms a day. She was surprised to see Giuseppina coping far better. "She carried on through the trial—with great pain and suffering but also with great strength," said Alessandra.

Alessandra knew Giuseppina drew most of her courage from the same source that had always inspired her: her children. A few days before Giuseppina testified, her eldest daughter, Angela, had given her a necklace with a silver cross on it. "That was another message," said Alessandra. "Angela was telling her: 'If you feel afraid, if you feel scared, touch the necklace and think of us.' During the trial, she had a moment or two when I thought she was collapsing. But she immediately recovered, and I know her strength came from thinking about her children and how she was doing this for them. That gave her all the strength she needed."

Alessandra pondered the affection she felt for Giuseppina, once again characterizing their connection as "umbilical." She wondered how it compared with the bond that still existed between Giuseppina and her family. The trial hearings would continue for the rest of 2012, and sentencing wasn't expected until May 2013. Few sights were more likely to rekindle a daughter's love for her parents than the spectacle of them in a cage. The day the case concluded, however, would likely be the last Giuseppina would ever see her parents and her family. Giuseppina needed to come to terms with their inevitable separation.

After the stress of testifying, Alessandra and Michele Prestipino left Giuseppina alone for a few weeks. At Paliano, it was summer and the tomatoes and eggplants were ripening in the penitentiary garden, ready for the *pentiti* to pick in the early evening to make giant trays of parmigiana in the kitchens. One hot July day, when they judged enough time had passed, Alessandra and Prestipino flew up to Rome and took the drive east out into Lazio and to Paliano. The two prosecutors arrived in the early afternoon. In their honor, warden Nadia Cersosimo had organized a surprise supper, attended by all the staff and inmates, cooked using vegetables and herbs from the garden. The guests ate and chatted amiably with the *pentiti*. Afterward, Giuseppina presented Alessandra and Prestipino with pickles and jams whose lids she had decorated with embroidered doilies: a simple design of cherries and apricots next to the initials of Paliano district. Regarding Giuseppina, it struck Alessandra that her witness had changed once more. For the first time, she wrote, "I had the distinct impression that I had replaced her family in her emotions." That family loyalty, that unquestioning bond—it was gone.

If anything, Alessandra began to realize, it was now she who was becoming too attached to Giuseppina. In quieter moments, she would admonish herself for imagining that their bond could ever be more than temporary. She would have to move on to other cases. Giuseppina would need to live her own life. Still, Alessandra's staff were incredulous when, a few weeks after her visit to Paliano and hours before she left on her annual August holiday, she took a call from Giuseppina on her office line, a number that an 'Ndranghetista should never have possessed. Giuseppina was upset over arrangements for her children's custody. Some bureaucrat was messing her around.

Alessandra's staff knew better than to interrupt their boss. Like any good mother, she never stopped worrying.

XXIV

W HEN THE LEA Garofalo trial collapsed in November 2011, it had seemed like a disaster. Within a week, however, a new judge, Anna Introini, was appointed and immediately added new urgency to the proceedings.

Introini was one of the most senior women in the Italian judiciary. A fifty-nine-year-old veteran of several mafia cases, as well as of attempts to prosecute Silvio Berlusconi, her experience had left her with little patience for defense gymnastics or procedural delays, let alone mafia misogyny. Mindful that Carlo's term of custody expired on July 28, 2012, Introini ruled, over the defense's objections, that no previous hearings need be repeated and that Denise's damning testimony still stood. She also instituted an accelerated timetable of two court days a week.

When hearings resumed in December 2011, the weight of testimony against Carlo and his *'ndrina* quickly mounted. A fellow prisoner at San Vittore in Milan testified—over Massimo Sabatino's shouted denunciations—that he had heard Sabatino describe how Carlo had asked him in May 2009 to dress as a washing-machine repairman and kidnap Lea in Campobasso.[1] A number of Carlo's acquaintances spoke of their fear of him. Others had such trouble with their memories that they unwittingly gave the same impression. Proceedings were further accelerated by Carlo's refusal to take the stand. One day, sending a message to the 'Ndrangheta that he was observing omertà, he cupped his hands over his ears. "The message was: 'There's no problem, don't worry, feel safe, I'm not going to talk,'" said Alessandra. Still, by not testifying, Carlo couldn't help but speed up his trial. By the time Matteo Cosenza wrote his letter to Denise in *Il Quotidiano* on March 8, Judge Introini had said she would announce a verdict and sentence on March 30, 2012.

When the day came, Introini passed word that she would deliver judgment at 8:30 P.M. Outside court, the hall was packed. On one side, relatives of the defendants whispered with their lawyers. On the other, student activists huddled around Enza Rando, passing her letters of support for Denise. Journalists hovered. In the caged dock Carlo, his brothers Giuseppe and Vito, Massimo Sabatino, Rosario Curcio, and Carmine Venturino greeted their relatives through the bars.

Just after 8 P.M., a court official announced proceedings were about to start. As the reporters squeezed into the press seats, Carlo chatted quietly with his *'ndrina*. When Judge Introini entered, the court fell silent. Introini took her seat. "In the name of the Italian people," she said, "the Court of Assizes condemns Carlo Cosco, Giuseppe Cosco, Vito Cosco, Rosario Curcio, Massimo Sabatino, and Carmine Venturino . . ." Judge Introini ruled that all six men had taken part in Lea's murder. She convicted all six of helping to dispose of Lea's body by dissolving it in acid and of pretending that Lea was alive and well and living in Australia. Introini gave life sentences to all. She specified that Carlo and Vito should serve their first two years in solitary, while the other four should serve one. All six men were also ordered to pay a total of €200,000 to Denise, €50,000 each to Lea's sister Marisa and her mother, and €25,000 to the city of Milan.

It was hard to imagine a tougher set of sentences. Alessandra was delighted. The 'Ndrangheta seemed shocked. In the public gallery, Carmine Venturino's mother and sister began to cry. Other relatives screamed in despair. "Are you happy now?" yelled one woman at the activists.

Outside court, Enza read a prepared statement. "The most important part of today is that a young girl of a murdered mother has had the courage to bear witness for justice," she said. "She broke through the fear and silence and made her contribution to justice and truth." Libera's founder, the priest Don Luigi Ciotti, added: "This sentence will go down in history. We must bow before this young girl who found the nerve to break omertà and restore dignity, truth, and justice to her mother."[2]

Denise had testified against a father who had murdered her mother and ordered her own death. By staying true to Lea, she had broken not just with omertà but with her upbringing, her family, and all Calabria. What her mother had started, she had finished. She was only twenty years old. She deserved the widest possible admiration.

When Calabria's prosecutors considered it over the next few months, however, Carlo's conviction felt anticlimactic. Going to jail, even for life, was something an 'Ndrangheta boss like Carlo Cosco accepted as the price of power. Even if the state had punished him, he had punished Lea for her disloyalty. The journalists writing about the case might focus on his sentence, but their stories couldn't help send the message that if you crossed the 'Ndrangheta or Carlo Cosco, you died.

And, of course, the way the 'Ndrangheta worked, Carlo might be in prison, but his stature inside the organization had risen. In the 'Ndrangheta's view, he had done the righteous and honorable thing by killing his unfaithful turncoat wife. He and his *'ndrina* had shown discipline in court. They hadn't talked. They'd barely recognized the court's authority. They even managed to torture Denise further by refusing to say how and where Lea had died or what they had done with her body. Carlo had been tested over and again and he had remained steadfast. In the 'Ndrangheta's eyes, he was already a *santista*, literally sanctified. Now he would be recognized as one of the biggest bosses in Italy, free to expand his empire from prison and plan for the day when he settled his score with Denise, just as he had done with her mother. Carlo was unshaken. The 'Ndrangheta endured.

BARELY THREE MONTHS after Carlo's conviction, however, came news that his organization had been smashed. At 9 A.M. on June 21, 2012, seventy policemen in riot gear descended on *il fortino delle cosche* at No. 6 Viale Montello. Breaking down doors, they evicted two hundred residents, including several 'Ndrangheta families and more than fifty Chinese and African immigrant families. In two hours, the mafia's forty-year occupation of one of Milan's most historic buildings was over. Carlo's base of operations was destroyed.[3]

Behind closed doors, other cracks were appearing in Carlo's empire. During their investigation of Lea's death, the carabinieri had discovered a secret diary that Lea had kept throughout her early years with Carlo. "I didn't know it existed," said Denise. "She kept it when she was pregnant with me. Reading it, I learned she was very much in love with my father." Her mother's words gave Denise a new perspective. "Our family's is a story about courage," she said, "but more than that it's about love. Everything began with the love my mother had for my father." To Denise, the way her mother wrote about her father, Carlo must have returned that love. "He had other motives for marrying her," she said. "But I think he did love her."[4]

Facing up to life in prison, Carlo's *'ndrina* was experiencing similarly mixed emotions. In July 2012, the prosecutor in the case, Marcello Tatangelo, received a letter from Carmine Venturino. "I want to confess what I know about the murder of Lea Garofalo," wrote Carmine. He went on to state that he had assisted in Lea's murder and lied about it afterward. He added that while under Carlo's command, he had had to obey "the law that exists in Calabria, which is

different from the one that governs the rest of the world." His lawyers had assured him he would be acquitted since without a body,
there could be no murder.

That had turned out to be incorrect. As a result, Carmine was
now following his own counsel. The trial had taught him, he wrote,
that "I am not a mobster. I am not a monster." He wasn't immune to
suffering, like Carlo and the other men. Rather, "the pain of losing
Denise leaves me no choice," he wrote. "It's a very delicate thing.
But I think everyone would like to know the facts of Lea's disappearance, especially Denise. I do this out of love for Denise. She was
brave. She is an example to me. I have to tell you the facts of what
really happened."[5]

CARMINE VENTURINO WAS thirty-three when he was sentenced
to life. He had been born in November 1978 in Crotone, on the
plain below Pagliarelle. He told Tatangelo in a series of interviews
over the summer and autumn of 2012 that one of his earliest memories was of how his family's attention, and love, was focused on his
brother, who was born disabled.[6] Carmine didn't blame them. He
described his family as "poor but honest." Like most Calabrians,
however, he said his parents would never have thought of crossing
the 'Ndrangheta.

When Carmine fell in with a crowd from Pagliarelle and began
smoking hash, heroin, and cocaine, his family let it happen. They
made no objection either when in September 2006, aged twenty-
seven, he moved to Viale Montello in Milan. At first, Carmine was
a user. Soon he was dealing for one of Carlo's cousins. Within a year,
he was working for Carlo, who had moved back into Viale Montello on his release from prison. With the money he was earning,
Carmine rented his own apartment. One day in 2008 Carlo showed
up at his door with a blanket and a pillow, asking if he could stay.

"He never left," said Carmine. His rapid promotion from drug user to lieutenant in Europe's biggest drug mafia was, said Carmine, "sweetness, followed by bitterness."

Carmine had heard about Lea Garofalo in Pagliarelle. "Everyone was talking about it," he said. "We all knew that Carlo had had to go away because of her and that that was why he wanted to kill her." In their apartment, Carlo told Carmine that Lea was trying to take Denise away from him. He was frustrated that Denise didn't try to fight her mother more. He didn't articulate, yet, what his plans were for Lea. Then again, said Carmine, he didn't have to.

Carlo's chances of exacting his revenge increased significantly in spring 2009 when Lea left witness protection for the second time. She sent a message via her sister, Marisa, asking Carlo if she and Denise could return to Calabria. Carlo had every reason to agree. Lea was playing into his hands. One day in April, said Carmine, "Vito Cosco came to me in Milan and told me that Carlo wanted to buy four sets of camouflage military gear, four balaclavas, and four sets of boots and gave me a note with a set of measurements on it. I asked what they were for, and Vito replied we would need the stuff to kidnap and kill Lea." Carmine added that he already knew where to buy the gear, because he had bought ski masks there for another murder.

Carlo told his 'ndrina that since he was already suspected of trying to kill his wife, he couldn't risk direct involvement in this new attempt. Instead, he wanted Vito, Carmine, and Rosario Curcio to murder Lea. Carmine duly bought the clothes with cash and loaded them into a stolen red Fiat van, together with an Uzi submachine gun equipped with a silencer and two magazines that he picked up from Viale Montello, all ready for the drive down to Calabria. But the plan was foiled when Carlo, having arrived in Pagliarelle to scout the attack, found that Lea had installed a new steel door on the house where she was staying, and that the police had stationed a car outside.

Carlo returned to Milan with a new plan. He'd spoken to Denise, and she'd told him she wanted to finish school in Campobasso. Carlo had rented her and Lea an apartment there. "That was where we were going to kill Lea," said Carmine. Carlo set May 5 as the date for Lea's murder. He recruited another 'Ndranghetista, Massimo Sabatino, to pretend to be a washing-machine repairman and gain access to the flat. Sabatino was to kidnap Lea. The other men, waiting outside, would then drive her to an isolated spot in Bari in the south, where they would kill her and get rid of her body. But on May 3, Carmine had a car accident. "I was drunk and high," he said. "I was so scared." With two stitches in his head, Carmine told Carlo he wasn't well enough to take part. Rosario Curcio, too, pulled out at the last minute, saying he couldn't leave his business unattended. "Stay well out of this," he advised Carmine. When Carmine told Vito he couldn't come, Vito slapped him across the face, knocking him to the ground. In the end, Carlo dispatched Giuseppe, Vito, and Massimo, only for Massimo to screw up the kidnapping. Carlo was incandescent. "You're all useless!" he shouted at Vito. "Do I have to do everything myself?!"

Evidently, Carlo decided he did. When Lea and Denise moved back to Pagliarelle for the summer holidays, staying with Lea's grandmother, he and Carmine drove down from Milan. Carlo began seeing Denise regularly. One night, he and Carmine took Denise out to a nightclub. They stayed out until 5 A.M. Denise's phone had run out of power, and she couldn't call her mother to tell her she would be home late. "When we dropped Denise back at her grandmother's house, Lea slapped Denise because she'd been so worried," said Carmine. "When we left, Carlo turned to me and said: 'That was totally uncalled for. That bitch has to die.'"

The next day, Carlo called Vito, Carmine, and Rosario Curcio together. He said they were going to kill Lea right away, as soon as possible, and he had a new plan for how to do it. Carmine would watch Lea's grandmother's apartment. As soon as Lea left to fetch water from the square, Carmine would call Carlo on a new burner phone that Vito had given him. Carlo would then arrive on the back of a motorcycle driven by Rosario and shoot Lea dead as they drove past; then he and Rosario would head immediately for the coast, dump the gun, and wash off any powder residue in the sea. In the event, Carmine did as he was told but Lea turned out to be buying cigarettes from the village shop. She was back in her apartment before Carlo and Rosario arrived.

Carlo just couldn't seem to kill Lea. He had tried and failed three times in five months. By now, his obsession was all-consuming. Enough people inside the 'Ndrangheta knew what he was planning so that if he didn't pull it off, he risked losing status. But as August turned to September, Carmine was surprised to observe a new calmness in Carlo. The reason, Carlo confided to him one day, was that he had finally figured out how to murder his wife.

Lea was beginning to trust him again, Carlo said. She was calling him and texting him all the time. "Carlo showed me text messages from Lea in which she had written that Nini—her nickname for Denise—wanted a little brother," said Carmine. "They were messages of love. I was amazed. Later they even went out for gelato together." Carlo calculated that if he could take his wife on a late-night date to Botricello, he could take all the time he wanted. The longer he waited, the more comfortable Lea felt, the easier it would be. "Carlo was very happy with himself," said Carmine. "He said now it would be so simple to kill her. He told me Lea was trapped."

In November 2009, Lea and Denise left for Florence to attend court. Initially Carlo thought he would try to kill Lea there. Then he told Carmine he had a better idea. He had convinced Lea and Denise to spend a few days with him in Milan. Carlo said they would kill Lea in the city where she had first betrayed him. There was a symmetry to the plan that pleased Carlo. He wanted all his men in on it.

ONCE LEA AND Denise arrived in Milan, said Carmine, "we followed Lea day and night, all the time." The plan, as in Campobasso, was to wait for the right moment, then kidnap Lea, try to find out what she had told the carabinieri in 1996 and 2002, then kill her and dispose of the body to make it look as if she had disappeared to Australia.

For four days, the gang played cat and mouse with Lea around Milan's streets. On one occasion, Carmine watched Lea enter a laundry and pulled over, ready to snatch her when she emerged, before deciding there were too many security cameras and the street was too busy. Another time, Carlo took Lea out to dinner and told his men to take her when she stepped outside for a cigarette, but it was a cold night and Lea stayed put. The following night, Carlo took Lea to dinner again and told Carmine, Vito, and Rosario to wait for the two of them in a quiet street near an underpass, ready to intercept the two of them and kill her on the spot when Carlo drove past. On the way over, however, Carlo ran a red light and was stopped by a carabiniere, so Carlo called it off. That was also the night that Carmine met Lea for the first time. A few hours after he was meant to have killed her, he found himself driving over to Lea's hotel at Carlo's request and giving her a small block of hash.

Carmine and Rosario began to think Carlo was about to be thwarted one more time. Rosario, for one, still believed that Lea was Carlo's private concern and not something with which the *'ndrina* should be involved. Maybe Carlo would kill her this time. Maybe not. Right now it looked like he was dating her. Every 'Ndranghetista knew the clan had its hot and impetuous side, its machismo. But its activities were also based on cold calculation, especially when it came to matters like the murder of a clan daughter. Carlo's planning was all over the place. He affected calmness, but you could tell he was in turmoil. This was the kind of thing that could sink them all, said Rosario. He and Carmine should play no part in it.

But Carlo was insistent. The gang would have their last chance on November 24. Lea and Denise were due to take the 11:30 P.M. train back to Calabria. Carlo told his men he had come up with yet another plan. He had asked his friend Massimiliano Floreale if he could borrow the keys to Floreale's grandmother's apartment on Via San Vittore, on the edge of Milan's historic center. He had also arranged for Denise to have dinner with her cousins so that Lea and he would be alone again. Shortly after 6 P.M., Carlo picked up Denise at the Arch of Peace, near Sempione Park, and dropped her off at her cousins.' Then he set off to fetch Lea.

Around the same time, Carmine drove Vito to the apartment on San Vittore in a Volkswagen Passat he had stolen that day. When the pair arrived, Vito entered the apartment. Carmine's job was to stay outside. If anything was wrong, he was to signal by turning on his hazard lights. While waiting, Carmine called Rosario to arrange a time and a place to pick him up. But when Rosario answered, he said he couldn't come. He was with his girlfriend and she was in one of her moods. Rosario said he couldn't shake her. It was clear he was lying. "You should stay out of it, too," he told Carmine.

Just after 6:30 P.M., Carlo picked up Lea from Sempione Park. After she climbed into the Chrysler, he told her he had to drop in briefly at an apartment a few streets away. Shortly before 7 P.M., Carmine saw Carlo and Lea pull up on San Vittore in the Chrysler. The pair parked and got out. Carlo rang the bell to the apartment. Vito buzzed him in. Lea entered, then Carlo.

Fifteen minutes later, around 7:15 P.M., Carmine saw Carlo exit the apartment, walk quickly to the Chrysler, and leave. "He didn't say a word," said Carmine. Vito left the apartment seconds later and climbed into Carmine's Passat.

"We did it," said Vito, breathing heavily.

Vito gave Carmine a mobile. It was Lea's, he said. "Get rid of it right away before anyone calls," Vito instructed. Vito then left on foot.

Carlo and Vito now had to construct their alibis. Carlo also had to try to persuade Denise that Lea had just upped and left. That left it to Carmine and Rosario to get rid of Lea's body.

Carmine exited the car, ripped the SIM card out of Lea's phone, and threw it into a drain, followed by the phone battery. He threw the rest of the phone in a trash can. He got back into the Passat and phoned Rosario. Carlo had evidently called Rosario in the meantime. Rosario now said he would help after all, and Carmine drove over to pick him up.

Looking for somewhere to dispose of the body, the two men spent more than an hour trying to locate the keys to a warehouse owned by a friend in San Fruttuoso on the outskirts of Monza, about half an hour away by car. Unsuccessful, they drove back to San Vittore and ascended the stairs to the apartment. Carmine opened the door, turned on the light, "and there was Lea Garofalo's body on the ground," he said. "She had a sofa over her."

Carmine wrenched back the sofa. He scarcely recognized Lea. "She had bruises all over her face. Her mouth was bloody, like it had been crushed. There was blood all over her nose and neck and a pool of blood on the floor. The clothes across her chest were ripped. There was a green cord around her neck with which she had been strangled and which had cut into her neck so deeply that it had disappeared. I knew the cord. It was from the curtains in my apartment."

Whatever doubts Carmine and Rosario had once harbored, the ferocity of Lea's killing erased them. They trussed the body with a sheet, just in case Lea was merely unconscious. Then they lifted it into a large cardboard box they had brought along. They scrubbed the floor with hot water and rags. Then they threw the rags into the box, used duct tape to seal it, and heaved it downstairs to the ground floor. Carmine waited in the hallway with the box while Rosario went to fetch the Passat. Then the two men lifted the box out through the apartment block's front door, down the street, and into the back of the car.

With nowhere to dump the body, Carmine and Rosario drove to the home of Floreale's parents. They dropped off the keys to the apartment, left the Passat locked in the street, and went home to change clothes. A few hours later, by which time it was nearly midnight, Carmine called Floreale and asked to meet him at the apartment on San Vittore. Once both men had arrived, Carmine apologized to Floreale that the floor of his grandmother's apartment might be a little dirty. Spotting a piece of the green cord on the floor, Carmine immediately burned it in an ashtray. He then noticed a spot of blood on the sofa and told Floreale that the two of them should dump the couch in the street, which they did, next to some rubbish bins. Floreale asked no questions.

Around 1:30 A.M., Carmine went to see Carlo at the Green Dragon. Carlo said Denise was asleep at Viale Montello. Carmine updated Carlo on the cleanup. Carlo said he now had the warehouse keys and that Carmine and Rosario should take Lea's body there the next morning. Carlo and Carmine then went back to Carmine's apartment. Before they turned in, Carlo asked if he could borrow some antiseptic cream for a cut on his finger. He showed Carmine the mark.

"Lea," he said, smiling.

THE NEXT MORNING, November 25, 2009, Vito and Rosario drove Lea's body in the Passat to the warehouse outside Monza. Carmine went in a separate van. By the time he arrived, Vito had left to clock in for work at a construction site. Rosario and Carmine took Carmine's van to fill up a ten-liter jerry can with gasoline. Then they drove back and lifted the box containing Lea's body out of the Passat and into the warehouse. "We took a large metal trunk that was in the warehouse," said Carmine. "We opened the box with the body in it and shoved the body into the metal trunk. You could just see her shoes sticking out. We shook some of the gas on the body and lit it. We threw the cardboard box on top."

Carmine said he and Rosario watched Lea's body smolder for an hour. "It didn't burn well," he said. "At one point, Rosario said that maybe it wasn't working because there wasn't enough air getting in. So I took an axe and knocked several holes in the bottom of the trunk. But even with the new holes, the body burned very slowly." Carmine left Rosario and went to find Vito to ask him for advice. Unsuccessful, he returned to find that Rosario had moved the body out of the trunk with a section of scaffolding and dropped it on top of some wooden pallets, placed more wood on top, then, after adding more gas, set light to everything again. "The body was much more destroyed now," said Carmine. "The head was almost gone. There was a lot of smoke and a strong smell of burned meat. Next door, there were some gypsies burning leaves and at some point one of them, a woman, came up to the fence and asked if we could give her a pallet for their fire. I passed them one through a hole in the fence. She couldn't have failed to notice the smell of cooking meat. She didn't ask any questions."

Neither Carmine nor Rosario had slept more than a few minutes the night before, and by 1 P.M. exhaustion was setting in. "Before leaving, we put what was left of the corpse in a small pit that had already been dug in the warehouse grounds. Only a part of her chest and her legs were left. But there were many bone fragments, which we collected with a shovel and dumped in the trunk. Finally, I chopped up what was left of the body into small pieces with the axe. It was all blackened bones and flesh. Then we covered it with earth and a metal sheet."

Carmine and Rosario left to sleep for a few hours. They returned that afternoon with Vito, who sent Carmine to buy five more liters of gas. The three men then shoveled what remained of Lea's body back into the metal trunk, loaded some extra wood on it, doused it in gas once more, and set light to it a final time. They watched it burn down to the embers, broke what remained into shards by beating it with the back of the shovel, and left.

That night, Carmine caught up with Carlo in the Green Dragon. He was with Denise. Carmine told Carlo Lea's body was nearly gone. Carlo told Carmine about Denise's five-hour interview with the carabinieri. That was another headache they would have to deal with, he said.

The next morning, Carmine and Vito returned to the warehouse one last time. They scooped the ash and burned embers into a wheelbarrow, washed and scrubbed the metal trunk, and threw all the remains they could find into a nearby manhole. The following day, November 27, Carmine met the friend who owned the warehouse to return the keys to him. "Finished?" asked the friend. "All done," confirmed Carmine.

Carmine never spoke again to Carlo or any of the other men about those three days. The only time Carlo brought up the matter was in March 2010, when he heard that Denise had spoken to the carabinieri and accused him of murdering Lea. If that was true, said Carlo, "then we all know what we have to do."

CARMINE OFFERED TO show the warehouse to Tatangelo and the carabinieri forensics team. It was October 2012, almost three years since Lea had died. The forensics officers took fragments of dust from the warehouse and, using a bulldozer, dug into the soil and excavated the manhole. Over several days, they were able to gather more than three kilos of material, which they transported to their laboratory in Milan. Processing the samples took several more days. But by early November, they were able to confirm the presence of 2,812 bone fragments, as well as a dental screw with which Lea had been fitted in 2007, and microscopic parts of the necklace and braided white-and-yellow gold bracelet that Carlo had given Lea when they first met.

Denise had initially been distraught at the knowledge that she had fallen in love with the man who had disposed of her mother's body. Now she found comfort in his contrition. When Tatangelo brought Carmine and the other defendants back to court in April 2013, Denise listened to his testimony throughout. Carmine didn't spare her feelings with his descriptions of what he had done to her mother's body. But it was clear he felt compelled by devotion to her. "I want to say that this is a very difficult day for me," he said. Carmine said that in prison he had learned that family was nothing without love, and that love conquered any other allegiance. "I am not accusing ordinary people or strangers but people with whom I shared three years of my life, some of them from the same family. I made this choice out of love for Denise. Her father does not love her. Her family does not love her. But she owns my heart. It sickens me to think that I am contributing to her pain, but it is also thanks to her example that I am here today." Carmine said he was aware he was signing his own death warrant by speaking. "I know I'm can-non fodder now," he said. "Sooner or later, Carlo will kill me." Still, he added, he had no choice. "I am really in love," he said.

Carmine's confession was striking as much for the reasons why he had spoken out as what he said. The code stressed discipline and the suffocation of feeling. Hardening their hearts was how 'Ndran-ghetisti won. By outkilling and out-terrorizing, they could outlast their rivals. And yet here was Carmine, a drug dealer working for one of the 'Ndrangheta's hardest men, speaking out because he couldn't contain his tenderness. Even in the 'Ndrangheta's darkest depths, a faint light still shone.

When Lea's former lawyer Annalisa Pisano read about Carmine's testimony in the newspapers, she found herself reeling for different reasons. For three years, she had dreamed about Lea calling out her name, surrounded by flames in a warehouse. "I thought I had to be wrong," she said. "I'm not the kind of person who believes in that sort of thing. But when I heard this was how it ended for her, in the worst possible way, of course I remembered my dream right away."

Initially, Annalisa was horrified by what her nightmare might mean. Had she deserted Lea? Had Lea died calling for her help? In time, however, she came to think of it differently. According to Carmine's evidence, Lea had died long before the flames consumed her. If there was any truth to her dream, Annalisa began to think it was as a testament to the bond between her and her client. "I began thinking that, in a way, this was some sort of consolation," she said. "If her last moments really were spent thinking about me, then maybe she knew that I loved her."

XXV

G IUSEPPINA'S EVIDENCE HAD led to the arrest and trial of sixty-four members of the Pesce *'ndrina*. So detailed was it, and so numerous the charges to which it led, that the trial lasted for a further year after she testified. But shortly after 6 P.M. on May 3, 2013, after seventeen days of deliberation, the three judges filed back into court in Palmi to deliver their verdict.

Twenty-two of the accused were acquitted. Forty-two were convicted. Three-quarters of the sentences were for more than ten years. The most severe went to Giuseppina's immediate family. Her uncle, clan head Antonino Pesce, was sentenced to twenty-eight years. Giuseppina's father, Salvatore, received twenty-seven years and seven months. Her husband, Rocco Palaia, was given twenty-one years and two months; her mother, Angela Ferraro, thirteen years and five months; her sister Marina Pesce twelve years and ten months; and her brother Francesco twelve years. Ten more Pesces, two more Ferraros, and one other Palaia were convicted. Even Giuseppina's eighty-year-old grandmother, Giuseppa Bonarrigo, was sentenced to a year and eight months for receiving stolen goods. The only clemency shown was to Giuseppina, sentenced to four years and four months for mafia association, most of which she had already served.[1] "The Pesces were destroyed," said Giovanni Musarò. "There was barely a single one left walking around Rosarno."[2]

While most of the family absorbed their ruin in silence, a few

Pesces found the humiliation too much. Giuseppina's younger sister, Marina, whom Alessandra described as blessed with "the face of an angel," began howling and screaming and tearing her hair when the sentences were read out. "She completely freaked out," said Alessandra. Outside court, grandmother Bonarrigo—one of the few Pesces allowed bail—growled to reporters that real Pesce women went with their men to the grave. Not long afterward, Alessandra arrived at work at the Palace of Justice in Reggio to find a group of 'Ndrangheta wives from Rosarno staging a protest outside. "It was surreal," she said. "They had signs which read 'Shame on you,' 'The sentences are unjust,' and 'The innocent are in jail.' Some had even chained themselves to the gates." In all seriousness, apparently, Europe's biggest mafia was presenting itself as a victim of the state. Alessandra assumed the demonstration was also designed to send a message. "The idea was to show that real Calabrian women were still with the 'Ndrangheta. But I saw it as a sign of desperation, of weakness. You really need to prove something that you shouldn't need to? You really need to demonstrate something that a few years ago everyone would have taken for granted?"

The Pesces were broken and their rule of Rosarno was over. Two weeks after the verdicts, Giuseppe Pesce, the last *'ndrina* boss still on the run, turned himself in to begin his sentence of twelve years and six months. "Enough," he said as he walked into the Rosarno carabinieri station. "I'm sick of running. Let's finish it here and now."

Still, the people of Rosarno took longer to digest their new reality. The Pesces had ruled the town for decades, and most of the bosses were still alive and still sending their boys to collect *pizzo* from shopkeepers and restaurant owners. But people noticed that the price of extortion was falling. A violent reaction from the Pesces was inevitable but when it came, it was pitiful: a grenade, which slightly injured the brother of Giuseppina's boyfriend, Domenico

Costantino, when he opened a farm gate to which it was strapped. Maybe the Pesces *were* finished. It was hard to believe. But then so was the sight, little more than a year after the end of the maxi-trial, of a bulldozer driving through the front door of Giuseppina's grandmother's old house, the family's former meeting place. The authorities had confiscated the house in 2011 but had struggled for years to find a contractor willing to do the work. Now Gaetano Saffioti, a builder from Palmi, told reporters he was delighted to raze the Pesces' palace to the ground. So happy, in fact, he had done it for free. "The fight for legality is won with deeds, not words," he said.[3]

Watching as one of Europe's most powerful crime syndicates was pulled apart brick by brick, Alessandra found herself wondering whether it was the Pesces' obsession with honor that had ultimately doomed them. It was almost as if the family had died of shame. "If a woman betrays her family, it has a huge resonance," she said. "It means the family is unable to control its women." To an 'Ndrangheta crime family, it seemed there was nothing worse.

LESS THAN A month after the Pesce convictions came new verdicts in the Lea Garofalo case. Carmine's confession had exposed Carlo's lie that Lea was still alive. When proceedings reopened in Milan on April 9, 2013, Carlo made a desperate attempt to regain the initiative, announcing from the dock at the end of the first day: "President, I wish to speak!"

His lawyer, Daniel Sussman Steinberg, appeared stunned. Carlo had been clutching a piece of paper all day. Now it was clear why: he, Carlo Cosco, was breaking omertà. After a brief consultation between Carlo and Steinberg, the lawyer announced that Carlo would like to make a "spontaneous statement," and Carlo was escorted to the witness box.

Speaking in halting Italian, he read: "Madam President, and gentlemen of the court, I accept full responsibility for the murder of Lea Garofalo."

In the courtroom, nothing moved.

"I wanted to do so during the original trial but circumstances prevented me," Carlo continued. "My daughter hates me and deservedly so, because I killed her mother. But I cannot endure the shame of the accusation that I want to kill her. For me, it is inconceivable that my daughter is under anyone else's protection. From whom? I would give my life for her. Woe betide anyone who touches my daughter!"

It was an astonishing outburst. There was, after all, no reason for it. Carlo had already been convicted of Lea's murder. Legally, his confession changed nothing. But psychologically, it changed everything. Carlo, it seemed, had cracked. The hardest of the 'Ndrangheta's hard men had let his feelings show. He was an 'Ndranghetista, a *capo*, a *santista*. He was a drug smuggler, an extortionist, and a murderer. But first and foremost, it now appeared, he was a father. "I hope one day that my daughter will forgive me," said Carlo. "I live in hope of her pardon."

Others, however, perceived an altogether different message. When Carlo began reading his letter, he had scratched his ear. Then he scratched his eye. A little while later, he touched his finger to his lips. To those able to read the signals, Carlo was sending another message to the 'Ndrangheta. *Listen to me*, he was saying. *Watch me. You'll hear and see that I will say nothing.* Carlo wasn't confessing. He was offering reassurance and proposing a bargain. *I am responsible for all this*, he was saying. *Whatever the price, I will pay it. But I will not collaborate. And in return, nobody touches my daughter.*[4]

Now that Carlo had finally opened his mouth, however, he seemed to find it difficult to close. Over the next few weeks, he spoke expansively about his early married life with Lea. He explained the attack in Campobasso by saying he had asked Sabatino to beat Lea to "teach her a lesson" after she threatened his mother. He described meeting his daughter again after seven years. "*This* became my obsession," he said. "To be with my daughter, to know where she was. Not to kill her mother. I never intended that."

Carlo's testimony was all about love. Carlo loved his daughter. Carlo loved his mother. When Lea hurt Carlo's mother, Carlo had only asked Sabatino to slap Lea around a little because, really, Carlo said, he loved Lea, too.

It was the same when Carlo killed her. "I really didn't mean to," he said. "That morning, November 24, 2009, I went to get Denise and her mother in the hotel. When I saw them, I had an idea to surprise Denise. She had told me she wanted to live in Milan. So I thought I'll ask my friends for a key to their apartment to give to Denise as somewhere where she could come and go."

A few hours later, Carlo took Lea to show her the apartment on Via San Vittore where their daughter could stay. But Lea had misunderstood. "When she saw the apartment, she was angry," said Carlo. "She told me I was a liar because I told her I had nothing, no money, and actually I had an apartment. The truth was that it wasn't mine. I lived with Venturino. But Lea told me that I was an asshole and that I would never see Denise again."

Carlo caught his breath.

"I had a fit of rage, Madam President," he said. "I punched her. Twice. She fell and hit her head on the couch. I grabbed her by the shoulders and this time she fell and hit her head on the floor. Even before I saw the blood, I knew she was dead."

It was all just a terrible accident, Carlo was saying. One of those things that happened when a bighearted husband and father was overcome by emotion. "All this happened because I loved Lea," said Carlo. "If I hadn't loved her, nothing like this would ever have happened. But when she threatened me with never seeing my daughter again, I couldn't see my love for her anymore.

Because I love Denise above all else. For me that's the greatest torment. Denise must know that I care for her. She must know the truth." Trying to rationalize his client's intervention, Steinberg, the lawyer, described Carlo as split by a "lacerating internal struggle," which prompted him to lash out at Lea but acquitted him of premeditated murder.

Prosecutor Marcello Tatangelo was unconvinced. "You're only talking now because Lea Garofalo's body has been found," he said. Carlo hadn't shown remorse at the time, he added. Quite the opposite. Days after Lea's murder, Carlo had hosted a party in Pagliarelle to toast her death under the guise of an eighteenth birthday party for Denise. But Tatangelo was curious nonetheless. "Why speak up now?" he asked.

"Eh," said Carlo with a shrug. "People said things that weren't right. You mentioned acid. You said I hated my daughter's mother. How could I let that go?"

Unmoved by Carlo's protestations of love, on May 29, 2013, appeals judge Anna Conforti, another of the most senior women in Italy's judiciary, confirmed life sentences against Carlo and his brother Vito, Rosario Curcio, and Massimo Sabatino.[5] Carmine's sentence was reduced to twenty-five years. Giuseppe Cosco was acquitted but remained in prison, since by now he was also serving an unrelated ten-year sentence for drug trafficking. Five months later, using evidence given by Lea seventeen years earlier, seventeen 'Ndranghetisti were arrested in Pagliarelle, Petilia Policastro, and Crotone, charged with seven murders, possessing illegal weapons, and drug dealing—charges that related to the clan feud that had raged in the Calabrian hills between 1989 and 2007.[6]

Outside court on the day Carlo's life sentence was confirmed, Enza told a crowd of supporters, "Denise thanks you all. That you are all here gives her strength." Denise could now finally bury her mother, added Enza, and the funeral would be in Milan. "This is the city where she was killed," said Enza. "But it's also the place where everyone finally mobilized to fight the mafia."

ONLY MARIA CONCETTA Cacciola's case remained unresolved.

Partial closure came in Palmi in early July 2013, in the same courtroom where the Pesces had been humbled. Giuseppina testified in Concetta's case, breaking down when asked to describe her friend and recalling how "terrified" Concetta was of her brother Giuseppe. "She told me if you knew him, then you knew he could kill her," she said. "She was forbidden to leave the house, to go out, or to have friends. She never went to a party. She was never allowed to have fun."

On July 13, 2013, Concetta's father, mother, and brother were found guilty of provoking her suicide. Michele Cacciola was given six years; Giuseppe, five; and her mother, Anna Rosalba Lazzaro, two.

If Alessandra and Giovanni were unhappy with the lightness of the sentences, the judge was, too. "The court had started doubting that Concetta's death was suicide," said prosecutor Giuseppe Creazzo. The judge indicated he had been dissatisfied at being unable to impose the kind of sentence that a conviction for murder would allow. "So he sent the case back to the prosecutors for them to investigate further if it was murder."

Sandro Dolce, who had interviewed Lea Garofalo in 2002 and was now assistant prosecutor in Palmi, was ordered to investigate the Cacciolas' two lawyers, Gregorio Cacciola and Vittorio Pisani. After seizing their computer terminals, he found proof that Concetta's statement had been through various drafts on their computers before she even returned to Rosarno—proof of a conspiracy to force her to retract. In February 2014, the two lawyers were arrested. On

September 8, Vittorio Pisani sent word that he wanted to confess. Alessandra and Giovanni had him moved to the *pentiti* prison at Paliano. They spoke to him a few days later.

Pisani told the two prosecutors that he had started working for the Cacciolas in June 2011, a few months before Concetta died. He said the family had initially approached him because they suspected Concetta was having an affair with a policeman. They wanted him to use his contacts on the force to investigate. "It was an abnormal request," said Pisani, "but I took it because I had money troubles and I didn't want to lose the chance of working for a family like the Cacciolas."

Later that month the carabinieri discovered one of the Cacciolas' bunkers, then a second. The Cacciolas and Belloccos were convinced the information had come from Concetta. The Belloccos insisted that she be made to return to Rosarno and retract. By this time, the Cacciolas, impatient for a result, had begun threatening Pisani. When Concetta returned to Rosarno, Pisani was under no illusion that she, too, was being coerced. On August 12, he witnessed Concetta record her retraction. When she died eight days later, he knew the family was responsible. For a year and a half, Pisani had tried to bury his conscience. The Cacciolas and the Belloccos were unimpressed, however, and Pisani became convinced he was in danger. "I was scared," he told the prosecutors. "And I needed to be able to look myself in the mirror again."

"Tell us, why was so much attention paid to this one woman?" asked Giovanni.

"As a warning," replied Pisani. "It was to say: 'Enough now.'"

The identity of Concetta's killer remained a mystery. But the case was still open and the prosecutors were inching closer. On July 30, 2015, the Court of Appeal in Reggio Calabria increased Michele's sentence to eight years and eight months, Giuseppe's to seven years and four months, and Anna Rosalba Lazzaro's to five years and six months.

XXVI

In October 2014, Alessandra and her husband packed up their tiny apartment in the roof of the carabinieri barracks in Reggio and moved back to Milan. Alessandra had been promoted to deputy public prosecutor in Italy's financial capital. Most of the rest of the anti-mafia team had already left Calabria. Giuseppe Pignatone, Michele Prestipino, Giovanni Musarò, and Renato Cortese, the flying squad chief, were all taking up more senior positions in Rome.

The reassignments made sense. Some of the biggest 'Ndrangheta clans had been smashed, especially on the stronghold of the Gioia Tauro plain. The cost to the prosecutors of their success was an increased threat to their lives. Alessandra, who like Pignatone and Prestipino had lived inside close protection for years, knew she had added new names to the list of those who wanted to kill her. Of those she knew about, there was Giuseppina's father, Salvatore, who had threatened her in court, and Concetta's mother, Anna Rosalba Lazzaro, who had been bugged cursing Alessandra as "that bitch, that bastard bitch. I want her dead!"

Giovanni Musarò was another prosecutor now forced to make peace with the idea that he was fighting for a nation in which he no longer really lived. In 2010, in an unrelated case, Giovanni had ordered the arrest of the entire Gallico 'ndrina in Palmi, a total of thirty-two 'Ndranghetisti, including an eighty-four-year-old grandmother. Subsequently, clan head Domenico Gallico suffered the humiliation of watching his 'ndrina turn their backs to him in court. In

October 2012, Gallico asked to meet Giovanni in his cell in Viterbo prison, north of Rome. Giovanni was mystified, but agreed nonetheless. "It was a very strange situation," he told a parliamentary inquiry later. "I was shown to a very small room. When Gallico entered, he was alone without an escort and uncuffed. He came around to my side of the desk and said: '*Dottore*, what a pleasure that we can finally meet face-to-face. May I have the honor of shaking your hand?'"

When Giovanni extended his right hand, Gallico pretended to do the same, then with his left hit Giovanni across the face, breaking his nose. "I fell from the chair," said Giovanni. "As I lay there up against the wall, he kicked and punched me maybe fifty or sixty times." During the attack, Giovanni remembered thinking: *If I don't block his punches, he's going to break my neck. He's going to kill me.* After thirty seconds, several guards pulled Gallico off, kicking and screaming. "Are you crazy?" asked one, pinning him to the floor. Gallico pointed at Giovanni. "Ask him what he did to me and my family!" he howled. "Ask him what he did to me!"

Bodyguards were posted outside Giovanni's door in the hospital that night. They had not left his side since. Not long afterward Marcello Fondacaro, an 'Ndrangheta informer, told Giovanni that the same Bellocco boss who had ordered Concetta be made to retract had also made a plan to kill Giovanni and his boss, Prestipino. "The Belloccos thought Maria Concetta Cacciola's retraction would have ended the story," said Giovanni. "They were very angry when that didn't happen. Giuseppe Bellocco, in particular, was known as a very dangerous human being who held grudges and harbored great resentment." According to Fondacaro, Bellocco planned to ambush Giovanni and Prestipino with gunmen and explosives as the two prosecutors drove to court. "He knew I drove to Palmi twice a week during a trial I was dealing with," said Giovanni. "He knew the route, the color of my armored car and my escort car, and that

Prestipino would have been following in his armored car, with another escort car with him. He'd even asked permission from the Gallicos to carry out the attack." The double assassination failed only because the trial in Palmi was unexpectedly adjourned. And while, to some, gunmen *and* explosives might have seemed like overkill, to the prosecutors it underlined how serious the 'Ndrangheta were about revenge. "In Calabria they do it well or not at all," said Giovanni.

It was time to get out. None of the anti-mafia prosecutors or their families could expect to live a normal life again. It was, in a way, their own life sentence. But Alessandra, for one, was finding inspiration from an unexpected source. "Giuseppina knows what she did is another death sentence," she said. "Her betrayal has to be punished with death and it has to be her brother, the same blood, who kills her to restore the family honor. And one day, he will get out." But Alessandra said it had been years since she had seen Giuseppina doubt herself. "For Giuseppina," she said, "what she did was an act of love toward her children." In the end, the contest between The Family and her own family had been no contest at all. "She's fine," said Alessandra. "Actually, I think she's happy."

FROM THE MOMENT 150 years earlier when a group of southern criminals met a band of revolutionary freemasons in jail and decided to veneer their thuggish criminality with myth and legend, the 'Ndrangheta had shown itself to be nothing if not adaptable. Calabria would always be the 'Ndrangheta's homeland. There were still plenty of *'ndrine* to pursue there and the trafficking, extortion, corruption, and murder would continue. But as the prosecutors' Calabrian campaign against the 'Ndrangheta began to wind down, new surveillance evidence made clear that the center of gravity for Italian organized crime was moving to the north of the country and even further afield. The change made sense. Italy was the only country in the world that even had a law of mafia association. Few other countries allowed such intrusive surveillance. Plenty of them made it far easier to legitimize criminal wealth by buying assets like bonds, shares, property, and businesses.

And if the 'Ndrangheta was moving, it was also changing shape. The Calabria prosecutors had made a point of mapping and destroying the 'Ndrangheta's command structure. For the organization, the intelligent response was to dismantle it. Prosecutors began reporting the emergence of a more informal, decentralized, diffuse group, a loose association, an ad hoc gathering, even something as ephemeral as a state of mind. They likened its penetration of Italy's legitimate economy and, beyond it, Frankfurt, London, and New York to liquid poured on a sponge.

And you couldn't squeeze the world. In their new positions, many of the prosecutors found their time in Calabria quickly began to feel like the golden years. Like the swordfish hunters of the Strait of Messina, the Calabrian prosecutors had harpooned a monster and forced it to the surface. But now the creature was disappearing back into the deep, vanishing into the folds of an international financial system that not only tolerated secrecy but, in the case of the $20 trillion offshore banking industry, actively depended on it. The prosecutors often felt like they were in a losing race against time. Hundreds of billions of 'Ndrangheta euros and dollars had been already successfully laundered beyond reach or reproach. And to the prosecutors' frustration, in the world of frictionless global money movements, their fastidious objections were often viewed as pedantry. Franco Roberti, head of Italy's anti-mafia and antiterrorism office, lamented the lack of cooperation his investigators received in London or New York or Hong Kong, let alone the centers of secret banking on paradise islands around the world. Foreign governments "don't want to believe that the problem of the 'Ndrangheta is their problem, too," he said. "They want to believe that their money doesn't stink." Roberti was pessimistic about the chances of beating a global mafia in a world where politics was subordinate to business. "Business dictates and politicians follow, and this has facilitated the absorption of mafia money and influence around the world," he said. A world in which any idea of the common good had been replaced with greed and yawning inequality was one, said Roberti, whose gates were wide open to mafiosi. He called it the Snow White syndrome. "Nobody wants to look in the mirror," he said.

That kind of thinking could lead a prosecutor down a dark path, as Alessandra knew. A world where financial and political scandal had become depressingly routine was one in which it was all too easy to conclude that what the prosecutors were really fighting was the night in human nature. The 'Ndrangheta wouldn't be able to corrupt business and politics unless businessmen and politicians already had the potential for it. Hadn't the serpent admirers of Milan understood centuries ago that enlightenment and darkness walked hand in hand? And if family itself was a form of corruption, as the mafia posited, then what chance did legality have in any country, let alone Italy? "We can't fight the 'Ndrangheta just by putting people in jail," said Alessandra. "We need a cultural change. We need a change in people's minds." The prosecutors had no way to assist that effort. Barricaded behind their steel doors and bulletproof windows, all they could do was watch.

NONE OF THAT would diminish what had been accomplished in Calabria. The 'Ndrangheta was reeling. However nimble they were, the clans could not adjust to betrayal. "That's an unacceptable issue for them," said Prestipino. "It's unbearable. It threatens their entire existence." The effect of the Calabrian campaign would be felt for generations. Prestipino's experience in Sicily had taught him that once a mafia's invincibility cracked, the floodgates opened. In Sicily, hundreds of mafiosi had come forward to testify. "They never recovered," he said.

In the hill villages and small towns of Calabria, the 'Ndrangheta was still ruthlessly punishing disloyalty. In February 2012, a thirty-year-old man called Fabrizio Pioli who was having an extramarital affair with a mafioso's daughter was beaten to death with sticks outside Rosarno. In August 2013, Francesca Bellocco and Domenico Cacciola, whose affair had scandalized two of Rosarno's biggest crime families, disappeared. Such violent reprisals discouraged the flow of *pentiti*. But a steady stream was under way. By the end of 2015, the judiciary could count 164 *pentiti* and twenty-nine witnesses who had testified against the 'Ndrangheta. That was hardly a cascade. But given that five years earlier even a single 'Ndrangheta *pentito* was almost unheard of, it felt significant.

Perhaps most remarkable was the number of 'Ndrangheta wives following the three women's example: fifteen, more than had ever testified in four decades of Cosa Nostra trials. Di Bella's youth court, in particular, had become a magnet for dissident 'Ndrangheta women. As sons—more than thirty by the end of 2016—turned against their fathers, mothers chose their children over their husbands. "It's a phenomenon we didn't predict," said di Bella. "Many women realize these measures are not punishing their children but protecting them. They come secretly and ask us to send their children far away." One woman who wrote to di Bella in confidence in November 2015 was typical. Her husband had been convicted of murder. Her father, cousin, and eleven-year-old nephew had all been killed. Her two teenage boys, she wrote, "are rebellious and violent, hanging around with bad guys, and fascinated by the 'Ndrangheta and guns. My son Rosario thinks jail is an honor that will win him respect. Please send my children away. The thought tears me apart but it is the only solution. In my family, there is no one—no one—I can trust."

This first act of rebellion by an 'Ndrangheta mother sometimes grew into something more. Di Bella said the youth courts could add another ten 'Ndrangheta women to the fifteen who had testified in the adult courts. As a result of his success, di Bella's program was being rolled out across Italy. It helped that at the same time, such global figures as Malala Yousafzai and Michelle Obama were making women's emancipation a worldwide issue. Di Bella found himself wondering whether Italy might have finally found its way to a mafia-free future. "We're opening up these disagreements inside families that were previously thought to be impenetrable," he said. "We're a crack in the monolith, a light in the dark, a bright threat to the whole mafia family system."

At times, the momentum was palpable. In June 2014, Pope Francis further splintered the mafia's consensus when he traveled to Calabria and, before a crowd of a hundred thousand, excommunicated all mafiosi, denouncing the 'Ndrangheta as an example of "the adoration of evil and contempt for the common good." Francis later followed his decree by condemning the Camorra in Naples and visiting *pentiti* at Paliano. The change felt seismic, said di Bella, and to the 'Ndrangheta more than anyone. "They can feel the ground moving under their feet," he said.

IN THEIR NEW offices in Milan and Rome, asked by their staff how it had been in the south, Alessandra and Giovanni would tell stories about Calabria.

Giovanni's favorite tale was about hope. He'd been listening to wiretaps of the Cacciolas one day, he said, when he heard them discussing a family called the Secolos, whom the Belloccos were gradually ruining through loan-sharking. It reminded him of a conversation he had had with Concetta. She had told him about the bind the Secolos were in and how the matriarch, Stefania Secolo, had asked Concetta if she could help them. Concetta had asked her father to intervene but he had dismissed her pleas. Giovanni wanted to know more. "So I called Stefania Secolo in for a meeting," he said. "And in the days before she was due to come in, we also began listening to her phone. Her brothers and everyone else were saying to her: 'Don't say anything! Don't honor the memory of someone who cannot come back to life! Don't be a hero! Heroes die!' But on February 28, 2012, she came to me and told me exactly what happened, and with her evidence, we arrested the Belloccos and put them in jail." Giovanni sighed. It was "such a beautiful story," he said. "Stefania Secolo spoke out because her friend Concetta had reminded her how a person should behave and how they could be free. Her friend had been killed for it. Yet Stefania still spoke." From his five years in Calabria, "that's the day that stays with me." There was all the hope in the world in that one day, he said.

Alessandra was happy to talk about Giuseppina. But when people asked, she would often tell them the story of Giuseppina Multari. Just before Christmas in 2012, a few months after Giuseppina Pesce had resumed her cooperation and was preparing to testify against her family, a letter addressed to her arrived at the Palace of Justice in Reggio. The writer "expressed her support for Giuseppina and urged her to believe in the institutions of the state and the people around her," said Alessandra. "The letter read: 'Go for it! Be brave!'" It was signed "Giuseppina Multari, protected witness."

"I was curious," said Alessandra. "Who was this woman who had sent this very special letter? She was in the witness program and I'd never even heard of her." Alessandra searched through the Palace of Justice archives, looking for records of a Multari. Eventually she found a letter Multari had written to the carabinieri in 2006 and some statements she had made in 2008. Alessandra read how

Giuseppina Multari was Concetta's cousin by marriage. Her husband, Antonio Cacciola, was notorious in the *'ndrina* for dipping into his own drug supplies. He was also having an affair. One night in November 2005, Multari and Antonio had a fight, Antonio stormed out—and Giuseppina never saw him again. "Officially it was a suicide, but Giuseppina Multari was convinced his family had killed him," said Alessandra. "And after her husband's death, she was kept at home by his family like a slave. She could not go out. She could not drop off her children at school. She was only allowed to go to the cemetery."

One night, the Cacciola men left the house to go to a wedding. Finally alone, Giuseppina fled. She walked to the coast. "She was going to drown herself in the sea," said Alessandra. "But suddenly her phone went off, and it was her brother Angelo. She told him she was trying to kill herself. He came and found her." By the time Angelo arrived, his sister was suffering from hypothermia. He drove her to the hospital. When Angelo asked her why she was trying to commit suicide, she told him about the Cacciolas and the beatings and how she was living in a virtual prison. "I am going to do something for you," Angelo replied. "I am going to help you."

"The brother left," said Alessandra. "And *he* never came back."

After six more months confined to her in-laws' home, Giuseppina managed to sneak a letter to the carabinieri. As a result, in 2008, she made several statements against the Cacciolas and was taken into witness protection. "But no one ever acted on her evidence!" exclaimed Alessandra. "I decided to go to see her. And when she saw me, she burst into tears. 'I've been waiting six years for someone to come and talk to me,' she said."

Giuseppina described the Rosarno clans and the Cacciolas' empire in a series of statements that eventually ran to several hundred pages. A dozen 'Ndranghetisti were later convicted. But what was especially striking about the case, said Alessandra, was Giuseppina

Multari's faith in herself. Even though the state had let her down, she had held on to her conviction and her courage. "The best part?" said Alessandra. "Some of the men who kept her in that house are now serving time for slavery." It was, she added, a medieval conviction for medieval men.

IT WAS LEA's story above all, however, that moved Italy. If Concetta represented tragedy, and Giuseppina Pesce embodied resilience, then Lea was both. Here was a woman born into the mafia who had tried all her life to escape it. Trapped even deeper by marriage, she discovered the strength to fight in her love for her daughter, before being let down by the state, and trapped by a husband pretending to fall in love with her again. It was an epic melodrama of such unbelievable twists and turns that people seemed to turn up at the commemorations of her life that were held across the country from 2013 just to check that what they had heard was true.

There was something else, though. After her death, a number of pictures of Lea and Denise found their way into the newspapers. There was Lea smiling through long, dark hair, or sitting on a rock by the beach with Denise on her knee, or holding Denise aloft in a city piazza, or smoking a cigarette in sunglasses on the beach, or at the stove in Bergamo on the run with Denise. People began to feel they knew Lea. Before them was a whole life, from girlhood to marriage to motherhood, from love to fear, in the city and on the beach, in the north and the south. In time, Lea's story became one of the few ever to truly unite Italy. Posters of her face became a staple on walls across the country. There were documentaries and anti-mafia rallies, marches and newspaper profiles, plays and books and a television movie. Parks, bridges, piazzas, and roads were named after her. Plaques were erected in Bergamo and Boiano and next to the warehouse outside Monza where she was buried. In Milan, a plot was selected for Lea's remains in the Cimitero Monumentale beside the city's most illustrious citizens.[1] A monument was erected in Petilia depicting a ball splitting a rock in two. In his speech unveiling the statue, the mayor declared Petilia would be forever after a beacon to "women of courage" across Italy.

On October 19, 2013, nearly four years after her death, thousands of Italians gathered on a chilly morning in Milan to remember Lea in the city where, as an expectant mother, she had once hoped for a new life. Buses rented to transport mourners from Pagliarelle and Petilia arrived ominously empty. Among the crowd bearing flowers and waving flags decorated with Lea's face, however, were hundreds of Calabrians who had made their own way. Enza Rando met one 'Ndrangheta wife who, following the service, walked immediately into a carabinieri station to make a statement against her family. "She said: 'Lea taught me to be brave,'" said Enza. "'Lea taught me to have courage.'"

Alessandra, unable to attend such a public event, watched on television. Lea's coffin was carried through the streets around Sempione Park by pallbearers who included the mayors of Milan and Petilia, and Don Luigi Ciotti, head of Libera. It was the size of the crowd that most caught Alessandra's attention. The roots of the 'Ndrangheta went back to 1861 and the unification of Italy. Everything that had followed since had sprung from that first refusal to accept an Italian nation-state. As a result, Italy had never really come together. It had always been north and south, state and mafia, Piedmontese, Lombardian, and Venetian against Campanian, Calabrian, and Sicilian. And it was in those rifts that malevolence and murder had thrived. And yet here, on the streets of Milan, was all Italy together. This was what a modern, lawful, united nation looked like. Was it possible that in the funeral of a mafioso's daughter there were glimpses of a nation finally made whole?

Lea's coffin was placed on a stand in front of the crowd. Over it

hung a banner that read "I see, I hear, I speak," a slogan that, alongside images of Lea, Giuseppina, and Concetta, had become a fixture
at anti-mafia rallies. Don Luigi then addressed a eulogy to Lea. She
needn't worry, he told her. Denise now had a family of thousands
to look after her. "Your heart and your conscience will forever be
wellsprings of freedom," he said. "You were a martyr to truth. Your
spirit will never die."

Don Luigi was followed by Denise.[2] She had been only a girl of
seventeen when, a few streets away, her mother had disappeared
into the night. Now she was a woman of twenty-one and a government witness who had sent her father and boyfriend to jail for murdering her mother. And finally she was able to say her good-byes.
The crowd stood in silence. Denise, close by but hidden from view
on her bodyguards' insistence, spoke to the crowd through loud-
speakers. "Today is a very difficult day for me," she began. After
a long pause, in a gentle voice, she spoke to her mother. "Thank
you for all you did for me," she said. "Thank you for giving me a
better life. Everything that happened, everything you did, I know
now that you did it all for me and I will never stop thanking you
for it." Denise's voice was cracking. There was no revenge here, no
honor, and no justice. There was just a daughter standing before her
mother, telling her she loved her. "Ciao, Mama," Denise said.

ACKNOWLEDGMENTS

AN EXTRAORDINARY SELECTION of people tried to suppress the story of *The Good Mothers*, and many of them did their best to frustrate the reporting and writing of this book. As with any investigation into the mafia, the 'Ndrangheta's violent enforcement of omertà ensured that many of its leading characters were unavailable. By the time I heard their stories, two of the three Good Mothers, Lea Garofalo and Maria Concetta Cacciola, were dead, killed for their courage in standing up to the organization; the third, Giuseppina Pesce, was unreachable in witness protection. Most mafiosi and those intimidated by them were also unwilling to speak. On those occasions when subjects did talk, their answers to my questions often contained warnings or veiled threats. That the book exists at all is due to the courage and determination of a rare few.

Foremost among those who stepped forward to be counted is my agent at Pew Literary, Patrick Walsh. Patrick was the first to spot the potential of this story, and he remains the greatest champion for whom a writer could ask, somehow combining charm and warmth with sage advice and commercial precision. Patrick forms an unbeatable team with Luke Speed, my film agent at Curtis Brown, who immediately saw the promise of *The Good Mothers* and whose consequent effect on my professional life has been nothing less than transformational. Arabella Pike at HarperCollins in London and David Highfill at HarperCollins in New York were both everything a writer wishes for in an editor: gracious in their welcome, generous in the time they allowed me to write, firm in their support against saboteurs, efficient and insightful in their editing—and providers of delicious lunches. In London, Katherine Patrick at HarperCollins UK organized a publicity campaign that could have conquered worlds, Leo Nickolls created the fantastic cover, and Iain Hunt ushered the final text to publication with the skill and collegial civility that has led to his universal acknowledgment as one of the best in the business.

In the U.S., Chloe Moffett's stoicism, precision, efficiency, and unflappable good humor kept me on track when many others might have given up. David Palmer's forensic eye for text saved me from several embarrassments. Lauren Janiec and Libby Collins attracted and corralled extraordinary press interest. And Tavia Kowalchuk made sure every bookseller and book enthusiast, library, and literary institution knew the story of *The Good Mothers*. My deep thanks, too, to publisher, Liate Stehlik.

Elsewhere, Tessa Ross and Juliette Howell at House Productions, who bought the film and television rights before there was even a proposal, let alone a book, have my everlasting gratitude for their brave and early support. I owe a large debt to Nick Trautwein at the *New Yorker* for championing an excerpt in the magazine, as well as gentle, meticulous, and insightful editing; Dorothy Wickenden and David Remnick for their enthusiasm; and Fabio Bertoni, Nick Niarchos, Stephania Taladrid, and Francesca Magnani for their forensic diligence. Thank you also to Philip Gourevitch for the introduction.

I first heard about the women of *The Good Mothers* on my first reporting trip to Italy (for a different story) when Laura Aprati, an Italian journalist whom I had asked to set up a couple of interviews, insisted that as part payment I watch a one-woman play she had written with Enrico Fierro. The play, *O cu nui o cu iddi* (*With Us or with Them*), was being staged entirely in Italian to an audience of teenagers in a run-down, heavily mafia area on the outskirts of

Rome. I picked up on the drama and the tragedy but little more. My confusion—and the audience's—was only heightened when Laura pushed me onstage to answer a few questions through an interpreter about my impression of the play, the mafia, and the past, present, and future of Italy.

Chastened by this exposure of my ignorance, I returned to my guesthouse knowing only the name of the woman on whose life the play was based: Maria Concetta Cacciola. Thus began the process of research and reporting that led me to her story, and those of Giuseppina Pesce and Lea and Denise Garofalo. There was a lot to read. Though the Italian press initially missed the story of the Garofalos, it later made up for its inattention with blanket coverage of Carlo Cosco's trial. By then, Lea and Denise were becoming heroes to a generation of young Italian activists. The arrest of the powerful Pesce clan, by contrast, was a big story from the start, especially when Giuseppina began testifying. As the press watched the unraveling of the Gioia Tauro 'Ndrangheta, Concetta's death also received significant coverage.

Still, many of the newspaper reports were frustratingly brief and incomplete. There are sound reasons for this: Italian journalists who report on the mafia in any depth are routinely forced to seek protection from the authorities. In addition, the 'Ndrangheta is a phenomenon whose scale and threat has only recently begun to be understood. Uncovering the detail of the criminal conspiracy that lies behind the story of *The Good Mothers* and exploring the history of the 'Ndrangheta required a painstaking two and a half years rummaging through the archives of the Italian judiciary, accumulating, translating, and assessing tens of thousands of pages of court documents. These were then supplemented by lengthy and repeated interviews with the participants as well as historians and academics.

Laura was my guide throughout this process, along with Giuliana Clementi, the interpreter who first translated my ramblings that night at Laura's play. Laura's deep knowledge and resourcefulness left few stones unturned. Giuliana's pinpoint and nuanced translation in a world that the 'Ndrangheta would prefer to remain as murky as possible was essential to the accuracy of my understanding. I am forever grateful for their assistance. I also benefited immensely from the insight and generosity of Enrico Fierro, Laura's professional partner for many years and an encyclopedia of mafia knowledge; and from the generosity and expertise of Lucio Musolino, whose contacts in Calabria are unparalleled and who continues to report daily on the 'Ndrangheta in the face of numerous threats to his life. I also owe deep thanks to Teo Butturini, Marta Clinco, and Francesco Creazzo for fixing and translating.

I would also like to acknowledge the generous assistance of Alessandra Cerreti, whose insight into the importance of women to the 'Ndrangheta and how feminism was the key to bringing down Europe's most powerful mafia informed the theme of *The Good Mothers*. Alessandra allowed me to interview her for a total of eight hours over the course of a year.

The openness of the Italian justice system, and its tradition of prosecutors presenting their entire case in official documents that contain transcripts of wiretaps and surveillance videos, as well as transcripts of interviews with key suspects and witnesses, is a treasure trove for any journalist, and those legal and evidential documents form the backbone of this book. As well as to Alessandra, I am indebted to numerous prosecutors in Calabria and across Italy for their assistance in providing the relevant documents and agreeing to lengthy interviews, particularly Franco Roberti, Michele Prestipino, Giovanni Musarò, Giuseppe Lombardo, Sandro Dolce, Giuseppe Creazzo, Roberto di Bella, Federico Cafiero de Raho, Marcello Tatangelo, and Gaetano Paci, and, despite a cold that had taken away his voice, the indomitable Nicola Gratteri. Renato Cortese took time out of his busy schedule to answer my questions. Raffaele Grassi, Reggio Calabria's steadfast police chief, was unfailingly solicitous on my visits to the city and granted me a rare and astonishing tour of the giant floor on the top of the police headquarters entirely given over to wiretapping, surveillance, and bugging. Like many on the Gioia Tauro *piano*, I am also indebted to Antonino de Masi and Antonino Bartuccio, mayor of Rizziconi, who continue to speak out—to me and others—despite the repeated threats to their lives.

Among the lawyers who also assisted me, particular thanks are due to Annalisa Pisano, Lea Garofalo's only contact in the outside world for many years, who broke seven years of silence to speak tearfully and honestly to me in a quiet corner of a courthouse café in Catanzaro. Vincenza "Enza" Rando, one of my first interviewees, dealt patiently with my frequently misjudged questions. Adriana Fiormonti, Giuseppina Pesce's lawyer, was charmingly instructive on her client and the workings of the 'Ndrangheta. Jules Munro at Simpsons Solicitors in Sydney, Beth Silfin at HarperCollins, and Nicola Landolfi in Rome all provided crucial legal advice.

I drew on a host of academic research in my investigation of the 'Ndrangheta. Among those who were especially helpful were Enzo Ciconte in Rome, Ernesto Savona in Milan, and John Dickie and Anna Sergi in London. Anyone interested in pursuing this subject could do worse than to peruse the considerable back catalog belonging to these four experts.

I also relied on a small army of readers to proof and offer suggestions, all of which were invaluable. My deep thanks to Max Askew, Colin Perry, and members of southern England's best book club: Venetia Ellvers, Serena Freeland, Cleodie Gladstone, Wiz Hok, Susie Honey, Cheryl Myers, Millie Powell, Louisa Robertson, Amanda Sinclair, Sally Turvill, and Anna Worthington. Deep thanks as ever to Tess, who read every draft, endured countless discussions, and offered limitless, incisive advice. None of it works without you, Tess.

To the many lawyers and various others on several continents who tried to frustrate this book—and whose tactics bore a marked resemblance to those employed by the 'Ndrangheta—I hope you can still enjoy it. A number of you made the argument that this was not my book to write, because I was neither Italian nor a woman. As someone who has worked as a foreign correspondent for more than two decades, I know the pitfalls of the profession only too well. The outsider is hindered by ignorance, language, and expense. A very fair question is often: who are you to tell this tale? My own view is that these obstacles are formidable but not insurmountable; that distance can sometimes lend perspective; and that empathy, imagining yourself in the shoes of another, is the duty of any writer and the basis of any good writing. If the story of *The Good Mothers* tells us anything, it is that to define human capacity by the accident of gender or skin color, religion, or nationality, is folly. The entire world gained because a small group of southern Italian women sought a different destiny from the one others had marked out for them. It is their example, above all else, that has been my guide in these pages.

NOTES

THE STORY OF *The Good Mothers* relies heavily on official court documents released during the trials of those charged with the murders of Lea Garofalo and Maria Concetta Cacciola, and the cases that followed Giuseppina Pesce's revelations. The Italian justice system is an invaluable tool for the reporter trying to reconstruct a story after the fact. At each stage of the trial process, the prosecutor will release, in printed form, all the evidence he or she intends to rely on in court, including all transcripts of tapped phone conversations and other intercepted communications. These documents are detailed and comprehensive: each set of trial documents for Giuseppina Pesce ran to more than one thousand pages, and more than two thousand in the latter stages of the process. They also carry an unimpeachable legal privilege, as do the trial transcripts. It's hard to imagine a legal system where more trouble is taken to ensure that justice is seen to be done.

For each of the three Good Mothers, as well as for other cases that feature in their story, my method was to digest the official documentation, then follow it up with supplementary interviews with the protagonists. Italy's anti-mafia prosecutors were unfailingly accommodating, and most direct quotations from prosecutors in the text are from those interviews, though I have marked the source where it might be unclear or where that is not the case. (A full list of those prosecutors who assisted me, along with my thanks, can be found in the acknowledgments.) Mafiosi, 'Ndranghetisti, and their legal representatives tended to be less forthcoming: such are the restrictions of omertà. I also interviewed a number of experts—academics, law enforcement officers, judges, lawyers, politicians, officials. Again, any quotations that appear in the text should be assumed to be sourced to my interviews unless I have indicated otherwise. Finally, as part of my research, I read thousands of articles in the Italian and international press, as well as a slew of books and academic articles, and I have indicated in the text where I have relied on them for points of information.

I

1 This chapter is based on official transcriptions of Denise Cosco's testimony in court on September 20 and October 13, 2011, judicial documents from the murder trial that followed, and transcripts of her interviews with the carabinieri on November 25, 2009, and March 5, 2010. I also conducted several supplementary interviews, notably with Denise's lawyer, Vincenza Rando; Lea's lawyer, Annalisa Pisano; and prosecutors Alessandra Cerreti, Giuseppe Creazzo, and Sandro Dolce.

II

1 Interview with the author, May 2016, Pagliarelle.
2 Estimates of the 'Ndrangheta's earnings vary wildly. This is partly because the 'Ndrangheta is such a secretive organization, partly because it is laterally structured, giving no one boss much knowledge of the 'Ndrangheta's finances beyond his own 'ndrina. Some variation is also accounted for by Italian researchers' habit of focusing only on revenues from inside Italy. Finally, some of the more spectacular figures seem to be explained by researchers, journalists, and prosecutors wishing to draw attention to the group.

Transcrime, a respected criminal research unit run by Professor Ernesto Savona, whom I interviewed at his offices at the Catholic University in Milan, estimates the 'Ndrangheta's annual earnings at $3.49 billion. In a paper published in *Global Crime* in 2014 ("Mythical Numbers and the Proceeds of Organized Crime: Estimating the Mafia Proceeds in Italy"), Transcrime also estimated 'Ndrangheta annual earnings to be in the range of $2.5 billion to $4 billion.

Most other estimates of the 'Ndrangheta's earnings are far higher, in the $40 billion to $80 billion range. In December 2008, for instance, the U.S.

consul general to Naples, Patrick Truhn, returned from a fact-finding tour to Calabria to file a report that began with the arresting opening statement: "If it were not part of Italy, Calabria would be a failed state. The 'Ndrangheta organized crime syndicate controls vast portions of its territory and economy and accounts for at least three percent of Italy's GDP (probably much more) through drug trafficking, extortion and usury" (Wikileaks released the cable: https://www.wikileaks.org/plusd/cables/08NAPLES96_a.html).

The figure of $100 billion comes from anti-mafia prosecutor Giuseppe Lombardo, who is based in Reggio Calabria and has studied the 'Ndrangheta's money, domestic and international, for a decade. Lombardo is not an individual given to exaggeration, and there are few people in the world who know more about the 'Ndrangheta's money. It is his figure that I have used here as an upper limit.

Why the variation in figures? And why use Lombardo's figure, which is one of the highest? Savona was keen to puncture what he considered to be the wilder estimates of mafia wealth, a laudable aim in an area prone to hyperbole. Still, anecdotal evidence such as the value of the European cocaine trade (€4.5 billion to €7 billion a year at wholesale prices, or €22 billion a year at street prices), the embezzlement and defrauding of billons of euros in European Union funds, and the uncovering of mafia money-laundering networks processing tens of billions of euros a year suggests Transcrime's figures are low. Possibly this is because, in its admirable effort to nail the facts, Transcrime focused only on documented domestic seizures and Italian police evidence of criminal revenues, plus academic and media reports. In other words, it concentrated only on the known and local and took no account of the unknown or foreign. It's worth noting that in a separate 2013 study, Transcrime itself estimated that 80 percent of the 'Ndrangheta's money is earned overseas. Lombardo, on the other hand, took a global view and has information on the 'Ndrangheta not available to academic researchers. His figures also accord much more closely with other international estimates of the value of global organized crime.

3 Milka Kahn and Anne Véron, *Women of Honour* (London: Hurst, 2017), p. 77.

4 Although Italian law recognized the imperative of defending honor until 1981, allowing the defense of reputation as mitigation for murder. See Pierfilippo Saviotti, " 'Le donne contro la 'ndrangheta,' Pavia incontra il procuratore Cerreti," Stampo Antimafioso, November 16, 2013: http://www.stampoantimafioso.it/2013/11/16/pavia-procuratore-cerreti/#sthash.zns0zKkt.dpuf.

5 Michele Inserra, "Quaderni del Sud, Locri la giornata della memoria Al cimitero di Rosarno per le donne 'sparite,' " *Il Quotidiano del Sud*, March 17, 2017:

http://www.quotidianodelsud.it/calabria/societa-cultura/2017/03/17
/quaderni-sud-locri-giornata-memoria-cimitero-rosarno-donne.

6 *Amanda Knox*, Netflix, 2016: https://www.netflix.com/title/80081155.

III

1 This section is based primarily on several interviews with Alessandra Cerreti conducted between July 2015 and May 2016, as well as supplementary
research.

2 "Profile: Bernardo Provenzano," BBC, April 11, 2006: http://news.bbc.co
.uk/1/hi/world/europe/4899512.stm.

3 "Imprenditore arrestato per frode all'erario E' accusato di aver sottratto
un miliardo," *La Repubblica*, February 9, 2007: https://www.repubblica
.it/2007/02/sezioni/cronaca/arresto-cetti-serbelloni/arresto-cetti-serbel
loni/arresto-cetti-serbelloni.html; "Islam, nell'aula del tribunale è polem
ica fra giudice e imputato sul copricapo," *La Repubblica*, February 26, 2009:
http://milano.repubblica.it/dettaglio/islam-nellaula-del-tribunale-e-po
lemica-fra-giudice-e-imputato-sul-copricapo/1596678.

4 Emanuela Zuccalà, "La 'ndrangheta esiste, che fatica dimostrarlo ogni volta," *Io
Donna*, October 9, 2012: http://www.iodonna.it/personaggi/interviste/2012
/alessandra-cerreti-pubblico-ministero-mafia-calabria-40999238466.shtml.

IV

1 This chapter is based on official transcriptions of Denise Cosco's testimony and of her interviews with the carabinieri on November 25, 2009,
and March 5, 2010, as well as supplementary interviews with Denise's
lawyer, Vincenza Rando; Lea's lawyer, Annalisa Pisano; and prosecutors
Alessandra Cerreti, Giuseppe Creazzo, and Sandro Dolce.

V

1 John Dickie, professor of Italian studies at University College London, is
a rare example of an outsider in a field—mafia history—dominated by
Italians. His studies of mafiosi, *Cosa Nostra*, *Mafia Brotherhoods*, and *Mafia
Republic*, draw on earlier work by Italian scholars but also Dickie's original
research. Alessandra read works by many mafia scholars, most of them
Italian. But it was Dickie's research that revealed to her the 'Ndrangheta's
early attachment to prostitution. It is a measure of Dickie's stature that
Alessandra later struck up a correspondence with him. In this passage,

I quote from Dickie's work as well as from a supplementary interview in London in June 2016.

2 John Dickie, *Mafia Brotherhoods* (London: Sceptre, 2011), pp. 171–74.

3 See for example the founding myths of the Chinese triads, the Japanese yakuza, or the South African prison gangs the 26s, 27s, and 28s.

4 León Arsenal and Hipólito Sanchiz, *Una Historia de las Sociedades Secretas Españolas* (Barcelona: Planeta, 2006), pp. 326–35.

5 Dickie, *Mafia Brotherhoods*, p. 5.

6 Antonio Zagari, *Ammazzare stanca* (Cosenza, Italy: Periferia, 1992; reprinted Reggio Emilia, Italy: Aliberti, 2008).

7 Interview with the author, May 2016, Rome.

VI

1 This section is largely sourced from repeated interviews with Alessandra Cerreti, Giovanni Musarò, and Michele Prestipino between July 2015 and November 2016.

2 Rachel Donadio, "Corruption Is Seen as a Drain on Italy's South," *New York Times*, October 7, 2012: http://www.nytimes.com/2012/10/08/world/europe/in-italy-calabria-is-drained-by-corruption.html.

3 Interview with the author, June 2016, Gioia Tauro.

4 Alex Perry, "Cocaine Highway," *Newsweek Insights*, November 17, 2014: https://www.amazon.co.uk/Cocaine-Highway-lines-habit-terror-ebook/dp/B00PSI1M42/ref=sr_1_1?ie=UTF8&qid=1481295939&sr=8-1&keywords=cocaine+highway.

5 Steve Scherer, "The Mafia and a Very Special Flower Arrangement," Reuters, April 11, 2016: https://www.reuters.com/investigates/special-report/italy-mafia-flowers/.

6 The best description of the 'Ndrangheta's structure and the evidence gathered for it can be found in the judicial documents supporting the case that eventually resulted from these inquiries, code-named Operazione Crimine. Copies can be found at the following web addresses: http://www.casadellalegalita.info/doc/sentenza-GUP-CRIMINE.pdf (939 pages) and http://www.casadellalegalita.info/doc/Decreto-Fermo-CRIMINE.pdf (2,681 pages).

These documents also detail the election of Domenico Oppedisano and give further detail on the carabinieri's surveillance methods.

7 For an account of the summit, see this interview with the center's manager, Paderno Dugnano: https://www.youtube.com/watch?v=xGsOuUHH0WA.

8 Stephan Faris, "Italy Braces for a New Mafia War," *Time*, October 14, 2010: http://content.time.com/time/world/article/0,8599,2025423,00.html; "It-

aly: Police Uncover Mafia Drug Ring in Milan Convent," AKI, May 12, 2010 (a reprint of the story, containing details of the government crackdown, can be found on a chat thread of the Gangsters Inc. blog at: http://z14 .invisionfree.com/GangstersInc/index.php?showtopic=1605&st=720); Nick Squires, "Italy Claims Finally Defeating the Mafia," *Telegraph*, January 9, 2010: http://www.telegraph.co.uk/news/worldnews/europe/italy/6957240 /Italy-claims-finally-defeating-the-mafia.html.

VII

1 Much has been written about Lea Garofalo's death. In this account, I have stuck to the official transcriptions of her testimony in 1996, July 2002, and April 2008; Denise Cosco's statements on November 25, 2009, and March 5, 2010, and her testimony in court on September 20 and October 13, 2011; and judicial documents from the murder trial that followed. I also conducted supplementary interviews with Vincenza Rando, Alessandra Cerreti, Marisa Garofalo, and Sandro Dolce in 2015 and 2016.

2 Milka Kahn and Anne Véron, *Women of Honour* (London: Hurst, 2017), p. 107.

VIII

1 The source material for most of this chapter is the same as for chapter 7.

2 I have supplemented quotes from my own interview with Enza Rando with some from this court report: Emanuela Zuccalà, "L'ultimo sms di Lea Garofalo: torno a Milano per ricominciare," *Corriere della Sera*, November 14, 2012: http://27esimaora.corriere.it/articolo/lultimo-sms-di-lea-garofalo -allavvocatotorno-a-milano-mi-rifaro-una-vita/.

IX

1 "Reggio Calabria, bomba al tribunale alto potenziale, danni, nessun ferito," *La Repubblica*, January 3, 2010: https://www.repubblica.it/2010/01/sezi oni/cronaca/reggio-bomba/reggio-bomba/reggio-bomba.html; Nick Pisa, "The Moped Mafia: CCTV Catches Bomb Delivery by Italian Mobster on Scooter Driven by His Moll," *Daily Mail*, January 8, 2010: http://www .dailymail.co.uk/news/article-1241682/The-moped-Mafia-CCTV-catch es-bomb-delivery-Italian-mobster-scooter-driven-moll.html. Though the driver was initially reported as being a woman, Prestipino said later investigations identified a man.

2 "Rosarno, polizia: 'Ndrangheta dietro a scontri. Via 1.100 immigrati,"

Reuters, January 11, 2010: https://it.reuters.com/article/topNews/idIT
MIE60A0AB20100111?sp=true.

3 Reports of the discovery of the car can be found on this Gangsters Inc. chat
thread: http://www.z14.invisionfree.com/GangstersInc/index.php?show
topic=1605&st=720.

4 The passages on the early life and friendship in Rosarno of Maria Concetta
Cacciola and Giuseppina Pesce are based on official court documents, dated
July 13, 2013, released by the Italian prosecutor, Giuseppe Creazzo, who
oversaw the case relating to Cacciola's death, as well as transcripts of Giuseppina's testimony to those proceedings, dated February 7, 2013. Supplementary material is available in official documents relating to the subsequent
trial of lawyers representing the Cacciola family, dated July 30, 2014, and a
custody hearing for Concetta's father, Michele Cacciola, dated February 4,
2012.

X

1 This chapter is based on official transcriptions of Denise Cosco's statements
on November 25, 2009, and March 5, 2010, and of her testimony in court on
September 20 and October 13, 2011; on judicial documents from the murder
trial that followed; and on statements made to police and in court by Carmine Venturino in 2012 and 2013.

XI

1 "Operazione 'All Inside,' colpo al clan Pesce di Rosarno. 30 arresti,"
CN24TV: http://www.cn24tv.it/news/30318/operazione-all-inside-colpo
-al-clan-pesce-di-rosarno-30-arresti.html.

2 Caterina Scaffidi Domianello, "Donne contro la 'ndrangheta," *Narcomafie*,
July–August 2013: http://www.liberanet.org/narcomafie/2013_07.pdf.

3 Julian Gavaghan, "Italian Mob Boss Arrested After 17 Years on the Run Is
Cheered by Crowd as Police Lead Him to Jail," *Daily Mail*, April 27, 2010:
http://www.dailymail.co.uk/news/article-1269304/Italian-mobster-arrested
-17-years-run-cheered-crowd-police-lead-jail.html.

4 Tom Kington, "Italian Police Arrest 300 in Raids on Calabrian Mafia," *Guard-
ian*, July 13, 2010: https://www.theguardian.com/world/2010/jul/13/cal
abria-mafia-arrests-italy; Stephan Faris, "Italy vs. the Mafia: Beheading the
'Ndrangheta," *Time*, July 13, 2010: http://content.time.com/time/world/arti
cle/0,8599,2003598,00.html.

5 Interview with the author, July 2015, Milan.

6 Interview with the author, July 2015, Modena.

7 Interview with the author, July 2015, Milan.

8 Ibid.

XII

1 Stephan Faris, "Italy Braces for a New Mafia War," *Time*, October 14, 2010: http://content.time.com/time/world/article/0,8599,2025423,00.html.

2 Author interview with Alessandra Cerreti, May 2016, Milan.

3 Clare Longrigg, "Women Breaking the Mafia's Rules," Mafiology, October 14, 2013: https://mafiologytest.wordpress.com/2013/10/14/women-breaking -the-mafias-rules/#more-556.

4 Ibid.

5 Cerreti spoke about her conversation with Giuseppina in several forums, such as in Rome in March 2014: "Experts Commend Mafia-Linked Women's Help in Crime Fight," Xinhua, March 15, 2014: http://china.org.cn/world/Off_ the_Wire/2014-03/15/content_31793448.htm. She also gave several accounts during more than seven hours of interviews with the author in July 2015 and February and May 2016. This quotation is a compilation of Cerreti's public remarks and her quotations in interviews.

6 Longrigg, "Women Breaking the Mafia's Rules."

7 Interview with the author, July 2015, Milan.

8 Ibid.

9 Ibid.

10 Interview with the author, February 2015, Rome.

11 Interview with the author, July 2015, Milan.

12 Interview with the author, July 2015, Rome.

13 Giuseppina Pesce's statement to prosecutors was sourced from official tran- scripts of her testimony included in several subsequent trial documents.

XIII

1 This chapter is based on numerous trial documents relating to the Lea Garo- falo case. In the earlier stages of the investigation, the carabinieri made some false allegations and were mistaken over some factual details, which were corrected as their inquiries proceeded at later stages of the investigation and the trial.

2 Author interview with Enza Rando, July 2015, Modena. See also Michele Bram- billa, "The Tragedy and Courage of a Mobster's Daughter," *La Stampa in En- glish*, April 17, 2014: https://www.lastampa.it/2014/04/17/esteri/lastampa-in

-english/the-tragedy-and-courage-of-a-mobsters-daughter-lrpU6aQB445i
f2MPCiJM9I/pagina.html.

XIV

1 This section is based on trial documents relating to Operation All Inside,
the prosecution of the Pesce clan, and statements made by Giuseppina Pesce
both to Alessandra Cerreti and during the subsequent trial.
2 Clare Longrigg, "Women Breaking the Mafia's Rules," Mafiology, October
14, 2013: https://mafiologytest.wordpress.com/2013/10/14/women-break
ing-the-mafias-rules/#more-556.
3 *Calabria Ora*'s website has since closed. I am grateful to the veteran journalist Franco Abruzzo, whose website is an invaluable archive on a diverse
range of matters, including the *Calabria Ora* controversy: https://www.fran
coabruzzo.it/public/docs/palmi-articolicommenti-9fb13.rtf.

XV

1 This chapter is based on official records of statements made by Maria Con-
cetta Cacciola to Alessandra Cerreti and Giovanni Musarò on May 25 and
June 28, 2011; trial documents relating to the prosecution of Michele Cac-
ciola, Giuseppe Cacciola, Anna Lazzaro, Gregorio Cacciola, and Vittorio
Pisani; and supplementary interviews with Giuseppe Creazzo, Giovanni
Musarò, and Alessandra Cerreti. I'm also grateful to Laura Aprati and Enrico
Fierro for a transcript of their one-woman play about Concetta, *O cu nui o cu
iddi*, which is also closely based on the official evidence.
2 Caterina Scaffidi Domianello, "Donne contro la 'ndrangheta," *Narcomafie*,
July–August 2013: http://www.liberanet.org/narcomafie/2013_07.pdf.
3 Interview with the author, May 2016, Milan.
4 Interview with the author, May 2016, Rome.
5 Clare Longrigg, "Mafia Witness 'Forced to Drink Acid,'" Mafiology, February 2, 2014: https://mafiologytest.wordpress.com/2014/02/02/mafia
-witness-forced-to-drink-acid/more#572.
6 Interview with the author, May 2016, Rome.

XVI

1 This section is based on the author's interview with Alessandra Cerreti in
May 2016 in Milan.
2 Interview with the author, May 2016, Milan.

3 Caterina Scaffidi Domianello, "Donne contro la 'ndrangheta," *Narcomafie*, July–August 2013: http://www.liberanet.org/narcomafie/2013_07.pdf.

4 Various reports of the correspondence between Giuseppina Pesce and her family can be found online. The most complete is Caterina Scaffidi Domianello's account in "Donne contro la 'ndrangheta," *Narcomafie*, July–August 2013: http://www.liberanet.org/narcomafie/2013_07.pdf. Others that proved useful include two reports on strill.it: http://www.strill.it/citta/2011/10/la-famiglia-scrive-a-giuseppina-pesce-le-lettere-ricevute-in-carcere/; and http://www.strill.it/citta/2011/09/le-lettere-di-giuseppina-pesce-collaboro-per-dare-un-futuro-ai-miei-figli/. Excerpts were also included in the judicial documents accompanying the trials that followed Operations All Inside and All Clean. Finally, Alessandra Cerreti read some of the letters to the author in an interview and at other times summarized their contents.

XVII

1 This chapter is based on evidence and transcripts presented in official judicial documents relating to the trial of Michele Cacciola, Anna Lazzaro, and Giuseppe Cacciola, and the subsequent trial of the two lawyers, Vittorio Pisani and Gregorio Cacciola. This material is supplemented by the author's interviews with Alessandra Cerreti, Giovanni Musarò, and Giuseppe Creazzo, as well as reference to the play *O cu nui o cu iddi* by Laura Aprati and Enrico Fierro.

2 Dario Crippa, "Sciolse la mamma nell'acido, nessuna pietà per mio padre," *Il Giorno*, July 4, 2011: https://www.ilgiorno.it/milano/cronaca/2011/07/04/537205-sciolse_mamma.shtml.

3 Santo Della Volpe, "Le donne e la lotta di liberazione dalle mafie," Libera, 2012: http://www.libera.it/flex/cm/pages/ServeBLOB.php/L/IT/IDPagina/6462 (no longer available).

4 The eleven-minute recording of Concetta's "retraction" is on the Stop'Ndrangheta website: http://www.stopndrangheta.it/stopndr/art.aspx?id=1419,La+ritrattazione+estorta+alla+Cacciola.

5 Clare Longrigg, "Mafia Witness 'Forced to Drink Acid,'" Mafiology, February 2, 2014: https://mafiologytest.wordpress.com/2014/02/02/mafia-witness-forced-to-drink-acid/more#572.

XVIII

1 This chapter is based on evidence and transcripts presented in official judicial documents relating to the trial of Michele Cacciola, Anna Lazzaro, and Gi-

useppe Cacciola, and the subsequent trial of the two lawyers, Vittorio Pisani and Gregorio Cacciola. This material is supplemented by the author's interviews with Alessandra Cerreti, Giovanni Musarò, and Giuseppe Creazzo.

2 Interview with the author, May 2016, Milan.

3 Interview with the author, May 2016, Rome.

4 "Orsola Fallara in condizioni disperate al Riuniti di Reggio dopo un tentativo di suicidio," CN24TV, December 16, 2010: http://www.cn24tv.it/news/16616 /orsola-fallara-in-condizioni-disperate-al-riuniti-di-reggio-dopo-un-tentativo -di-suicidio.html.

5 Carlo Macrì, "Il suicidio della testimone anti clan," *Corriere della Sera*, August 23, 2011: http://www.corriere.it/cronache/11_agosto_23/il-sui cidio-della-testimone-anti-clan-carlo-macri_7e7fbc74-cd49-11e0-8914 -d32bd7027ea8.shtml.

6 The full letter can be found here: http://www.sdisonorate.it/wordpress/wp -content/uploads/2014/03/Le-testimoni-di-giustizia-calabresi.pdf.

7 Ibid. *Calabria Ora*'s front page can be seen a few pages further on.

XIX

1 This chapter is based on official transcriptions of Denise Cosco's statements on November 25, 2009, and March 5, 2010, and of her testimony in court on September 20 and October 13, 2011, as well as judicial documents from the murder trial that followed.

2 Milka Kahn and Anne Véron, *Women of Honour* (London: Hurst, 2017), p. 118.

3 Marika Demaria, *La Scelta di Lea* (Milan: Melampo Editore, 2013), p. 26. I am indebted to Ms. Demaria, the only reporter to stay in court throughout the nine months of the trial, whose persistence allowed for a complete, public account to be given.

XX

1 This section is based on trial documents relating to Operation All Inside, the prosecution of the Pesce clan, and statements made by Giuseppina Pesce to Alessandra Cerreti and during the subsequent trial.

2 Much of the Pesce correspondence is also reprinted in full in Caterina Scaffidi Domianello's invaluable articles in "Donne contro la 'ndrangheta," *Narcomafie*, July–August 2013: http://www.liberanet.org/narcomafie/2013_07.pdf. Excerpts from Giuseppina's letter of August 23, 2011, are also reprinted here: http://www.strill.it/citta/2011/09/le-lettere-di-giuseppina-pesce-collaboro -per-dare-un-futuro-ai-miei-figli/.

3 Domianello, "Donne contro la 'ndrangheta."

4 Piero Gaeta, "Condannati a 20 anni Vincenzo e Ciccio Pesce," *Gazzetta del Sud*, September 21, 2011: http://www.calabrianotizie.it/condannati-anni -vincenzo-ciccio-pesce-sentenza-esemplare-del-gup-roberto-carrelli-palombi -che-ieri-sera-condannato-undici-imputati-ordinato-maxi-risarcimento/.

5 Paolo Toscano, "Giuseppina Pesce si è pentita di nuovo," *Gazzetta del Sud*, September 22, 2011: http://www.calabrianotizie.it/giuseppina-pesce-pentita -nuovo-dopo-avere-interrotto-collaborazione-con-magistrati-della-dda-reg gina-figlia-del-boss-salvatore-ripreso-riferire-vicende-della-cosca-figli/.

6 Ibid.

7 'Ndrangheta. "Giuseppina Pesce domani al processo di Palmi," CN24TV, September 22, 2011: http://www.cn24tv.it/news/32497/ndrangheta-gi useppina-pesce-domani-al-processo-di-palmi.html; "Clan pesce, Palaia scrive alla moglie pentita: 'stai rovinando te stessa ed i tuoi figli,'" CN24TV, November 23, 2011: http://www.cn24tv.it/news/32639/clan-pesce-palaia -scrive-alla-moglie-pentita-stai-rovinando-te-stessa-ed-i-tuoi-figli.html.

8 "Operazione 'All clean 2'. I dettagli," CN24TV, October 13, 2011: http://www .cn24tv.it/news/33781/operazione-all-clean-2-i-dettagli.html.

9 "Processo al clan Pesce, la testimone di giustizia sarà sentita da un luogo segreto," CN24TV, October 21, 2011: http://www.cn24tv.it/news/34338/processo-al -clan-pesce-la-testimone-di-giustizia-sara-sentita-da-un-luogo-segreto.html.

10 Nick Pisa, "Judge Hands 1,000-Year Prison Sentence to 110 Mafia Mobsters in Massive Show Trial," *Daily Mail*, November 22, 2011: http://www.daily mail.co.uk/news/article-2063932/Judge-hands-1-000-year-prison-sentence -110-Mafia-mobsters-massive-trial.html.

11 Author interview with Alessandra Cerreti. Also see the account in Francesca Chirico, "Rosarno, donne e 'ndrangheta: il processo del contrappasso," Stop'Ndrangheta, November 25, 2011: http://www.stopndrangheta.it/stopndr /art.aspx?id=1215,Rosarno%2c+donne+e+%27ndrangheta%3a+il+processo- +del+contrappasso.

XXI

1 This section is based on two interviews with Roberto di Bella at his offices in Reggio Calabria in July 2015 and May 2016, as well as a visit to the hostel housing 'Ndrangheta children in Messina and interviews with the staff there.

2 Riccardo Francesco Cordì, "Voglio una vita normale," *Corriere della Sera*, May 8, 2014: http://www.corriere.it/cronache/14_maggio_08/voglio-vita -normale-6f0f1dc2-d672-11e3-b1c6-d3130b63f531.shtml.

1 Translation from the United Nations Office of Drugs and Crime, *Review of Implementation of the United Nations Convention Against Corruption*, Italy, p. 4: https://www.unodc.org/documents/treaties/UNCAC/WorkingGroups /ImplementationReviewGroup/26-27November2013/V1387842e.pdf.

2 *Il Quotidiano della Calabria*'s front page for February 10, 2012, can be seen here: http://www.stopndrangheta.it/file/stopndrangheta_1381.pdf. The page includes the start of Matteo Cosenza's editorial, as well as stories on Maria Concetta Cacciola, Giuseppina Pesce, and Lea Garofalo, perhaps the first time that the three women and their stories had been reported collectively. The full editorial is here: http://19luglio1992.com/il-simbolo-dell8-marzo-tre-donne -coraggiose/.

3 For example, see Giuseppe Baldessarro, "Lea, Concetta, Giuseppina è l'8 marzo della Calabria," *La Repubblica*, March 2, 2012: https://www.repubblica.it /cronaca/2012/03/02/news/donne_ndrangheta_8_marzo-30721686/.

4 Ilaria Calabrò, "Reggio, 8 marzo: dagli studenti una lettera alla Pesce, 'nel tuo riscatto è possibile il riscatto di tutti,'" strettoweb.com, March 8, 2012: http://www.strettoweb.com/2012/03/reggio-8-marzo-dagli -studenti-una-lettera-alla-pesce-nel-tuo-riscatto-e-possibile-il-riscatto-di -tutti/25999/#07DWLhJEL6JRX3w0.99.

5 Matteo Cosenza, "Vicini a Denise che ha scelto la verità e la giustizia," *Il Quotidiano della Calabria*, March 8, 2012: http://www.stopndrangheta.it /file/stopndrangheta_1485.pdf.

1 This section is based on official transcripts of the court proceedings held in Palmi, May 21 to 26, 2012.

1 Marika Demaria, "Processo Lea Garofalo, riprendono le udienze," *Narcomafie*, December 2, 2012: http://www.acmos.net/processo-lea-garofalo-ripren dono-le-udienze.

2 "Sei ergastoli per l'omicidio di Lea Garofalo la testimone sciolta nell'acido," *Il Fatto Quotidiano*, March 30, 2012: https://www.ilfattoquotidiano .it/2012/03/30/milano-ergastoli-lomicidio-garofalo-testimone-sciolta-nel lacido/201316/. See also Tom Kington, "Italian Mobster Condemned by Daughter's Evidence," *Observer*, April 1, 2012: https://theguardian.com /world/2012/apr/01/italian-mobster-jailed-by-daughters-evidence.

3 Simona Ravizza, Cesare Giuzzi, and Redazione Milano online, "Viale
   Montello 6, sgomberato dopo 40 anni il 'fortino delle cosche,'" *Corriere della Sera*, June 21, 2012: http://milano.corriere.it/milano/notizie/
   cronaca/12_giugno_21/viale-montello-fortino-cosche-sgombero-polizia
   -cosco-lea-garofalo-201694845491.shtml. *Corriere della Sera* also has pictures of No. 6 Viale Montello as it was when Carlo ruled it and how it
   might be renovated here: Elisabetta Andreis, "Una 'corte' moderna nell'ex
   fortino della mafia," August 29, 2016: http://milano.corriere.it/notizie
   /cronaca/16_agosto_29/viale-montello-fortino-mafia-stabile-abbandonato
   -progetto-demolizione-41cb3f10-6d58-11e6-baa8-f780dada92e5.shtml.

4 Michele Brambilla, "The Tragedy and Courage of a Mobster's Daughter,"
   La Stampa in English, April 17, 2014: https://www.lastampa.it/2014/04/17
   /esteri/lastampa-in-english/the-tragedy-and-courage-of-a-mobsters-daugh
   ter-lrpU6aQB445if2MPCiJM9I/pagina.html.

5 This account of Carmine Venturino's confession is based on official court
   documents. There are also numerous press reports of Carmine Venturino's letter. See for instance Sandro De Riccardis, "Il verbale dell'orrore sulla
   pentita Garofalo: 'Bruciai il suo corpo finché rimase cenere,'" *La Repubblica*,
   March 20, 2013: http://repubblica.it/cronaca/2013/03/20/news/il_verbale
   _dell_orrore_sulla_pentita_garofalo_bruciai_il_suo_corpo_finch_rimase
   _cenere-54945861/?ref=search; Alessandra Coppola and Cesare Giuzzi, "Uc-
   cisi Lea Garofalo, il coraggio di Denise mi ha spinto a collaborare," *Corriere della
   Sera*, December 4, 2012: https://www.senzatarga.wordpress.com/2012/12/04
   /lea/; Marika Demaria, *La Scelta di Lea* (Milan: Melampo Editore, 2013).

6 This section relies chiefly on official records provided by prosecutor
   Marcello Tatangelo of his interrogation of Carmine Venturino on October 3 and 11, 2012, as well as later transcripts of Carmine's questioning
   by Tatangelo in court. Once again, I am also indebted to Marika Demaria of *Narcomafie*, who doggedly followed the case and published in-
   termittent reports as well as her book, *La Scelta di Lea*. Also useful were
   various other press reports, as indicated.

XXV

1 "All Inside, il dispositivo della sentenza (I grado)," *Narcomafie*, May 3,
   2013: http://www.stopndrangheta.it/stopndr/art.aspx?id=1709,All+In
   side%2c+il+dispositivo+della+sentenza+(I+grado).

2 When the final sentences were delivered four years later, on March 29, 2017,
   sentences were confirmed against thirty-four accused: "'Ndrangheta, diven-
   tano definitive le condanne inflitte al clan Pesce di Rosarno," *Zoom 24*,

March 29, 2017: http://www.zoom24.it/2017/03/29/ndrangheta-pesce-con
danne-rosarno-45842/.

3 Giuseppe Baldessarro, "'Ndrangheta: nessuno demolisce la casa del boss, ac-
cetta solo l'imprenditore sotto scorta," *La Repubblica*, September 16, 2014:
https://www.repubblica.it/cronaca/2014/09/16/news/calabria_ndran
gheta_boss-95872877/.

4 Barbara Conforti, *Mafia, la trahison des femmes* (documentary), Canal+,
March 2, 2014.

5 "Omicidio Lea Garofalo, in appello confermati 4 ergastoli. Un assolto," *Il
Fatto Quotidiano*, May 29, 2013: https://www.ilfattoquotidiano.it/2013/05/29
/omicidio-lea-garofalo-in-appello-confermati-4-ergastoli-assolto/610120/.

6 Vincenzo Ruggiero, "Omicid di 'ndrangheia. 17 arresti a Crotone e in altre
4 regioni. Decisive le dichiarazioni di Lea Garofalo," CN24TV, October 29,
2013: http://www.cn24tv.it/news/77515/omicidi-di-ndrangheta-17-arresti
-a-crotone-e-in-altre-4-regioni-decisive-le-dichiarazioni-di-lea-garofalo
.html.

XXVI

1 Vincenzo Ruggiero, "Omicid di 'ndrangheia. 17 arresti a Crotone e in altre
4 regioni. Decisive le dichiarazioni di Lea Garofalo," CN24TV, October 29,
2013:   http://www.cn24tv.it/news/77515/omicidi-di-ndrangheta-17-arres
ti-a-crotone-e-in-altre-4-regioni-decisive-le-dichiarazioni-di-lea-garofalo.
html.

2 There are several videos of Lea's funeral online that include Denise's
short speech. See https://www.youtube.com/watch?v=4oR9kFYFVcs or
https://www.youtube.com/watch?v=I9jxIMRQlT8.

ILLUSTRATION CREDITS

Lea Garofalo. The picture is undated but seems to capture Lea in her early twenties, just after she became a mother. The image became iconic. (*http://www.wikimafia.it*)

Lea, on the left, and Denise captured by CCTV in Milan in their last minutes together on the evening of November 24, 2009. (*Milan Carabinieri*)

Alessandra Cerreti, pictured in her office in Reggio Calabria. (*FILIPPO MONTEFORTE/AFP/Getty Images*)

Reggio Calabria, as seen from the hills to the southeast of the city, looking northwest across the Strait to Messina. (*Anna Quaglia/Alamy Stock Photo*)

San Luca. For decades, the 'Ndrangheta have convened an annual meeting on September 2 in this Aspromonte hill village, using a religious festival as cover. (*ROPI/Alamy Stock Photo*)

Carlo Cosco in a police mug shot taken after his arrest in February 2010. (*Lanese/Epa/REX/Shutterstock*)

Giuseppina Pesce the day after her arrest in April 2010. (*ANSA*)

Domenico Oppedisano being driven through the streets after his arrest in Rosarno in July 2010. (*Franco Cufari/Epa/REX/Shutterstock*)

Giuseppina Pesce in her mug shot after her arrest. (*ANSA*)

Maria Concetta Cacciola. As she was confined to the family home for weeks at a time, only one other picture of her has ever surfaced. (*ANSA*)

The gate of the warehouse in San Fruttuoso, Monza, where Lea's remains were discovered in October 2012, three years after her death. (*Fabrizio Radaelli/Epa/REX/Shutterstock*)

Breaking a lifetime of omertà, Carlo speaks in court on April 9, 2013. (*Corriere TV*)

Giuseppina's mother, Angela Ferraro, and sister, Marina Pesce. (*ANSA*)

Concetta's mother, Anna Rosalba Lazzaro, and father, Michele Cacciola. (*ANSA*)

Lea's funeral on October 19, 2013. Thousands from all over Italy turned out for a woman who, four years after her death, united the nation against the mafia under the slogan "I see, I hear, I speak." (*Marco Aprile/NurPhoto/Corbis via Getty Images*)

INDEX